THE PRACTICAL GUIDE TO CONCEALED CARRY

PRACTICAL GUIDES
BOOK 5

TOM MCHALE

IPG

CONTENTS

1. INTRODUCTION   1
  Training   2
  Planning   3
  Case Study: Self Defense Isn't Just About You   4

2. THE CONCEALED CARRY LIFESTYLE   5
  Situational Awareness   7
  Case Study: An 'Innocent' Distraction   15
  Find the Armed Citizen   16
  Spotting Suspicous People   21
  Case Study: Anger Management   30
  A Polite Lifestyle   31

3. SHOULD YOU CARRY A GUN?   33
  What Do Guns Actually Do?   35
  Guns and Physiological Factors   36
  Case Study: What Stops an Attacker?   40
  'Knockdown' or 'Stopping' Power   41
  Effects of Different Types of Guns   47

4. SELF-DEFENSE LAW   52
  Knowing the Law   52
  Is Self-Defense Homicide?   53
  Reasonable Person Doctrine   54
  Case Study: No Shots Fired   55
  Imminent Bodily Harm   56
  Case Study: He Was Unarmed!   57
  Castle Doctrine   58
  Stand Your Ground   59
  Monday Morning Quarterbacking   60
  When and Where Can You Carry?   61
  State Reciprocity and Traveling with Firearms   62
  Legal Defense Networks   63

5. LESS LETHAL OPTIONS   65
   Can a Flashlight Save Your Life?   66
   Pepper Sprays, Streams and Powders   70
   Tasers and Stun Guns   75

6. GUNS   77
   Choosing the Right Handgun   78
   Types of Handguns   90
   Semi-Automatic Pistols   91
   Revolvers   98
   Derringers   100

7. HOLSTERS   101
   Why the Right Holster is So Important   102
   A Word on Belts...   103
   Buying a Good Holster   104
   Carry Method Tradeoffs   105
   Carry Methods and Holster Types   108
   Inside the Wasitband   109
   Appendix Carry   116
   Outside the Waistband   123
   Body Carry: Shirts and Belly Bands   127
   Pocket Holsters   131
   Ankle Carry   135
   Off Body Carry   137
   Spare Magazine Carriers   140

8. AMMUNITION   142
   Defensive Ammunition   143
   Practice and Match Ammunition   145
   Reloaded Ammunition   147

9. SIGHTS, LIGHTS AND LASERS   149
   "Iron" Sights   149
   Standard Target Sights   154
   Fiber-Optic Sights   155
   Tritium Sights   156
   Red Dot Sights   156
   Laser Sights   159
   Lights   171
   Hand-held Lights   172

Weapon Lights   173
Case Study: The Importance of Light   174

10. BASIC SHOOTING SKILLS   176
Case Study: Gun Safety Always Matters   177
Gun Safety Rules   177
Gun Handling Etiquette   182
Case Study: Range Safety and Etiquette   184
The Foundation: Stance   185
Grip   190
Sight Picture   198
Trigger Press   200
Natural Point of Aim   201
Ready to Shoot!   203
Drawing from a Holster   213
Ongoing Practice   219

11. DEFENSIVE MINDSET   231
Finding A Reputable Defensive Training Program   232
Mission: Escape   233
Case Study: You Were Right! You Lost Everything...   235
Mental Defense   236
Action vs. Reaction   241

12. BASIC DEFENSIVE SKILLS   249
Case Study: A "Non-Range' Situation   251
Myths or Strategies?   252
Gun Control and Operations   259
Shots on Target   260
One-Handed Shooting   262
Drawing Your Gun From Concealment   266
Moving   269
Communication   273
Changing Magazines   274
Reloading a Revolver   284
Go Fast, But Don't Miss   288
Case Study: Unarmed Fighting Skills   289

13. ADVANCED DEFENSIVE SKILLS   290
Cover and Concealment   290
Using Lights   296
Case Study: Two Is Better Than One   302

Team Defense   302
Active Shooter Situations   308

14. AFTERMATH   311
Case Study: Getting Shot By the Police   311
On the Scene   312
Case Study: Subway Good Samaritan or Villain?   318
What Happens Next   319
Self-Defense Liability Protection   322

15. PARTING SHOTS   324

About the Author   327
Also by Tom McHale   329

1

INTRODUCTION

Y ou may have heard it before. A seemingly innocuous comment by someone who has not (yet) embraced the reality that the world can be a dangerous place.

"Why would anyone need to carry a gun in a coffee shop?"

Sounds innocent enough, right? The problem is that the perspective is all wrong. As a legally armed citizen, you don't want your gun or any other to become a factor in a coffee shop visit. You have no intention of using your gun in a coffee shop or anywhere else, for that matter. So what's the problem?

The problem is this. Whether or not you "need" a gun in a coffee shop is not your decision. That decision is made by one person and one person only—someone who intends to inflict harm. If you got to choose where and when people committed crimes and whether you'd even be present, we'd have a chronic shortage of victims. Who in their right mind would go to a place where they knew a crime would occur?

Sure, you can stack the odds in your favor by not going to places where crime is a higher probability. You can decide not to wander dark alleys with a stack of $20 bills hanging out of your back pocket. You'll certainly reduce your chances of becoming the next armed robbery statistic. But if some creep out there decides to rob the local coffee shop, and you happen to be there, you're now involved, like it or not. And therein lies your choice. You can recognize that while some places have a lower likelihood of criminal activity, you don't get to decide whether there will be a criminal encounter. That's up to the other guy.

The point here isn't to "prove" you need a gun in a coffee shop, figuratively speaking. The point is this.

You don't get to decide where you do or don't need a gun.

The criminal is solely responsible for that decision. Sure, logic says you shouldn't need a gun at the grocery store or playground, but criminals don't adhere to your definition of logic.

Your choices are simple. You can play the odds by frequenting places where "no one would possibly need a gun" and hope for the best. That's your call. You can also choose to prepare, knowing that you don't get to pick the battlefield.

If you have decided to prepare, then this book is for you.

There are two things under your control that will help improve your odds of going through life without becoming a statistic, and neither of them is simply "having a gun."

Training

If nothing else, this book will reinforce the importance of learning. Not just a one-time study reading this or any other resource on the topic of self-defense and concealed carry, but a lifelong commitment to maintaining a risk-reduction lifestyle.

As we will discuss, *buying and carrying a gun means virtually nothing.* Without training in a host of areas, only part involving gun handling, you'll have significant gaps in your personal and family protection strategy.

So, we're going to encourage you to go out and get credible and professional hands-on training. Carrying a gun is an enormous responsibility, and it's up to you to treat that commensurate with its potential for life and death consequences.

When you take a personal defense training class, I hope it scares you. A good class should make you realize how much you don't know. That's the right starting point for your concealed carry journey.

Planning

Good planning leads to success, and the best way to start your planning journey is to embrace reality ruthlessly.

We'll discuss strategies for living a more "switched-on" and observant lifestyle in more detail, but for now, consider your daily routines, potential problems, and what you would do about them.

We would all respond to an emergency in a fantasy world by rising to the occasion and doing something heroic to save the day. But we only tend to succeed at things we've already done before. Humans rarely "rise to the occasion" but rather fall back to their lowest level of training and preparation. The chaos of a life-and-death encounter isn't the time or place to figure out a defensive strategy.

Sheer desperation rarely makes up for lack of preparation.

I'm not suggesting you go through life as a twitching and paranoid jumble of nerves. In realistic and rational terms, I suggest you think about things that could go wrong and what your response would be.

When I was in school, CPR training was part of the curriculum. While I've yet to use that particular skill, I'm confident I know enough about it to take positive and helpful action if the need ever arises. If I never had that class, would I have the vaguest idea of what to do if someone clutched their chest and fell to the ground?

As you read this book, consider scenarios that might apply to your life. What would you do if you were in a convenience store and the guy in front of you pulled a gun and demanded money from the cashier? How about if you were walking down the street and gunfire between two individuals erupted nearby? What if you're in a restaurant, and someone presents a gun and starts making threats?

Making decisions in advance about possible events might save your life. Suppose you've already thought about bolting through a restaurant kitchen and out the back door during an emergency. In that case, you're far more likely to overcome social and embarrassment inertia should such an occasion ever arise. By considering such things in advance, you'll be far more likely to respond in a decisive manner.

Case Study: Self Defense Isn't Just About You

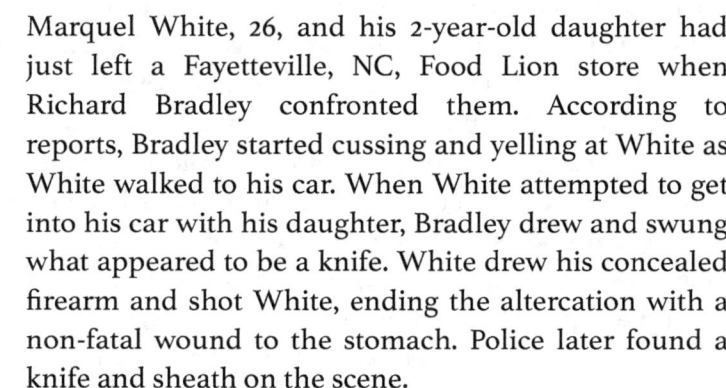

> Marquel White, 26, and his 2-year-old daughter had just left a Fayetteville, NC, Food Lion store when Richard Bradley confronted them. According to reports, Bradley started cussing and yelling at White as White walked to his car. When White attempted to get into his car with his daughter, Bradley drew and swung what appeared to be a knife. White drew his concealed firearm and shot White, ending the altercation with a non-fatal wound to the stomach. Police later found a knife and sheath on the scene.

Lessons

Cases like these bring up difficult questions. Self-defense encounters don't happen at convenient times and places; you may have family members or children with you. How would you balance protecting your child while fending off an attacker in a situation like this?

2

THE CONCEALED CARRY LIFESTYLE

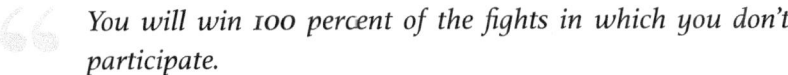 *You will win 100 percent of the fights in which you don't participate.*

Yes, it's that simple. Yes, you can learn skills and take action to reduce the odds of becoming a participant in a fight. No, there's no guarantee; no matter how good you are at avoidance, you still might be caught up in a violent encounter.

It's all about the odds. Hopefully, most of us don't plug 19 extension cords into the same outlet and run an open flame fire pit in the TV room. Sure, actions like this may not immediately set your house on fire. However, by doing "less than safe" things, you have certainly increased the odds of a fire, haven't you?

There's an old hardware store saying. The wise shop owner tells their fresh new employee, "No one ever wants to buy a 1/4-inch drill bit. They want to buy a 1/4-inch hole." That concept applies to concealed carry, too. No rational person wants to shoot another human in self-defense. *They wish not to die should they ever face an unavoidable violent encounter that threatens their life.* It's a critical distinction.

These ideas may sound trite, but when you start reading cases about unfortunate armed citizens whose lives have been ruined even though they did the "right" thing in trying to protect their loved ones, you'll appreciate the reality.

If you decide to carry a gun for self-protection, it's your mission and responsibility to do everything in your power to avoid using it.

To adequately cover the topic, we'll discuss ways to maintain constant awareness and look for suspicious behavior. However, it's also important not to overreact. Don't be a paranoid freak. That takes all the fun out of life.

You can dramatically improve your general awareness level by adding a few new habits and breaking some bad ones—like keeping your nose buried in your phone anytime you're in public. That action alone will increase your general safety level by a significant percentage.

One lifestyle change will do more than anything else to help improve your situational awareness: put away the phone while navigating public spaces.

You may even find that a more switched-on lifestyle improves your daily life experience. By paying more attention to your surroundings, you'll discover new things and experiences to enjoy and appreciate. By paying more attention to people and remembering that 99.9 percent of them aren't out to hurt you, you might make some new friends and acquaintances.

Here's the bottom line. Keep perspective. Being alert improves your odds of avoiding a criminal encounter and makes you a less attractive potential victim. That doesn't mean you have to become paranoid. Most people are not actually out to get you.

In the next section, we'll discuss strategies and tactics you can use to avoid trouble in the first place.

Situational Awareness

Situational awareness is precisely what it says: knowing what is happening in and around your immediate environment. While human beings are pre-wired with senses like sight, smell, and hearing alerting us to impending danger, situational awareness requires one to actively "switch on" their danger radar.

Maybe someone in your life can walk through a room and, afterward, recall each person's wardrobe choice. Perhaps you're that person. Some people are just naturally observant and can effortlessly pick up on such details. Most of us aren't wired that way. Even those who are could use some training and guidance on what types of things are essential to observe from a self-defense perspective.

For those of us who might not have the Sherlock Holmes observation gene, some practical tips can help you stay "switched on" during your daily travels.

The "Normal" Baseline

Wherever you go, there is a "baseline" of normalcy. Not to say that things are "normal" in the broad sense, but instead, there are constants and rhythms in every situation.

People in specific environments will dress, act, and speak in specific and detectable ways. Knowing the "normal" state of affairs during your daily routines is the easiest way to spot the abnormal. That's why it's essential to use your observation skills to pay attention to the normal state of being wherever you go. What you usually see, hear, and feel will establish the baseline to alert you to the abnormal.

At the beach, the normal baseline will be reflected by people wearing bathing suits, shorts, and t-shirts. You'll see people carrying large bags filled with towels and toys. People will read books, play games, and go swimming. Those are all normal and expected things for that time and place. A guy wearing a suit and dress shoes would not be typical, nor would a man wearing a trench coat.

While the beach is an extreme and obvious example, the principle applies everywhere.

A woman pushing a cart and dragging a child in a grocery store is perfectly normal and expected. So is a man waiting at the deli counter. However, someone standing at the front of the store near the checkout lines without a cart or basket may not fit into the regular grocery store activity rhythm.

When outdoors on a summer day, it's not at all unusual to see people wearing short-sleeved shirts, sundresses, or shorts and flip-flops. A trench coat? Not so much.

At a church, you're likely to see plenty of couples and families. A man or woman carrying a bag or pack isn't the least bit unusual—if a small child is present. On the other hand, a man walking in the door alone with a large bag or pack might be unusual. If he's also carrying a well-worn bible, maybe he does fit into the normal baseline.

Being transactional in nature, ATM locations have a normal state, too. Those there to use it stop, withdraw or deposit money, and leave. Someone loitering near an ATM is likely not there to use it, otherwise they already would have.

Convenience stores are characterized by people coming and going quickly after paying for gas or buying a few items. You'll see business suits and construction attire, but the common element will be the "quick stop" behavior. Individuals hovering outside the door out of sight of the employees may be part of the baseline, but it is a suspicious one.

You get the idea. Whether you consciously know it or not, *you already see and process baseline activity for every place you frequent.* The first step to actively increasing your situational awareness is to catalog the baselines of places you go. That will help you spot the people and activities that are out of place.

A realistic observation strategy focuses *on the anomalies of those people outside of the environmental pattern*. To do that, you must filter through the rest of the nearby folks and discard or ignore them. Suppose you walk into a convenience store and see an adult holding a gallon of milk while dragging a three-year-old away from the candy counter. In that case, those are two people you can probably delete from your observation and tracking radar. Rather than worrying about noting and remembering their physical descriptions, perhaps focus on the guy fidgeting off to the side. The more familiar you are with your local environment, the easier it will be to observe, process, and ignore people who fit within the usual pattern.

Establishing the norm and focusing on anomalies outside that pattern makes a lot of sense. That allows you to quickly discard as potential threats the 99+ percent of people you encounter each day who mean you no harm.

Switch On

The simple act of...*being active* is arguably the single most important thing you can do when going about your daily business. In the old days before smartphones, you might have seen the occasional person walking down the street reading a paper or talking on a flip phone. Now, we have far too many new inventions distracting us. What percentage of people you see in public are buried in their smartphones? Would you say 50 percent? Maybe 75 percent? Higher? Can we agree the majority of people in this day and age are not paying a whit of attention to their surroundings?

So, step one is to pay attention to your surroundings. It's a conscious decision not to allow yourself to be distracted or zoned out while in public. Saying and doing that are two different things, so let's consider some strategies to help maintain active awareness.

Put Away Your Phone

The easiest way to prevent self-destruction is to step away from the primary device that causes it. While we all like to think we're first-class multi-taskers, the human brain isn't wired that way. Until you have an Intel Quad Core logo inked on your forehead, your brain will do one thing at a time. Sure, you can switch back and forth quickly, but not nearly so rapidly as you might believe.

Let me prove it to you. With my phone in my pocket and using average speed, it takes me about seven seconds to retrieve it, unlock it with my fingerprint or face identification, and check a new message. That's the time to check just one text, social media post, or short email—the minimum time required to respond to one "ding" from your mobile device. I'll bet you a ribeye steak (medium-rare, please) that on very, very few occasions do we check "just one thing" when the phone comes out. So, in reality, seven seconds is an exceedingly optimistic best-case scenario.

What can happen in just seven seconds? Many life-changing events can occur just that fast.

Someone intent on attacking you can cover over 20 yards. We're not talking about Usain Bolt's speeds either—those figures assume a rate of just seven miles per hour. Sprinters move at over 20mph.

A car moving 70 miles per hour can travel 700 feet—a good bit over two football fields or a very long par three hole on a golf course.

If you happen to be standing in line at a fast-food joint or waiting to pay at a convenience store, someone who's not even in the building can open the door, get inside, and commence robbing the place.

Those are just a few examples of things that can go down during a quick peek at just one item on your phone. Now, imagine what can happen when you start typing a response or reading other incoming messages. Better yet, rather than guessing, look around the next time you're out and see how long the average person is looking down at their phone before they raise their head to see where they are. Seriously, time a few, and you'll probably be shocked at how much time elapses. While you're at it, imagine you are a criminal looking for victims. Would you choose someone from the "nose in the phone" committee as an ideal victim candidate?

Notice People

No matter where we live or what language we speak, we human beings share some common biological traits. When we're stressed or fueled with adrenaline, we exhibit certain behaviors. When we're worried about getting caught doing something against the will of others, we tend to become furtive. We'll come back to these visual cues later, but for now, know that in many cases, there are hints and clues to be had if we only know what to look for—and if we are paying attention.

Noticing everyone we encounter in our daily travels may sound like a herculean task, but it's not. Here's why. In today's day and age, with smartphones and music players, most people go about their daily activities blissfully unaware of almost everything going on around them. Many in the concealed carry community believe only two groups of people are aware of their surroundings: the switched-on good guys and the bad guys. And when I say good guys, I'm referring to those of us who have consciously decided to assume responsibility for protecting ourselves and our loved ones.

Half of the battle is committing to take note of the people who intersect with our lives. The other half is knowing what to look for.

Ignore People

So we just talked about the importance of noticing people, but now we're going to discuss ignoring them? Yes.

This tip may sound counter-intuitive, but it makes sense when you think about it. What's the natural response when you try to focus on being observant? It's to suck in every detail of all the people and things within a 12-mile radius like a giant Hoover vacuum, all while trying to commit every detail to memory. Unless you're a modern-day Stephen Hawking, that won't work. It's just too much information to process, and you'll be reduced to writing REDRUM on Motel 6 mirrors in short order. *To be situationally aware without causing a brain meltdown, observing, evaluating, and discarding quickly and efficiently is essential.*

Consider this example. While walking down the street, not having your nose buried in your phone, you notice a young mother pushing a two-seater stroller with a couple of toddlers. Should you take in every detail of the family's wardrobe and the stroller's year, model, and make? Just in case? I suppose it's possible this mom is a stealth terrorist highly trained in the art of progeny disguise, but the odds are in your favor if you choose to discard this group as a non-threat and move on to processing the next person you encounter. Be sure to smile and wave at the kids—we're not here to become paranoid freaks and frighten people.

That's what "ignoring people" is all about. Using observation skills and some behavioral rules, quickly discard those operating in the "norm" from your active radar so you can focus on those who aren't.

Read the Signs

No, I'm not being clever in telling you to discern others' intentions from non-verbal signals. *I'm suggesting that you literally read the signs.* And the ads. And the store names. And the bumper stickers. And everything else that passes you by.

I'm not a natural Sherlock Holmes or super spy from an action novel. I usually can't tell you if the person I just met had nicotine-stained hands or a shoelace missing. I have to work hard at observing the details in my surroundings. One of the best ways I've found to stay switched on and notice things is to keep my eyes busy. Think about it. Whether outside or in a restaurant or store, there's an infinite amount of reading material. I'm not suggesting you try to assimilate it or memorize the content. I'm just suggesting that it may help you keep alert if you're like me. If your eyes are at work with purpose, so is your brain. Besides, by noticing you're on the 300 block of Kickapoo Drive, you can give the folks at 911 a good location or tell your friends exactly where that great new restaurant is located.

There's a secondary benefit to actively engaging your eyes. Crooks intent on doing some form of no-no are less likely to choose you as a participant in the *Let's Make a Robbery* game. If you were going to mug someone, wouldn't you prefer a victim who was obviously zoned out?

If that's not enough reason to read the signs, know that you'll be shocked at how many new things you notice that you've bypassed a thousand times. Whether it's something new in the grocery store or a new window display, it's nice to find new things, right?

Count the Doors

At the risk of repeating a pithy self-defense aphorism, pay attention to the exits wherever you go.

If you're in a public facility of any kind, the fire codes are your friend because they force architects and builders to design and build many different ways to exit a building quickly. The purpose is to get everyone out efficiently in the event of a fire. However, these exits are just as useful for escape during other emergencies, like violent encounters.

If you're like me, you might hear the "identify all the exits whenever you enter a building" adage, but perhaps, like me, you often fail to do that. As I do with reading signs, I force my brain into gear to find the exits. Rather than relying on a good habit of identifying the exits, *try counting how many ways you can exit a room or building when you go in*. It's a little self-motivation trick that will help you quickly find all the doors. If you've counted it in your total, you know where it is.

Remember, doors aren't always the only way to exit a building. If push comes to shove, and you have no other reasonable option, the "chair through the window" approach may work. Save that one for last-ditch efforts, as many windows are storm-rated and may not break as easily as you'd expect, even using the "chair toss" method.

Shoe Shopping

Noting specific details is always more effective than issuing a general "pay attention" commend to your brain. Think of it this way. At the range, you can shoot at the target as a whole, or you can zero in on a specific bullseye and aim for that. Which yields better results?

When watching and evaluating people you encounter, one detail that's unusually distinctive is their shoes. If you ever have to provide a description later, shoes are a great focal point. They're often unique and easy to describe. If you're dealing with a sophisticated crook who changes shirt or jacket after their crime spree, shoes are hard to change while on the run.

Shoes can also be an indicator of the potential threat level. If you spot someone who doesn't look right, peek at the footwear. If they're wearing flip-flops, high heels or cowboy boots, they may not be anticipating running anytime soon. Perhaps that's a cue that they're not dressed for bad behavior. Or perhaps not. Cues are just that, not perfect leading indicators.

Last but not least, a deliberate look at a specific focal point (shoes or some other feature) helps keep your observation brain in gear and prevents zoning out from a sea of faces.

Pay Attention to Time

Smartphones are great at telling time, so who needs to wear a watch in this day and age? You do, and here's why.

Awareness of the current time and the passage of time is a critical component of an "awareness lifestyle." If you rely on your smartphone for time-keeping chores, you'll probably get distracted by another app or message and violate the "put away your phone" advice.

Wearing a watch allows you to monitor not only the current time (that might be handy to know if you're ever a witness to an event of any kind) but also allows you to mark the passage of time. Unless you're paying attention to time, it's far too easy to lose track of how much slips by before you know it. Has that guy been sitting in his car in front of the convenience store for ten minutes now? Didn't your significant other say they would be in the store or fast food joint for just a few minutes? That was 15 minutes ago. You get the idea. It's a good habit to be aware of time.

Oh, there's one more reason to wear a watch. Asking for the time is a favorite distraction tactic for some criminals. If you find yourself unable to brush off or ignore those types of requests from strangers, a watch allows you to answer without looking down to dig a cell phone out of your pocket. Of course, asking for the time is a common tactic of people trying to close distance with you, but that's a whole new topic.

Case Study: An 'Innocent' Distraction

 A 71-year-old man was working part-time in a Tennessee laundromat to pass the time and get out of the house. One evening, a 13 and 14-year-old in the laundromat near the change machine called the man requesting help. As the two distracted the worker, a third 14-year-old armed with a rifle approached the man from behind.

The man made a decision to fight back, unarmed, and struggled with the teens but was quickly knocked to the floor, where the teens repeatedly butt-stroked him with the rifle and kicked him in the head. Two of the teens broke into a video game to steal the money while the third continued the beating.

The man died several days later from his injuries, while the teens were later charged with murder.

Lessons

Those intent on committing violent crimes don't share the same value system as you and me. Using an "innocent" ruse and asking for help as a means of mounting a surprise attack is a common strategy. This is why it's so important to remain "switched on" even if circumstances seem relatively benign.

Find the Armed Citizen

You might have noticed several of the situational awareness hints involve looking for a specific attribute. Focused activity means a focused brain.

Across the United States, there are over 20 million legally armed citizens with concealed carry permits. That doesn't count those in states with constitutional carry provisions not requiring a state-issued license to carry a gun. That means, not counting criminals, somewhere over seven out of every 100 people you see may be carrying a defensive firearm. Of course, that's a national figure, so it includes those states where concealed carry is much less prevalent. Depending on where you live, the ratio is likely to be higher. For example, there are about 325,000 active carry permits here in South Carolina and an adult population of about 3.5 million. That means close to one out of ten people may be carrying legally.

Looking for others who are carrying a firearm is a great awareness exercise. As the numbers show, there are plenty of people to find just among the legal carry population. That doesn't count those who don't follow the law.

Why bother? Spotting law-abiding concealed carriers is a great way to stay in tune with your environment by keeping your eyes and brain engaged. It's also a great way to fine-tune your own concealed carry techniques. When you spot others making mistakes in their carry approach, you can learn what not to do and improve your carry tactics.

Spotting someone carrying a gun for less than legal reasons can yield a safety benefit. If nothing else, it might be a hint to raise your alertness level or even get the heck out of there.

Here are a few clues that someone is carrying a concealed firearm.

Unusual Touching and Checking

When carrying an object of significance, they tend to touch and verify its presence and security frequently. You might notice the individual touching an area around the beltline, either on the side, front or back. This behavior is instinctive to make sure the gun is still in place.

Also, observe how people rise to a standing position from a car seat or chair. If they're carrying on the waist, they likely have developed a habit of holding the shirttail down as they stand to prevent showing their handgun.

Protective Arm or Hand Position

You might notice someone holding their hand or arm close to their side. In particular, the elbow will be close to the grip of a gun carried on the waistline, so look for someone "anchoring" their elbow to their side. Often, this is a way to "hide" the shape of a firearm and provide security to prevent dropping or losing their handgun.

This behavior is pronounced when someone is walking. Humans usually tend to let their arms swing at least a little. If someone has one arm drawn in closer to the body while the other moves naturally, perhaps they have an injury. Or maybe they're shielding a hidden firearm. This type of positioning also happens during windy conditions if someone is wearing a handgun covered with a sports coat or jacket.

The good news for you as a spotter is that these actions tend to happen subconsciously. Unless someone is very experienced and accustomed to carrying a gun, they'll likely exhibit these types of behaviors without even knowing.

Odd-Shaped Bulges

Whether from an inside-the-waistband holster or carrying a gun tucked into the belt, there will be a telltale bulge in the covering clothing. It may be subtle, but even compact handguns add one to two inches to the beltline.

Many people carry a subcompact pistol in their pants pockets. While good pocket holsters help break up the visible profile of the gun, you may still notice an unnaturally large pocket bulge. Even a small handgun presents a larger profile than a wallet or smartphone, especially if it's holstered.

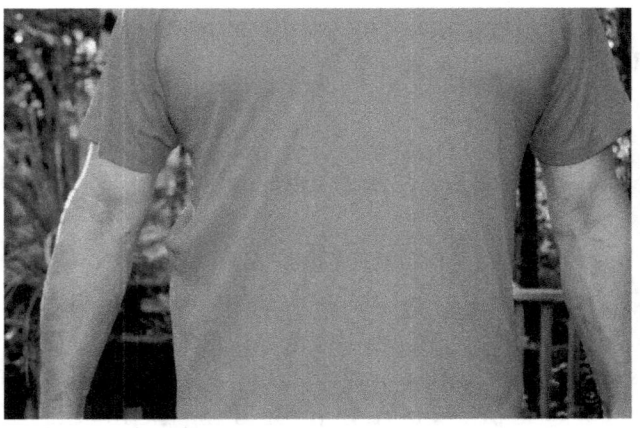

This is a less-than-ideal shirt for concealed carry as it is too clingy. However, it does illustrate how a covered gun and holster can create a visible bulge in your clothing.

Leaning Forward

If someone is carrying a concealed handgun in a belt holster on the side of their body, you may be able to observe the grip "printing" when they lean forward. Typically, people bend at the waist out of habit when drinking out of fountains, picking something up, or looking more closely at something on a store shelf. If they bend at the waist, the grip of a belt-carried handgun will "point" out the back and create a visible tent in shirt or jacket fabric.

Belt Clips

Some inside-the-waistband holsters are "tuckable." The holster and handgun ride inside the pants or skirt. The unique belt clip design allows the wearer to tuck in the shirt or blouse over the firearm's grip and between the holster body and pants or skirt. Once the cover garment is tucked correctly, only support clips on the belt's exterior are visible.

Most people wouldn't spot these or know their significance. As a concealed carrier, you'll see them immediately. Of course, you'll also be able to confirm your suspicion by observing the shape of the pants or skirt fabric underneath.

Unusual Gait

A loaded handgun can easily weigh a couple of pounds and influence one's natural walking motion when carried on one side. Also, people tend to walk more carefully and favor the "gun side" when carrying in a subconscious effort to make sure the gun stays in place. A trained eye can detect a minor anomaly like this, but it takes practice.

The Heavy Purse

Purses can be extra-heavy for many reasons, but a firearm packs on a couple of pounds. That might be a clue if you see someone constantly switching sides on which they carry a purse.

If you have sharp eyes, you can also look for separate external compartments accessible with a snap or zipper. That just might be the gun storage area on a concealed carry purse.

Pants Leg Flashing

Ankle holsters are perhaps the most common carry option for backup guns. It's also a viable carry method for those who spend much of their day seated or driving. Although fast access in an emergency isn't one of the benefits, ease of concealment and convenience are.

If someone is wearing an ankle holster, they have an extra pound or so strapped onto one leg, so you might notice a slightly off-kilter gait. You also might spot a more obvious bulge or irregularity in how the pants fabric drapes on the lower leg. If the person is sitting down, there's a great chance you may be able to spot at least the bottom of the ankle holster, as pants legs tend to ride up when you sit. Most ankle holsters are black and designed to match dress socks.

The Phake Photographer

If you've watched enough National Geographic specials, you've seen photographers wearing tan vests outfitted with a billion and a half pockets for various types of gear.

Since these vests are handy for carrying all manner of stuff and are made of thicker material, they're also effective as a cover garment for concealed carry. Many armed citizens use them even though they violate all rules of common fashion decency. So, if you spot someone wearing one of these at the mall, and they don't have a camera or press badge, there's a good chance it's an armed citizen. I feel confident most gang bangers aren't using these to hide their firearms.

Lopsided Jacket or Sweatshirt

A jacket or sweatshirt pocket is a great place to carry a gun, like a small revolver. It's easy and convenient to conceal, and you can even place your hand on the grip if you sense potential danger.

However, even a compact handgun weighs a pound, give or take, so it will cause one side of the jacket to droop noticeably. A smart concealed carrier will put other things in the opposite pocket to even out the weight, but a crook may not be so forward-thinking.

Inappropriate Fanny Packing

There are some places where you expect to see lots of fanny packs, even though we should all be able to agree they should be banned. For example, theme parks and tourist attractions are perfectly normal places to see many fanny packs. In warm weather, people don't have the luxury of fall and winter clothing pockets and tend to use gear like this to store spend-the-day-as-a-tourist supplies.

If you see fanny packs in other less natural places, such as the mall, the movie theater, or a restaurant, it may be a clue, especially if the wearer doesn't fit the tourist fanny packer profile.

Spotting Suspicous People

Yeah, I know. In a previous section, we told you to ignore people, but now I'm talking about the remaining ones you chose not to ignore. Perhaps they don't quite fit the pattern of the current environment. Or maybe they're looking at you funny, acting suspiciously, or wearing a University of Shawshank football jersey. Whatever the cause for keeping them on your watch list, it helps to look for specific cues.

Before we go into practical tips that can help you spot pending bad behavior, we're going to point you to another book. The topic of human behavior can fill sets of encyclopedias, hence the referral to a more in-depth resource. Developed to help active military units spot impending trouble, the *Left of Bang* course delves into the science of making snap decisions with good outcomes. Fortunately, the course material is documented in a book of the same name. While the text is chock full of valuable takeaways, a big one is this. Learn what to look for, then apply your situational awareness tools to spot those cues.

Human behavioral cue observation is a big topic, so get the book. It's a great read. For now, consider these types of behavioral cues.

Intuition

The word masters at Webster define intuition as "direct perception of truth, fact, etc., independent of any reasoning process." The formal definition goes on to include "keen and quick insight." I'm not going to argue with the folks who write dictionaries, but the technical definition doesn't include factors influencing what drives the keen and quick insight of intuition.

The answers we get from intuition are partly based on our previous experiences and things we've learned in the past. For example, we all understand that if we hear a noise in an abandoned and dark building, we know better than to walk backward into the scary room without first calling for help. This isn't intuition; it's knowledge based on years of experience and learning from watching bad horror movies. Yes, when we looked and saw nothing but dark shadows while hearing creepy music, we just knew Michael Myers was hiding in there. It seems like the magic of intuition, but it's a snap judgment based on experience.

But seriously, far too many people who are witnesses to or victims of an attack relay afterward that they "knew something was off." Even without having had the benefit (if you want to call it that) of numerous past violent crime encounters, their intuition told them something was not right. Still, since they had no past experience of the results of such a feeling, their brain didn't signal an "intuitive" command to run or fight. The moral of the story is simple. If something doesn't feel right, it's probably not a random and meaningless sensation. Your brain has associated visual, audio, and other current sensory inputs with something you've experienced or learned in the past. Don't ignore it.

Behavioral Anomalies

You also might pay attention to behavioral anomalies. Someone wound up to commit a crime may show signs of stress like rapid blinking, foot tapping, increased swallowing rate, or even head bobbing. On the other hand, someone about to attack might blink very little as they focus on their target. In either case, the blinking may be outside of normal bounds on either side of the "normal" spectrum. The key observation is that the behavior is outside the usual scope of your expectations for that situation. In a calm and relaxed environment, someone's burning of nervous energy is worth a second look.

While serving as a safety volunteer at my church, I was recently called to investigate a single male who managed to bring a backpack into the worship service. We usually discourage that, but this particular gentleman made it through. Anyway, as I approached, I noticed he was burning a lot of nervous energy. His head was bobbing back and forth rapidly, moving only an inch forward and back. He was tapping his feet and fidgeting in his chair. The combination of a lone man, backpack, and nervous behavior certainly was cause for suspicion in this environment. To be sure, I decided to watch him discreetly from behind his seat. Unaware of my presence, the man proceeded to listen to the pastor's message. The longer the message went on, the more the man calmed down. During this time, I did not observe him looking around the room. Even initially, he was focused on what was happening on stage. To make a long story short, this was simply a case of someone having a tough time, and he needed to be there.

This story illustrates the importance of considering the collection of behavioral signals. While some of his actions were suspicious, others weren't. His lack of interest in the people immediately surrounding him was a clue that maybe he wasn't preparing to initiate violence. His attire was appropriate for the situation. He wasn't sweating, nor were his hands active. I also paid attention to his breathing pattern. He wasn't breathing rapidly, nor did he appear to be actively trying to control his adrenaline by slowing down his breathing. After a few minutes, my intuition told me he was likely OK.

And there is the gotcha. It was intuition and a "best guess" based on all the available clues that allowed me to relax. Is that ever a sure thing? No. Can you be positive someone is about to do something bad based on behavioral cues? No. It's an inexact science.

Autonomic and Subconscious Behaviors

Our bodies do some things automatically, whether we like it or not. For example, the face may suddenly flush during an adrenaline dump. Under extreme stress, humans begin to sweat and breathe rapidly. Body responses like these are physiological and largely unavoidable under certain conditions.

It's essential to keep observed physiological responses in perspective. Witnessed on their own, they may or may not indicate suspicious or even aggressive behavior. Let's consider some examples.

If someone suddenly becomes flushed, they may be in the middle of a pre-attack adrenaline dump. Or they may be having a medical incident. Or they may be embarrassed.

Sweating? There are many possible reasons for that, even in moderate temperature conditions and when there is no vigorous physical activity. The person might be nervous because they're about to do something stressful, or maybe they're just nervous in front of strangers. Social anxiety is a common stressor for many.

The same things apply to an increase in breathing rate. While that could indicate a pending aggressive action, it may also be nerves, anxiety, or a medical incident in progress.

On a related note, you might take note of someone who is taking long, slow, and deliberate breaths. They might be trying to "calm themselves down" before executing some plan of attack or action. The human body naturally exhibits stress in that situation, and many will perform various "calming" actions to keep level until they strike.

Other "calming" actions that might indicate that someone is trying to lower their stress over a pending action include behaviors like face touching, neck rubbing, hair adjustment, and similar actions. On the other hand, these tics may be completely benign.

Involuntary and subconscious body responses and actions can be a warning signal about impending danger. But they are often associated with other more benign causes or medical conditions. Don't consider these types of cues on their own. If you observe them in combination with other suspicious behavior, that's a different story.

And there is the key. *Consider the entire collection of observable inputs before making a judgment.*

Looking Around—Too Much

Most people go through life not paying attention to their surroundings. Yes, that's unfortunate, but it's a fact. On the positive side, the tendency of most people to disengage from their surroundings provides an opportunity to spot abnormal and potentially suspicious behavior.

Suppose you see someone constantly scanning surroundings, especially looking behind themselves. In that case, that might be a cue they're trying to make sure the area is clear of threats before performing some illicit action. Think of it this way. If you were going to steal a Shake Weight from the local big box store, you'd most likely look for nearby people, cameras, or security officers who might spot or catch you in the act, right?

On a related topic, you might notice someone is noticing you. Someone watching you is not unusual on its own; we all tend to engage in some harmless people-watching from time to time. If that person looks away when you spot them doing it, there are two possibilities. Maybe they're embarrassed that you caught them staring, or perhaps they're trying to avoid alerting you to their plans to mug you. The first step in a crime is to scope out the victim. If they're spotted, they may immediately glance away. Often, people tend to look away immediately before an attack.

Hands Up!

Police and other professionals who regularly deal with potentially violent encounters are trained to watch the hands. Societal manners program us to look people in the eye when we meet or talk to them. While the eyes can undoubtedly provide cues such as behavioral anomalies, eyeballs cannot draw a weapon or sucker punch you in the gut. As we all know, hands are required for those types of actions.

If you have any reason to suspect pending foul play based on your intuition or observable behavioral cues, watch the position of the hands. When standing around or walking, most of us allow our hands to hang naturally because it requires extra energy to keep them supported up higher relative to our body. If your observation subject has their hands held up higher, perhaps they're getting ready to use them.

Also, look for hand motion. If you watch sports, whether action-shooting events, baseball, or most any other, you'll notice athletes who are preparing for a play or action will move and flex their hands. A great example is watching someone draw from a holster in a timed shooting competition. Before the start buzzer goes off, you will likely see their fingers flexing and getting ready for action. The same may apply to a mugger preparing to draw a weapon or attack you physically.

You also might take note of the location of high-hand movement. If a person is gesticulating wildly and their hands and arms are "outside" the boundaries of their body, expressive communication or venting frustration might be all there is to it. If those movements are closer to the body, the movement may be preceding an attack.

The lack of visible hands can be a cue but practically speaking, only in the presence of other indicators. Many of us naturally keep one or both hands in pants or jacket pockets. Whether it's for comfort, supporting the weight of our arms or warding off cold, this is not an unusual activity on its own. Combined with other indicators, you might look for a concealed hand carrying a weapon.

Strange Multitasking

When someone gets busted for texting in a business meeting, the natural response is to say something like, "It's cool. I'm naturally good at multitasking..."

Well, in reality, and according to science, not so much. While people can do multiple tasks simultaneously, multitasking is more a function of purposely switching back and forth between activities.

When engaged deeply in one thing, the brain tends to tune out other inputs. A typical human trait is our relatively poor ability to truly multitask. While we may claim to do it well, we're hard-wired the opposite way. Computer science engineers call the concept "time-slicing," meaning we allocate a slice of time to one task and then switch to another.

If you're keeping an eye on someone who happens to be engaged in some innocuous activity solely for disguise, they're not going to be able to do whatever it is they're doing naturally. For example, if someone is pretending to read their phone or a newspaper but is there to scope out a robbery, their "reading" won't look smooth or regular. You may notice that person flicking their eyes to and away from their phone or paper.

The easiest way to spot the difference between manufactured or "fake" activity and genuine activity is to watch someone doing the real thing. When we're reading something on our phones, we're absorbed in the process. How often have you called out to someone engaged in reading or watching a video, and they don't even hear you, or if they perceive the call, they'll ask you to repeat what you said?

The takeaway is to make a note of a lack of focus.

Just a Quick Question...

Most people are wired to be friendly and have a natural aversion to being rude to strangers. That's a good thing, as it makes for a more polite and enjoyable daily experience for all of us. How often do you see a stranger hold a door open, help pick up dropped items, or offer minor assistance somehow? Hopefully, a lot.

Unfortunately, criminals often seize on this good side of human behavior as an opportunity to distract. A favorite tactic of someone trying to get close enough to you to inflict robbery or harm before your alarm bells start going off is to ask a simple question.

Do you happen to have the time?
Hey, do you have a light?

Do you know where 4 Privet Drive is?

Can you spare a dollar for _____?

You get the idea. On their own, these aren't threatening questions that would raise suspicion. However, questions like these offer two benefits to a criminal. First, it allows them to close distance from you without being overtly threatening. You're just talking, right? Second, most of these are intended to distract you, either mentally or physically. Most people carry a phone and don't wear a watch, so giving someone the time requires looking down to retrieve a smartphone. At the very least, it requires you to look away from the potential question-asking mugger to check. The combination of getting close and creating a second or two of distraction is all it takes for an experienced thug to impose their will.

So, what to do? Although an impolite one, the safest answer is to step aside with a firm verbal "no" or to issue a stern command to step away. This is hard for most people to do because most encounters like this won't involve bad intentions. It's also hard for most people to be overtly rude and uncooperative. Depending on how you're wired, you might consider other strategies that are less blunt. Casually step backward or to the side without breaking eye contact while you offer a polite "sorry, I can't help you" comment. If it's a simple request for the time, perhaps raise your watch hand to eye level so you don't have to break eye contact.

The important thing is to think about how you want to handle situations like this in advance. You may also add parameters to your planned response. If you're in a familiar environment like your church, office, or school, and someone asks for the time, you're probably safe just giving it to them rather than shouting for them to back off. If you're on a dark street and two shadowy figures ask the same question, it's a different story altogether.

Group Behavior

Like hyenas, criminals frequently act in groups. While one or more may be the designated "action guys," others might be responsible for keeping an eye out, driving a getaway vehicle, or serving as a backup if things go wrong. Someone nearby may be a "mentor" observing how the prospective member handles himself in a gang situation.

Suppose you enter a convenience store, and your intuition (trust it!) tells you the guy hovering in the fountain drink section is acting skittish. Your brain will want to focus on him as a potential threat, but how do you know his business partner isn't in another area of the store serving as a lookout or backup for a forthcoming robbery?

Or maybe you're walking down a street and notice someone talking on their cell phone. That's no big deal, right? What if this particular person follows you with their eyes while speaking in hushed tones? Is it possible they're giving their partners around the next corner a heads-up that you're on the way, and no other witnesses are in the immediate vicinity?

Maybe you're about to enter a store and see a running car near the front entrance. That's not necessarily unusual unless the driver acts furtively, perhaps looking around in all directions and tapping the steering wheel to burn off nervous energy. Maybe he's waiting for his partner to finish the stickup and get out of the store.

Once, while stopping at a highway Cracker Barrel location, I noticed a running car at the front door, a driver in the car, and someone wearing a Jason / Friday the 13th hockey mask in the passenger seat. If that didn't look like a robbery in progress or about to go down, I don't know what does. Needless to say, we stopped in our tracks and started to back up toward our car. Just then, a third person walked out the front door, casually carrying a delivery order and entering the back seat of the car. That sure seemed suspicious at first, but sometimes people are just weird. I guess one learning from that incident is not to drive around town wearing a Jason mask in your car—you'll freak people out.

You get the idea. As hard and unnatural as it is, it's important to remember that criminals don't necessarily act alone. Staying observant of cues like this might help alert you—in advance—to a situation you can avoid. Conversely, if you find yourself facing a violent encounter, your life might depend on your ability to break your concentration away from the primary threat to check for others.

Case Study: Anger Management

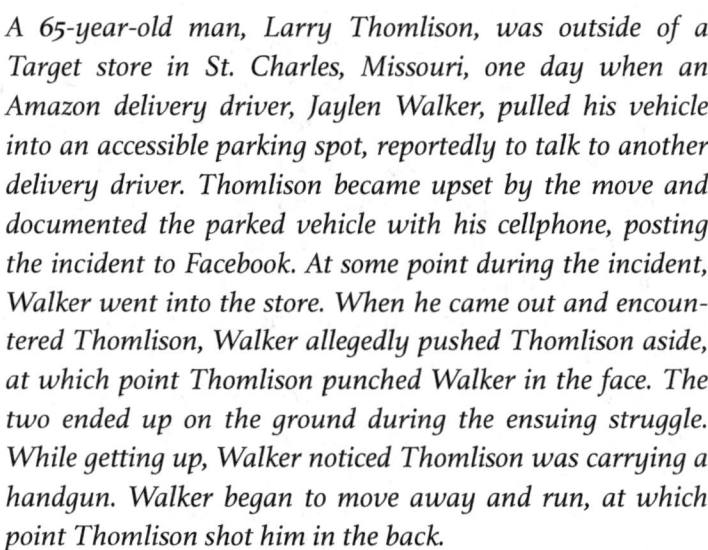

A 65-year-old man, Larry Thomlison, was outside of a Target store in St. Charles, Missouri, one day when an Amazon delivery driver, Jaylen Walker, pulled his vehicle into an accessible parking spot, reportedly to talk to another delivery driver. Thomlison became upset by the move and documented the parked vehicle with his cellphone, posting the incident to Facebook. At some point during the incident, Walker went into the store. When he came out and encountered Thomlison, Walker allegedly pushed Thomlison aside, at which point Thomlison punched Walker in the face. The two ended up on the ground during the ensuing struggle. While getting up, Walker noticed Thomlison was carrying a handgun. Walker began to move away and run, at which point Thomlison shot him in the back.

Thomlison was arrested and charged with first-degree assault and armed criminal action, for which he faces 10 to 30 years in prison. Walker sustained spinal cord injuries and may be paralyzed for life.

Lessons

This is an example of a violent encounter that should never have happened. While details are still sketchy, it certainly appears that Thomlison had every opportunity to avoid a physical confrontation. Arguments can far too easily escalate to pushes and shoves, which can quickly spin out of control. Early reports indicate Walker was shot in the back while trying to escape the situation. If that turns out to be accurate, Thomlison is unlikely to be able to claim he acted in self-defense. The opposite may turn out to be the case. He may be found guilty of instigating the entire situation when the case comes to trial.

If you choose to carry a concealed weapon for self-protection, remember that's what it's for—self-defense. An armed citizen does not assume enforcer duties—that's a law enforcement job. If the parking upset Thomlison that much (he did have a handicapped parking permit himself), all he had to do was report the incident to the proper authorities. As a result of losing his temper, he may spend the rest of his life in prison, and the victim may be confined to a wheelchair with a permanent disability. All over a parking spot dispute. A. Parking. Spot.

A Polite Lifestyle

While you can't control everything, you can control many things. If a mugger has selected you as the supplier of his next opioid fix, you may be able to discourage a confrontation using avoidance and mannerism skills. The more alert and "switched on" you appear, the less likely you are to become the target—an obviously easy victim is always preferable. While you can do things to decrease the odds of becoming the next assault victim, you have more control over situations with escalation potential.

Here's the bottom line. If you decide to carry a gun for self-protection, your responsibility is to become the most polite and forgiving person in any environment. As a responsibly armed citizen, you won't take the slightest risk of escalating a verbal or minor physical disagreement into something bigger. Let's consider some everyday examples.

Some jerk cut you off in traffic or flipped you a bird because you did something wrong or were driving too slow for their tastes? Great. Ignore it and go on about your business. Forget the hand gestures. You can even skip the smile and wave, which everyone knows to be a sarcastic, passive-aggressive reaction.

How about the slightly too-drunk guy who spills a beer on you or your spouse? Or maybe they're an angry drunk and just want to pick a fight, even a verbal one. Nope. Don't bite there, either. Clothes can be washed, and you can't win a debate with someone toting around 10 or 12 internal beers. If you're carrying (or even if you're not), that's an excellent opportunity to shrug your shoulders, wish that person a lovely evening, and be on your way.

We could go on all day with examples, but you get the idea. When you're unarmed, the worst consequence of a minor disagreement is that it escalates into a punch in the nose one way or the other. When carrying a lethal weapon, the consequences can be much, much worse. Is "winning" a bar fight or road rage incident worth a human life? Is it worth you dying over? Is it worth bankrupting your family and spending the remainder of your life in jail? Remember, if you're sitting in a jail cell, you're no longer serving or protecting your family, so it's not just about you.

Your job isn't to "win" a confrontation; it's to survive one. The best way to do that is to ensure that a conflict doesn't start in the first place. The second best way is to toss a cold blanket on those temper flames when they begin to smolder. The third best way is to... leave.

Exercising pride muscles rarely improves one's health and well-being.

3

SHOULD YOU CARRY A GUN?

W ill carrying a handgun make you safer? If you choose to carry a defensive firearm, you'll be safe, right? If something terrible happens, you can just retrieve your firearm and wave it around, only firing if you absolutely must, right? Nope.

Having a firearm might help you. Or it might not.

The presence of a gun doesn't guarantee anything, at least on its own. Consider the following hypothetical situation.

You're standing in line at the local McRonald's, deciding whether to order the Sugar Shake with Jimmies or a diet alfalfa juice. Suddenly, the customer in line behind you is waving a gun at the back of your head and the cashiers, demanding money, or everyone is going to die. You have a gun in your inside-the-waistband holster. Or maybe you're carrying a pistol in a purse holster. Whatever your gun choice and carry method, simply having theoretical access to a firearm isn't going to help you one whit in this situation because you're already way too far behind the power curve of the criminal encounter.

Even though this is a hypothetical example, it's a far more realistic scenario than what most of us envision as a defensive encounter. We could go on and on talking about real-life assaults and robberies, but you get the idea. In real life, criminals don't announce their presence from a comfortable distance while standing there waiting around to get shot.

One of the biggest traps to overcome is the false sense of security that comes with concealed carry. As newly-minted concealed carry permit holders, we tend to envision this foggy and not-very-detailed mental picture of how we would use a firearm in self-defense. The violent criminal would be standing there, far enough away to allow us some reaction time to draw a gun. And the bad guy would have the decency not to move around too much—making an easy target. While we may not develop the mental picture to that degree of detail, there's an underlying assumption that "if something bad happens, I'll simply rely on my gun to fix it." As with most things in life, the devil is in the details.

Simply carrying a defensive handgun may make you safer. It also might put you more at risk. Or carrying a gun may have no meaningful impact on the outcome of a defensive encounter. Having a fire extinguisher in the laundry room won't help you in the event of a gas line explosion. It won't even help you if that stir fry SPAM catches fire —unless you know how to use that extinguisher and react decisively.

Having a gun and investing in education, training, and ongoing practice is what can improve your odds of prevailing in a defensive encounter. And we're not just talking about gun handling skills. You can be the World Champion Action Pistol competitor, but that won't help you at all if you got caught by surprise in the McRonalds scenario we just described.

If you choose to assume responsibility for protecting yourself and your loved ones, buying a gun and learning how to shoot is only a tiny part of the overall strategy that can improve your odds in a dangerous world. For example, as an armed citizen, you'll always be more clued into your surrounding environment. Instead of answering texts on your phone while in line at the fast-food joint, maybe you noticed that the guy who came in the front door after you was furtively looking around, acting fidgety and sweating, even though it's a cool day. With your "threat radar" engaged, maybe you decided to step off to the side until you figured out what was going on. Or perhaps you turned around and left, choosing another brand of cheap lunch. Are you beginning to see how just "having a gun" may not be the dominant factor in your overall defense strategy?

What Do Guns Actually Do?

The question, "What do guns do?" is just a bit unfair because there are many gun types with widely varying performance characteristics. Rifles and shotguns are almost always far more powerful than handguns. Shotguns are powerful and effective for defensive purposes because they shoot larger and heavier projectiles or many projectiles at once. Rifles are generally more potent than handguns because they launch bullets at a much higher velocity than handguns. A projectile traveling at two or three times the speed of a handgun bullet can have very different effects on organic targets. As this book is about concealed carry, we'll focus on common handguns as we talk about what guns do. Fair enough?

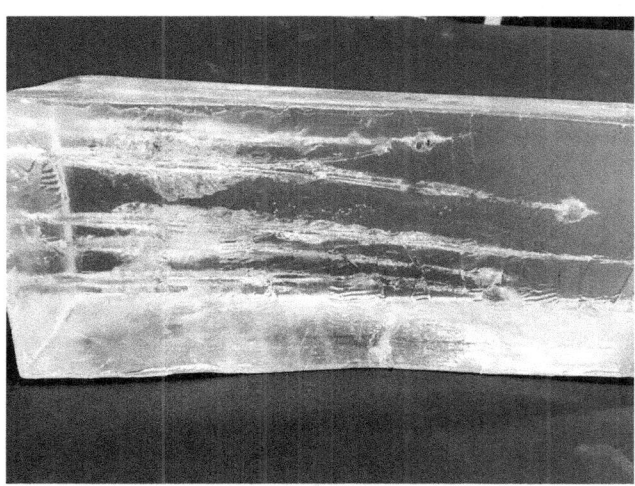

Five shots of .357 Sig pistol ammo penetrating a ballistic gelatin block. For scale, the side where they entered is only 6x6", so you can see the "holes" aren't as dramatic as one might expect.

With that said, guns aren't magic talismans. The only time they operate, like in the movies, is when they're resting in a holster doing nothing. Handguns only do one thing. Ready?

They make holes.

That's it. They don't send bad guys flying into walls or through windows. They don't instantly stop evildoers. They may or may not frighten someone into stopping whatever they are doing.

Next, let's look at precisely what firearms do and why. That will set the stage for defensive concepts you need to learn.

Guns and Physiological Factors

When considering the factors that might stop a determined attacker, it's essential to recognize there are an infinite number of variables at play.

Attackers have different physiological characteristics. Attacker "A" and attacker "B" might be siblings, but each might react to a gunshot wound in the same location in entirely different ways.

Mental toughness and the will to fight vary widely from person to person. One might give up from a moderate dose of fear alone, while another will fight to the death.

Drugs may be involved. Whether deadening pain or amping up the energy level, drugs may completely change one's resistance to armed defense.

The shot location alone can dramatically affect the outcome. An inch variance can mean the difference between the end of an encounter and no visible impact on the attacker, at least not immediately.

In short, predicting the impact of one or more shots against an attacker is impossible. There's no magic caliber that will end a fight. There are no gimmicks or tricks guaranteed to end a defensive encounter. The best thing you can do is recognize the inherent uncertainty and plan and train accordingly.

That said, a handgun can deliver "stopping" power for several reasons, acting independently or in concert.

Blood Pressure Loss

Since guns make holes, a gunshot wound stops an attacker by generating enough blood loss to reduce the body's ability to function. That blood loss can be internal or external. If the blood doesn't remain in the circulatory system, it doesn't transport oxygen, and things stop working.

When a person donates blood, they will generally give eight to ten percent of their total supply. A Class 1 hemorrhage represents up to 15 percent of the total blood volume and can result in feeling faint.

A Class 2 bleed represents losing 15 to 30 percent of total blood volume. The heart begins to beat more rapidly to get oxygen to the body and brain. The patient will feel weak and clammy but can still function.

A Class 3 hemorrhage is defined by losing 30 to 40 percent of one's blood supply. An even faster heartbeat is accompanied by blood pressure loss, and the body desperately tries to circulate what remains.

The worst, a Class 4 hemorrhage, causes over 40 percent blood loss and requires immediate medical care and transfusion. Not enough blood is available to keep organs alive or the patient conscious.

If your goal is to stop an attack—fast—relying on blood pressure loss doesn't sound all that promising. In the most severe scenario, where a major artery is damaged, a victim might start to lose consciousness in 20 to 40 seconds. A human can continue to fight or attack for much longer in many other situations.

Structural Damage

The human body has structural supports, like a building. If these supports are damaged or broken, our ability to move can be severely compromised.

If a leg is damaged, it inhibits walking or running. If an arm is damaged, it is still theoretically mobile. However, if the pelvis is damaged, it's a much bigger deal, as the body can't remain upright without critical foundational support.

While structural damage is debilitating and can prevent movement, in theory allowing you to escape, it doesn't necessarily prevent an attacker armed with a gun from continuing to shoot.

Electrical Damage

It's no secret the brain controls everything a body does, both voluntary and involuntary. Whatever the cause, there are two ways that the body's "electrical system" can be disabled.

Not the interior outline extending from the face and down into the torso. That's the primary neurological zone, which presents a very small target.

If the brain itself is damaged, then it's possible, and even likely, it won't be able to perform essential functions like accepting sensory input, processing it, and issuing physical instructions. Since the brain gets input and issues instructions through the body's neural highways, damage to those can disrupt the travel of brain signals to various parts of the body. So, from a self-defense perspective, one might disable an attacker in either of those ways.

While blood pressure loss takes time, and physical damage may not ultimately end the fighting ability of an attacker, electrical damage tends to be more instantaneous. It's also the most difficult to target, as instant capacitation requires a direct hit to the brain or upper areas of the spinal cord.

Fear and Loss of Will to Fight

One reason some attackers cease aggression after a single gunshot (or, in some cases, just seeing a gun) is fear.

No rational person wants to get shot. Unlike the movies, where the hero or bandit wraps a bandana around the wound, grits their teeth, and keeps on going about their business, real gunshot wounds are massively disruptive, resulting in severe tissue damage, broken bones, and organ destruction.

While it's hard to think of violent criminals as rational, some are certainly less committed to the cause than others and might just give up the fight by going down before the point where physical damage causes a cessation of hostilities. Whether a conscious or subconscious decision, the criminal who keeps fighting after being shot five or ten times may just have a much stronger will to fight than one who succumbs after a single hit.

When you hear "my huge caliber is best" anecdotal stories about how a single shot ended a deadly conflict or about how someone else stopped their attack after being shot once with a relatively small and weak .22 LR, remember the fear factor. It explains much of the wide variance in perceived handgun effectiveness or lack thereof.

The Net-Net

While there are many ways a gun can help end an attack, no

certainties will apply in your defensive encounter. If you're exception-ally fortunate, the sight of armed resistance may encourage your attacker to choose a different victim. Unfortunately, you can't count on that, nor can you rely on a "laser dot on their chest" or a warning shot (a terrible idea we'll discuss later) to end a violent attack. You also can't count on a single hit on your attacker to end the fight, so it's essential to train your mind and body to keep fighting until the attack ends and you are no longer in mortal danger.

Case Study: What Stops an Attacker?

Jacksonville, Florida, police officer Peter Soulis learned first-hand that "one-shot stops" can be a myth. After approaching a suspicious vehicle in a gas station parking lot, Joseph Kevin McGrotha opened fire on Soulis with a 9mm handgun.

During the protracted one-on-one gunfight where the suspect and officer maneuvered around both cars, Officer Soulis was hit five times. McGrotha was hit 22 times with premium defensive rounds from Soulis' department issue .40 S&W pistol. Even after absorbing 17 center-mass gunshot wounds throughout the ordeal, the suspect, later found to be wanted for murder in another state, continued to fight and survived for four minutes after the last shot was fired.

Lessons

Shooting an attacker with a handgun might stop them. Or it might not. Stay in the fight until the aggression stops. Then, it's up to you to stop your response immediately.

'Knockdown' or 'Stopping' Power

Physics always wins.

The last time we checked, the world was still ruled by the laws of physics. Objects will fall to the ground unless supported. Not even juicy gossip can travel faster than the speed of light. And every action has an equal and opposite reaction. That last one is important for our discussion on the potential effects of handguns on an attacker.

To steal a Hollywood example, consider the movie *Men in Black*. In one scene, the grizzled veteran alien enforcer "K" (Tommy Lee Jones) gives his rookie trainee "J" (Will Smith) a space-age pea shooter that's about the size of a container of Tic-Tacs. After the obligatory "Are you serious?" look, J fires it at an alien villain and is promptly thrown about 30 feet backward into a truck from the recoil.

While probably unintended, the scene illustrates a true lesson in real-world physics. If a gun, real or alien, has enough power to knock the target (of similar mass as the shooter) down, the shooter will also get knocked on their butt. Every action has an equal and opposite reaction.

If someone tells you about the knockdown power of a given cartridge, immediately run to the nearest library and ask to borrow a copy of *Physics For Dummies*. In it, you might find mention of a guy named Isaac Newton.

While his brother Wayne was busy developing a fine singing career in Las Vegas, Isaac focused on important issues related to object motion. Among his other accomplishments, he developed the "equal and opposite reaction" theory. If you want to know his exact wording, translated into English, it's this.

> "To every action, there is always opposed an equal reaction: or the mutual actions of two bodies upon each other are always equal, and directed to contrary parts."

This means that if an action (force) is going one way, an equal amount of action (force) is coming back the other way. If that bullet you fired has enough force (more on that in a second) to knock someone down, then there's enough force coming back in the opposite direction to knock the shooter down—just like Agent J in *Men in Black*.

So, if you rely on TV and movies to understand what guns do, you're in for some major disappointment. Contrary to what we see on the screen, guns don't cause bad guys to get knocked off their feet or fly through plate glass windows. In the movies, guns have "knockdown" power—literally. In real life, things don't quite work that way. In real life, guns make holes.

That's it. There's no magic or mystical force. Are there cases where dramatic results occur? Yes, but for different reasons than you might think. Before we get into a real-life "stopping power" discussion, let's finish this topic with a quick look at what types of energy guns do have.

Kinetic Energy

We're going to take this short diversion because you'll see these figures on ammunition boxes, and you'll certainly hear lots of discussion about them on internet forums.

Kinetic energy is the most commonly used measure of ammunition's relative power level. You can think of kinetic energy as destructive power. To use a simple analogy, you might compare kinetic energy to the effects of a high-speed drill. There's lots of commotion when you stick a drill into a piece of lumber. Sawdust will fly, and it'll make a hole. One wouldn't want to grab a spinning drill bit because of its destructive power, right? However, introducing the spinning drill to a piece of wood won't send that board flying across the room.

As a reference, let's look at the relative kinetic energy measurement of different calibers of firearms. These numbers will vary with the specific type of ammo used and the gun from which it's fired, but you'll get the idea. The numbers below are reflected in the kinetic energy measurement of foot-pounds.

.22 rifle: 120
.32 ACP pistol: 165
.380 pistol: 180
9mm pistol: 350
.40 S&W pistol: 440
.45 ACP pistol: 370

Those numbers sound impressive, don't they? Remember that they don't represent the ability to knock things through walls. Consider PGA Tour pro Bubba Watson can drive a golf ball with 127 foot-pounds of energy, and you'll get the idea. Or, if you're more into baseball, the fastest Nolan Ryan pitch on record generated 128 foot-pounds of kinetic energy—a little more than a .22 rifle shot.

Momentum

Kinetic energy represents destructive power, and momentum represents the ability to move objects. An object with lots of momentum can move or knock other objects down.

The kinetic energy numbers get big and look impressive because they put lots of mathematical weight on velocity. To determine foot-pounds of kinetic energy, you square the velocity measurement, hence the big numbers.

On the other hand, momentum emphasizes the mass of an object. Let's review our previous kinetic energy examples in terms of momentum. As a side note, momentum is measured in pounds-feet per second.

.22 rifle: 6.7
.32 ACP pistol: 10.5
.380 pistol: 12
9mm pistol: 20
.40 S&W pistol: 27
.45 ACP pistol: 28

To put those numbers in perspective, our Major League Baseball pitcher can crank out 52 pounds-feet per second of momentum while Bubba Watson drives a golf ball with 29. Does an errant baseball pitch knock the batter into the box seats? No. It hurts but it doesn't have the required momentum to do that. Handgun bullets can't do it either with less than half that level of momentum.

So the point here is that barring a million other factors, handgun bullets don't have enough energy to knock someone out of their shoes and through a plate-glass window.

Don't believe me? Next time you have an opportunity, take a 25-pound bag of sand to the range and prop it up on a stool. Heck, you can even stick something on the front so the bullet doesn't pass through, thereby delivering all its "oomph" to the sandbag. Guess what'll happen when you shoot it? Not much. It won't even tip over. Yes, we've tried it.

The Reality of Stopping Power

As an armed citizen, your goal in a defensive encounter is simple. *You want to stop your attacker from doing whatever they're doing as quickly as possible—so you can get to safety.* That's it.

The goal isn't to kill or shoot them "x" times. Ideally, it's to protect yourself by escaping a dangerous situation. A handgun can help you do that by leveling the odds against your attacker. If you weigh 105 pounds dripping wet and haven't yet earned even a macrame belt in martial arts, and your attacker tips the scales at 220 and is wearing a championship MMA ring, a firearm can help balance the scales. It does that by inflicting enough damage to make them stop their aggressive activity.

For this reason, I prefer to think in terms of "stopping power," recognizing, of course, that no handgun is guaranteed to stop anyone. As real-life post-shooting analysis shows, sometimes handguns are very effective at stopping an attack quickly. Other times, they're not. Some criminals stop their act at the sight of a defensive firearm.

Others have been shot 10, 20, and even more than 30 times before they stopped fighting.

With that said, it is safe to think in relative terms of potential stopping power. After all, we can probably agree a BB gun is much less likely to stop an aggressive attacker than a .45 pistol, right?

Caliber Myths

Is there a magic handgun caliber guaranteed to stop an attack immediately or with one shot?

No.

You'll hear lots of discussion to the contrary. When you do, be sure to separate anecdotes from data. Anecdotal stories about "that guy who went down after getting shot once with a .45" or "it took ten shots from a 9mm to make him stop attacking" mean little.

Earlier, we discussed the impossibility of predicting the effects of handguns on determined humans. Too many variables are at play to make meaningful predictions about what one caliber will do compared to another.

That said, there have been long-term studies on caliber effectiveness as measured by post-event analysis of real-world defensive and law enforcement encounters. Greg Ellifritz, a law enforcement officer and noted self-defense trainer, accumulated data from nearly 2,000 real-world shootings to see how different calibers fared on the street.

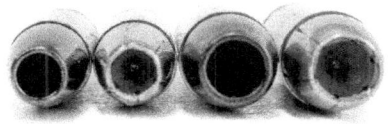

With all the hype about 9mm (the two on the left) vs. .45 ACP (the two on the right), you'd expect more difference in street performance results.

The findings were surprising. Ellifritz analyzed and recorded data on each shooting and captured data on the number of one-shot stops, the average number of rounds to incapacitate, the percentage of people that were not incapacitated at all, and other data points. Here are a few of the highlights.

One Shot Stops by Caliber
.22LR: 31%
.380 ACP: 44%
9mm: 34%
.38 Special: 39%
.40 S&W: 45%
.357 Magnum / .357 Sig: 44%
.45 ACP: 39%

Average Number of Shots to Incapacitate
.22LR: 1.38
.380 ACP: 1.76
9mm: 2.45
.38 Special: 1.87
.40 S&W: 2.36
.357 Magnum / .357 Sig: 1.7
.45 ACP: 2.08

Percentage of Failed Incapacitations
.22LR: 31%
.380 ACP: 16%
9mm: 13%
.38 Special: 17%
.40 S&W: 13%
.357 Magnum / .357 Sig: 9%
.45 ACP: 14%

You can find the complete study on the Buckeye Firearms

(buckeyefirearms.org) website, but the bottom line takeaways are here. First, don't put too much emphasis on the specific numbers in this report or any other. It's not intended to be a caliber selection guide. Instead, it's an illustration that shows how unpredictable the results of a defensive shooting can be. Also, there is no magic caliber that will work reliably. There's no horrible caliber that will be completely ineffective.

With that said, most will agree that the ability to put accurate put shots on target is the most critical factor. So, choose the largest caliber with which you can reliably do that.

Effects of Different Types of Guns

Different firearms have varying effects on organic targets like people and animals. If you're going to consider using a gun for personal protection, you don't need to become a ballistics expert. Still, you need to understand why some types of firearms create very different outcomes than others. Let's look broadly at the differences between rifles, shotguns, and handguns. Of course, there is a range of power and performance within each of these very broad categories, but the generalities will still apply.

Rifles

The most significant difference in ballistic performance between rifles and handguns comes from velocity.

While exceptions exist, most common centerfire (not .22 Long Rifle or similar calibers) rifles fire a projectile at speeds between 2,000 and 3,000 feet per second. Many factors, like barrel length and bullet weight, impact the muzzle velocity. Common calibers like .223 Remington or .308 Winchester operate in the range of 2,700 to 3,000 feet per second. "Bigger" caliber rifles don't necessarily shoot bullets faster than this; they just shoot heavier bullets at similar speeds.

Rifles like these will fore projectiles somewhere between 2,600 and 3,200 feet per second depending on caliber and specific ammunition type.

Here's why velocity is important for self-defense scenarios. At speeds over 2,000 feet per second, when a bullet enters an organic (living being) target, its pressure causes soft tissue to expand faster than the tissue can hold itself together. Gun gurus refer to this effect as hydrostatic shock, but we don't need to get into all that ballistic science to make the relevant point.

Imagine pressing your finger against a full water balloon slowly and steadily. As you press into the balloon's surface, the rubber and water inside move out of the way, and to a certain point, you can apply finger pressure without bursting the balloon. When you withdraw your finger, the balloon and water inside return to their original shape and position. No permanent harm has been done.

Now, imagine if you could accelerate your finger to 2,500 feet per second against the side of the balloon. The speed of the intruding pointer finger would be more than the rubber balloon wall could withstand, and the water couldn't move out of the way fast enough to prevent damage. The balloon would burst and, therefore, be permanently damaged.

While not a perfect illustration, this is what happens when a bullet hits a living target at high velocity. A slower handgun bullet makes a hole, and any tissue on the periphery might expand out of the path but return to its original shape and position. A rifle bullet will move faster than the body's tissue can handle, and therefore, the result will be more permanent damage.

You also might think of drilling into a bowl of Jello with a hand-operated drill spinning at 30 revolutions per minute. It'll make a hole and mess up your dessert, but not nearly so much as a 2,000 rpm power drill will do.

Many other factors are at play, but at a high level, this explains why a rifle is so much more effective on a living target than a handgun.

Shotguns

Shotguns differ from handguns and rifles for a couple of different reasons.

First, it's important to recognize that shotguns can fire a wide variety of ammo. Some shotgun loads contain hundreds of tiny pellets, each significantly smaller than a typical BB. Others have 8, 9, 12, or 15 larger "pellets," each approaching the size of a small marble. And other shotgun shells might fire a single, very large projectile called a slug.

Second, shotguns operate at velocities higher than many handguns but not nearly in the same speed range as rifles. The most common shotgun loads, whether small pellet, target pellet, or slug, come out of the barrel at speeds between 1,100 and 1,600 feet per second.

Generally speaking, shotguns' power and effectiveness come from either the size and weight of their projectiles or the use of multiple pellets per shot.

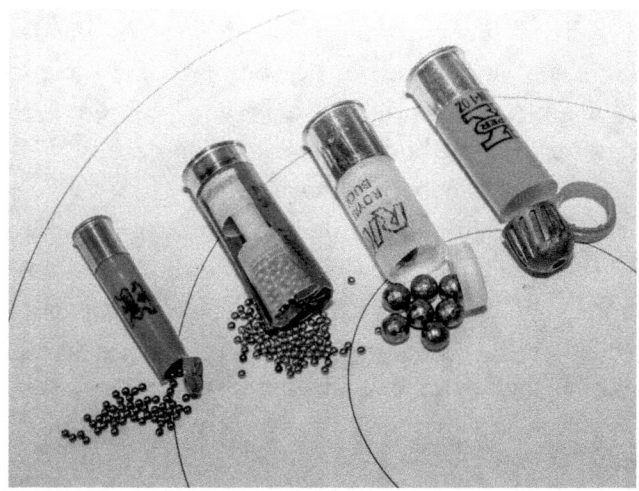

Shotguns can fire many types of projectiles depending on the cartridge design. On the right is an example of a single slug adjacent to a 00 buckshot load.

Handguns

Handguns make deliberate compromises for the sake of portability and convenience. The small form factor required for personal carry limits their ammunition's power and the projectiles' size and weight.

While a rifle can launch a bullet at velocities between 2,000 and 3,000 per second (and sometimes more), most handguns generally operate in the 850 to 1,300 feet per second velocity band. There is no hydrostatic shock effect at these lower speeds as with rifles. Hence, handgun bullets have to rely on different mechanisms to achieve the result of stopping a determined attacker.

We'll get into the details of ammunition types later in the book. For now, know that handguns make holes in their target. They don't offer "knockdown" power. They (generally) don't fire multiple projectiles with every shot, as does a shotgun. As destructive as they can be, handguns are at the bottom of the firearms effectiveness chart. As discussed earlier in this section, a handgun may or may not stop an aggressor quickly. That's why the training and techniques we'll discuss later in this book are so important.

4

SELF-DEFENSE LAW

W e will discuss some legal concepts related to concealed carry and self-defense. But remember, this is a Practical Guide, not a legal library. Also, we're not lawyers, nor do we play lawyers on TV. You should not rely on anything in this chapter as legal advice.

Knowing and understanding the law is your responsibility.

The concepts we discuss here are intended to provide a high-level overview of concepts you may need to investigate, learn, understand, and follow.

At the end of this chapter, we'll talk about legal defense networks that will help you connect with professional legal resources. In the meantime, please read this section and use it as a springboard to dive into the statutes applicable to your state, county, and city. Don't forget federal laws—they will apply to you as well.

Knowing the Law

Are you ready to study for the world's most challenging exam? Good, here we go.

There are over 20,000 gun-related laws on the books in the United States, and you're responsible for following all of them.

Sound like an insurmountable task? In fairness, many are local laws irrelevant to your home or work city or state. On the other hand, if you travel to any of those places, you will be responsible for knowing and following them.

Hang on to your shorts; it gets worse. Not knowing a law isn't a legal defense, nor does it offer any excuse for violating it. You must thoroughly understand self-defense statutes. If you're tracking with this discussion, there are more laws than you can ever hope to learn, but the law requires you to know them anyway.

Is Self-Defense Homicide?

If you use a gun in self-defense and fatally shoot someone, you've technically committed homicide. There's no getting around it. Someone has been killed, and you did it.

Here's where things get interesting. In a criminal situation, the defense strategy would be to find a way—any way—to prove someone didn't do something. Whether you did it or not isn't in question in a self-defense scenario. Your attorney might be making an argument like this.

"Yes, my client did shoot Mr. AssaultAndBattery. If he were placed in the same situation, with the information he had at the time, he would do it again, and here's why."

Sound strange? The difference between a criminal act of murder and a legitimate self-defense case rests on the concept of justifiable homicide. Everyone agrees you shot and maybe killed someone, but everyone also agrees you had no choice under the circumstances. You might think of justifiable homicide as an excuse for the action you took. Let's consider an illustration to make the point.

Have you ever seen the movie *True Lies*? If you haven't, it's highly recommended as a brilliant combination of comedy and action. In the film, Omega Sector Secret Agent Harry Tasker (Arnold Schwarzenegger) is chasing a terrorist through a hotel in downtown Washington, DC. To make a long story short, Tasker engages in a whopper of a gunfight in a hotel men's room and shoots the urinals to bits while killing two naughty guys who were involved in a plot to set off nuclear bombs in the United States.

I don't know where you come from, but here, shooting up hotel bathrooms is definitely against the law, not to mention frowned upon by hotel management. In the movie, and likely in real life, Harry Tasker wasn't and wouldn't be prosecuted for reckless bathroom renovation because his actions, even though illegal, were done in the context of protecting millions of people from serious harm and death. In other words, he gets a pass from the legal system because by breaking the law, he saved a whole bunch of people and made a fantastic movie in the process. The District Attorney (probably) isn't going to prosecute him for murdering those two terrorists or for porcelain property damage. Harry committed justifiable homicide.

Now, back to reality. In a purely hypothetical scenario, suppose you are outside minding your own business and giving free bacon treats to homeless puppies. If some evil guy suddenly springs up and tries to kill you, and there is no way to escape or avoid his ruthless attack, you might have to fight back. You might even have to use lethal force to save your own life. If you kill him in the process, you might find yourself in a similar justifiable homicide situation. You had no choice but to fight back to protect your own life and maybe those of others around you.

The difference between criminal defense and self-defense cases is that you will mount an affirmative defense. You're probably not disputing what you did, but you are making an affirmative case that you did it for a good and justifiable reason.

Reasonable Person Doctrine

After the fact, your actions will likely be judged based on the reasonable person doctrine. Law enforcement officers, judges, lawyers, or even jurors, all of the Monday morning quarterbacks, will evaluate your decisions and actions against what a "reasonable person" would have done in the same circumstances. Would a reasonable person have fled the situation if possible? Would a reasonable person use some other means of protecting themselves? Would a reasonable person have used potentially lethal force because they had no choice? If your actions are found to vary from what a "reasonable person" would have done, you might find yourself in serious trouble.

Case Study: No Shots Fired

 Jean Boujekian, a Pasadena, California jeweler, was working in his store when two men came in to look at Rolex watches. The men were fidgety and aroused suspicion, so when they asked Boujekian to take some watches out of the case for a closer look, the jeweler asked for identification. At this point, one of the two men drew a knife and demanded the watches.

As the robber lunged at Boujekian, he blocked the knife while his nephew, positioned nearby, drew a concealed handgun from behind the counter. Upon seeing the gun, the armed robbers fled the scene. No shots were fired during the escape.

Lessons

As the men immediately turned tail and ran when the good guy's gun entered the scene, the nephew made the right call by not shooting at the fleeing robbers. Did the men intend grave bodily harm? By drawing a knife and lunging at Boujekian, they certainly turned this robbery into an incident that very well may have justified the use of lethal force. However, when the nephew presented the gun, the men ran so the jewelers were no longer in imminent danger.

Another lesson can be learned from this case. In the closed-caption store security video, Boujekian can be seen talking to the men while he is positioned on their side of the counter—in front of it. As his level of suspicion increased, it would have been a good move to shift his position, if possible, to get the counter between him and the two men.

The nephew can be seen on the video drifting towards the part of the counter where the gun was stored. At a couple of points during the encounter, he appears to reach for the gun, then backs off. Clearly he was suspicious and deciding whether the two intended to rob the store. In hindsight, he was right, and the fact that he was able to draw his gun within a split second of the knife coming out may have saved his uncle's life.

Imminent Bodily Harm

During that split second, when you must decide if potentially deadly force is warranted, you'll need to prove you (or perhaps others) were in danger of imminent bodily harm or death. Period. Saying, "I was in fear for my life!" isn't going to cut it. You'll have to prove it. Protecting property or preventing a crime that's not about to cause imminent bloody harm won't cut it either.

The only time you should ever consider using a firearm for self-defense is when there is no other option to avoid death or serious bodily harm.

So, how exactly is imminent bodily harm defined? Three standard criteria must be met for a "reasonable person" to act in response.

Ability

The attacker must have the ability to inflict harm or death. This has nothing to do with weapons. If a 6'6", 300-pound Ultimate Fighting Champion attacks, you're experiencing imminent bodily harm and risk of death. After all, more people are killed with fists and feet every year than with rifles of any kind. If an attacker is larger or more skilled at violence than you, they have the ability to inflict harm or death. If an attacker has a weapon of any type, that could also meet the ability to inflict harm criteria. The ability criteria can be met regardless of who is armed and who isn't.

Opportunity

Does the attacker have the opportunity to inflict serious harm or death? If our example Ultimate Fighter is 200 yards away, they don't have a realistic opportunity to hurt you. If they are five feet away and winding up to kick you in the head, they do.

Opportunity might also be partially defined by movement. If a threat is moving towards attacking you, that increases opportunity. If they are running in the opposite direction, it wouldn't be realistic for you to claim that you were in imminent danger because they no longer have the opportunity to inflict harm.

Jeopardy

Jeopardy is the catch-all. Suppose our mythical fighter was warming up, flexing, or even holding a baseball bat (ability) and standing right next to you (opportunity). There is still no imminent danger in that case because you're not in jeopardy. That person may be minding their own business or asking you for the time. However, if they physically attack you, you're in jeopardy. You probably aren't in physical jeopardy if that person is only saying mean things.

Case Study: He Was Unarmed!

On May 26, 2018, Bratislava resident Juraj Hossu and very large man, was hassling women on a street corner. A Filipino expat, Henry Acorda, was living in the city and working for IBM. After asking Hossu to leave the women alone, Hossu chased Acorda and threw a single punch to the face. Acorda stumbled and ended up on one knee on the ground. At that point, Hossu delivered a single kick to Acorda's head. Acorda sustained massive brain damage and died.

Lessons

In this case, a single punch followed by a kick killed the victim. No weapons were involved except hands and feet. The lack of visible weapons is no guarantee that you or others can't be in mortal danger.

Entering a violent or escalating situation as a Good Samaritan bystander is always risky. You simply don't know the participants' frame of mind, and the situation can quickly spiral out of control.

It's unclear what the words were between Acorda and Hossu. It appears that Hossu was unhinged and may have attacked regardless of how much Acorda tried to de-escalate the situation. With that said, de-escalation skills are a must for anyone who chooses to carry a concealed weapon.

Castle Doctrine

Legally, one's home has been considered a special "safe space" since Roman times. Brought to the United States as a part of English common law, a man's home is considered his castle. The doctrine exists as law or precedent in all but a few states.

Simply put, the castle doctrine principle reduces or eliminates a duty to retreat from an aggressor when in the presence of one's own home. The concept of "home" can sometimes extend to cars, recreational vehicles, and other locations. Under castle doctrine, an individual has a right to feel secure in their residence, to the point of defending themselves using deadly force if warranted and justified.

State laws and precedents vary widely. In some cases, castle doctrine grants some immunity from criminal prosecution and civil judgment. However, in almost all situations, castle doctrine law works hand in hand with common self-defense law. It's not a blanket permission slip that allows homeowners to shoot trespassers, burglars, or even home invaders. Like stand your ground, Castle doctrine does not "create" or expand any "rights" to use deadly force other than those already covered by principles of justifiable self-defense. In many scenarios, if you are not in danger of imminent bodily harm or death, then castle doctrine laws alone may not support an affirmative defense if you shoot.

Be sure to carefully research your state's laws regarding castle doctrine and duty to retreat. Don't rely on generalized definitions discussed here to inform your understanding of the matter. No matter how complex the laws are, it's your responsibility to know them, and you'll certainly be held accountable.

Stand Your Ground

The media makes little effort to understand and accurately communicate the concept of "stand your ground." That's because there's nothing sensational about it. It's essentially the "to go" form of the Castle Doctrine principle. There's nothing special or even surprising about the concept or its associated laws.

The "stand your ground" principle does not:

Grant permission to shoot strangers in public.

Allow you to pick fights and claim a defense of "standing your ground."

Remove or alter the standard provisions of self-defense justification.

If a confrontation doesn't meet the legal principles set forth by overriding concepts like the reasonable person doctrine and the threat of immense bodily harm, then a stand-your-ground law will not help you.

To illustrate the need for stand-your-ground clarification, let's consider an example.

In some countries, it's considered one's duty and responsibility as a victim of crime to retreat from a threat or attack. Yes, you heard that right. If you're standing around minding your own business when a thug threatens you with a knife, saying, "Don't move while I rob you!" it may be your responsibility to run away while not inflicting harm on your attacker. If you whack your mugger on the head with a nearby garden tool, you just might be prosecuted as an aggressor for assaulting the criminal who threatened your life. It doesn't seem to matter whether or not you had a safe opportunity to escape. If the thug says, "Don't move, or I'll stab you!" it can still be your responsibility to get away from the situation—or comply. How dare you mind your own business in public while someone is trying to make a dishonest living at your expense!

The stand-your-ground concept states that you have as much right as your attacker to stand around and mind your own business. If someone threatens you with imminent bodily harm, you aren't obligated by law to retreat. If you deem your best odds of surviving the encounter lie with fighting back, you do you and solve the problem. There's an important nuance here. Instead of a legal duty to retreat, the stand-your-ground principle implies you can retreat if that's the best option, or you can fight to defend yourself if that's the best option. Sounds rational, right?

Consider Florida's wording of the principle as one example.

> A person who is not engaged in an unlawful activity and who is attacked in any other place where he or she has a right to be has no duty to retreat and has the right to stand his or her ground and meet force with force, including deadly force, if he or she reasonably believes it is necessary to do so to prevent death or great bodily harm to himself or herself or another or to prevent the commission of a forcible felony.

Did you catch the key phrase, "if he or she reasonably believes it is necessary to do so to prevent death or great bodily harm...?" Does this sound like some license to kill, as the media portrays?

As always, research and understand the specific laws in your state with the utmost care and attention to detail.

Monday Morning Quarterbacking

It's essential to recognize that an army of Monday morning quarterbacks will scrutinize every action you take during a self-defense encounter. Whether in a police station or courtroom, other people will look at the chain of events and determine what you should or should not have done during every split-second of a self-defense encounter. They'll have the luxury of time, multiple opinions, witness testimony, and maybe even video on which to base their judgments.

On the other hand, you get none of that and will have to make split-second life-or-death decisions and live with the consequences. Fair? Nope, not at all. That's why it's so crucial for you to educate yourself, think in advance, learn, and train. After a self-defense encounter, you'll be held to an unfair and arguably unreasonable standard.

When and Where Can You Carry?

Having a concealed carry permit doesn't mean you can carry anywhere. Nor does living in a state that allows constitutional carry— concealed or open carry without a permit.

Every state has different laws that define where carry is and is not allowed, so it will be up to you to learn and follow the regulations applicable to your home turf. With that said, there are some types of places where concealed carry is often prohibited. Again, this list will vary depending on your state, so be sure to check.

Schools and school events.
Government buildings and facilities.
Bars and restaurants.
Post offices.
Hospitals and medical facilities.
Private businesses where no-carry signage is posted.
Personal residences where you don't have explicit permission from the owner.
Workplaces, depending on state law and company policy.

The list goes on. These are just some of the more common places to serve as examples. While studying prohibited areas in your state, be sure to check the penalties for non-compliance, as they can be severe, including revocation of your permit, fines, and even jail time.

So, how do you find out where you can carry and where you can't? Going directly to your state's legal statutes is always the best bet as it's first-hand information. The National Rifle Association also maintains a directory of state gun laws. Just be aware that laws change all the time, so you'll want to verify information on the NRA website or any other. Fortunately, the NRA directory includes direct links to state statutes.

Here's where you can start: www.nraila.org/gun-laws

State Reciprocity and Traveling with Firearms

Unlike a driver's license, a concealed carry permit is not recognized automatically in other states. So, when you travel, you must research the laws in your destination state and any states you pass through in transit, at least if you plan to carry a firearm.

Fortunately for the legally armed citizen, a well-established concept of reciprocity between states exists. It's not a national policy but rather a set of voluntary agreements between states on how they will or won't recognize each other's concealed carry permits. Since it's voluntary, there is no blanket coverage. This is a great time to mention that even if you live in a state that requires no permit, it can be a good idea to get one anyway for purposes of reciprocity. You'll need that permit if you visit other states that recognize your home state's permit.

So, if you live in South Carolina and are driving to Georgia for a vacation, you'll have first to check to see if Georgia recognizes South Carolina concealed carry permits. If they do, you've only completed step one.

Once you've established a reciprocity agreement between your state and the state or states where you plan to travel, you'll need to understand and follow the specific gun laws in each state. The Founders believed that the United States model of government should put most of the power at the local level, so even though the Second Amendment of the Constitution protects a natural right to keep and bear arms, each state is responsible for the particulars of how that works.

Once again, you can look to the National Rifle Association at www.nraila.org/gun-laws for assistance understanding reciprocity agreements and state laws that apply to your travel. And, once again, it's up to you to continue to the source of each state's regulations to ensure you understand them clearly.

Sadly, too many people have found themselves in prison simply for carrying in a state where their permit isn't recognized or where the carry laws are different. States like New York, Maryland, and New Jersey (among others) seem to have made this type of prosecution a pastime. Don't make that mistake. As a gun owner, you have to be more responsible than the average Joe, so research before you go.

Legal Defense Networks

Over the past few years, several legal defense networks have emerged to assist legally armed citizens facing a self-defense legal nightmare.

Nothing is clear-cut with the law, and even if you do everything right in a self-defense encounter, you still might find yourself in serious trouble. There are far too many cases where local politics and overly ambitious prosecutors looking to make a name have prosecuted citizens who did nothing more than protect themselves and their families. That's the criminal law risk.

Conversely, you might find yourself defending against a civil lawsuit. If you caused the injury or death of a criminal, nothing is preventing that person or their family from suing you, too. Even if you're right and ultimately win the case, you'll have spent tens or hundreds of thousands of dollars on your legal defense. Good luck getting that money back.

You can be right and still lose everything if you face criminal or civil proceedings. If you're in prison while proving your innocence, you'll probably lose your job. To make bail, you may have to forfeit your savings and home. People will look at you differently, perhaps as a murderer. If you didn't lose your house to bail or attorney's fees, you'll likely lose it due to unemployment.

To protect against these eventualities, companies like the United States Concealed Carry Association have created protection plans. While not technically insurance, they operate on a similar principle. For some nominal monthly fee, the organization agrees to assist if you're involved in a self-defense encounter. Plans vary, but most offer immediate bail money assistance, immediate access to a lawyer well-versed in affirmative defense strategy, legal fee funding, and much more. Certainly not least in the benefits column, these plans offer a single 800 number for that one phone call you may be allowed. Remember, even if you did everything right, you might still find yourself arrested and in jail, at least for a while.

As you explore the pros and cons of various self-defense liability programs, be sure you understand the details. Some plans offer cash assistance immediately. Others operate more like a reimbursement plan. The program will reimburse you if you're declared innocent of wrongdoing. Just know you may be responsible for fronting tens or hundreds of thousands of dollars in the meantime. As long as you know how your chosen plan operates, you won't be surprised if you ever have to use it.

5

LESS LETHAL OPTIONS

To a hammer, every problem looks like a nail. To a gun, every problem may seem to require shooting. To a legally armed citizen, every problem requires carefully evaluating the right strategies and tools before implementing a response.

Are there self-defense situations warranting the use of force via a firearm? Yes. Do all "street encounters" warrant the use of a firearm? No.

I like to tell new concealed carriers to train as if they'll need to use their firearm but plan their life strategies so they'll never have to. Everyone wins if you can find ways to keep your gun safely holstered.

If you carry a gun for self-defense, it's your responsibility to consider the possible spectrum of problems you might encounter and develop strategies and tactics appropriate to different scenarios. There's a universe of tools and skills available to you representing a range of possible responses to potential threats, so be sure to place as much, or ideally more, emphasis on non-lethal and even non-offensive tools and tactics.

If you carry a handgun for self-defense, you should also strongly consider a non-lethal option like pepper spray. It would also help if you carried a powerful flashlight at all times—even during daylight hours. In the next section, we'll explain why.

Can a Flashlight Save Your Life?

Before exploring the basics of less-lethal defense options, I want to discuss non-lethal and non-offensive tools and strategies.

What self-defense skills and tools do you possess that won't hurt anyone? How do you deal with an individual encroaching into your personal space? What if they won't listen to verbal commands like "Please give me some space, OK?"

A reliable defensive flashlight can be an effective tool to help the responsibly armed citizen bridge the uncertainty gap between an encounter where things don't feel quite right and a criminal attack. It can also help you evaluate an unknown situation, forcing the other party to clarify their true intentions.

The Streamlight Wedge in the center is perfect for everyday carry with its flat profile. The simple on or off switch delivers 300 lumens or, with an extra firm push, 1,000 when needed. The Pocket Mate USB keyring light is a bit underpowered for defensive use, but sure is handy.

A Flashlight Scenario

Imagine you're walking from a downtown restaurant back to your car. You see a man hunched over, leaning into a doorway nook of a closed business. He appears to be giving back some of the many drinks he polished off at one of the nearby bars. There's traffic on the road, and the sidewalk is narrow, so you have to pass him to get to your vehicle. You spot another man edging into the scene from between two nearby parked cars as you get closer. He's wearing a hooded sweatshirt, so you can't get a good look at him. He puts his right hand into his sweatshirt pocket as he steps onto the sidewalk. Glancing back at the drunk, you notice he seems a bit soberer.

Your hackles are hackling. What do you do?

You can't, and at this point, shouldn't, draw a gun. There's been no threat of imminent bodily harm. If you pull a gun at this point, you very well may find yourself explaining to police officers why you brandished a firearm and threatened two people on a public street. If you had a small canister of pepper spray, perhaps you could discreetly palm it as you get closer—just in case. But you don't. Now what?

You're suspicious. Is this a strange coincidence, or are these guys varsity members of the mugging tag team squad? You don't know, but it sure would behoove you to do something proactive, wouldn't it?

A Non-Lethal Response Option

Here's an idea. If you have a defensive flashlight in your pocket, you might draw it, turn it on, and aim it at the street in front of these characters. You haven't introduced a "weapon" into an unknown situation. You have alerted both men you're paying attention. You've provided welcome illumination to see exactly what's going on. If anything becomes slightly more questionable, you can quickly raise that light to eye level, providing a moment of disorientation and hopefully a bit of degraded vision. If you want to be even less "threatening," you can always accompany your action with comments like,

"It sure is dark, isn't it? Are you OK?" Take your pick based on what vibe you want to exude while you're still unsure about the strangers' intent.

If the men were, in fact, strangers to each other and meant no harm, you might have created some annoyance bordering on rude use of a bright light. But what are they going to do? Call 911 and say, "Some guy just pulled out a flashlight! And he aimed it right at me!"

If these two characters were scoping out potential victims, you just put them on alert that you're on the ball and ready to respond, reminding them there are easier victims out there. Even if they don't leave you alone, you've interrupted their cycle and bought yourself a second or two to evaluate and respond.

This training curriculum at WOFT Training in Orlando, FL, shows how high-powered lights can be used to create or preserve space, delay or disorient others and serve as a "less offensive" tool. Image: WOFT.com.

The nifty thing about using a high-powered flashlight in this type of scenario is that it works in the daytime, too. While you won't be lighting up the area, nor is it necessary, a bright light in the eyes during daylight hours can create spots and a certain degree of temporary visual impairment. If you don't believe me, experiment on your own with a 500 or 1,000-lumen flashlight. Just be careful, OK? We don't need anyone burning their eyeballs out.

Think of how many scenarios in everyday life could be either wholly innocent or a clever setup for a criminal attack. A stranger enters your space on a public sidewalk, asking for the time. A beggar bumps into you, persistently asking for some spare change. A couple of guys ask for directions to a local bar. These encounters happen daily and are innocuous the vast majority of the time. They're also favorite strategies to close distance with a prospective victim without raising suspicion. The challenge for you is figuring out which scenario is true before it's too late.

Flashlight Selection Considerations

Modern defensive lights can be described as "miraculous." Very few years ago, giant Maglites full of D-cell batteries, weighing a couple of pounds, output a beam of light measured in tens of lumens. Today, the Streamlight PocketMate on my keychain generates 325, and it's about the same size as a stack of three or four quarters. While not really a defensive light, it's nothing to sneeze at, and you'll always have it readily available.

First and foremost, buy quality and don't skimp. This isn't something you're going to use to find the fusebox when the power goes out. We're talking about a tool you might rely on to save your life. Not only does it have to work correctly every time, but it must also stand up to all the knocks and dings it'll get from everyday carry. So, skip the LED light multipacks at the local Warehouse Mart and buy something good from a defensive light manufacturer like Streamlight, Surefire, or Fenix. There are others, but you get the idea.

Consider size and shape. A larger and heavier light may output 2,000 lumens and be capable of signaling the International Space Station. Still, if it's too bulky for all-day, everyday pocket carry, you'll leave it at home, where it will do you precisely no good. Plenty of lights on the market are compact and can spit out shocking amounts of light.

The market has evolved regarding battery vs. USB-rechargeable lights. In the early days of rechargeables, there were reliability issues and a spotty reputation for holding charges and battery life. No more. Modern USB-rechargeable lights are reliable enough for tactical and defensive use. As long as you pay attention to charge status and top it off as needed, they're a perfectly reliable option.

Remember, simpler is better. To differentiate product offerings from the competition, manufacturers are often tempted to add all sorts of whiz-bang features into their lights. Skip it. Find one—if you can—with only a simple on/off switch. Forget modes, strobing, and SOS programs. You won't be inclined to navigate through a half dozen brightness or operational modes in a defensive situation. You'll want your bright light on. Or off. Period. I've been shocked at how often my more complex lights start doing unexpected things in shoot house and close combat scenarios. Keep it simple.

Pepper Sprays, Streams and Powders

If a high-powered flashlight falls into the category of "less offensive," pepper spray takes a significant step up the spectrum toward deadly force.

Many refer to pepper spray as a "non-lethal" self-defense tool. I prefer to use the more accurate term "less lethal." Non-firearm tools like pepper spray, Tasers, and the like can and have killed people before. As a responsibly armed citizen, you need to appreciate the difference. When bringing a less-lethal tool into a defensive encounter, there is a risk of permanent harm or even death. Yes, less lethal tools like pepper spray are designed to provide a tool where deadly force isn't appropriate, but don't use them lightly. If you're not in danger of injury or serious harm, don't introduce less-lethal tools into a situation either. A high school kid in my area went to prison for decades after a "less lethal" encounter—a simple fistfight in a parking lot. He punched another youth exactly once, and that blow killed the other boy. Weird things happen.

In addition to providing an option for encounters that may not warrant lethal force, pepper spray offers another potential use case. There are many locations where firearms are prohibited. Think hospitals, schools, churches, federal or state properties, etc. Some-times, pepper spray may provide a legal substitute, giving you some force capability should you be caught in an attack. As always, do your research before carrying less-lethal tools into non-firearm permis-sible environments.

You also might benefit from having pepper spray products to defend against wildlife. If you walk the dog late at night, it's nice to have something other than a gun to deal with surprises. In my suburban neighborhood, we've got foxes and a growing population of coyotes. For situations like these, I'd rather have and use the spray, if necessary, than explain why I felt compelled to pull out a firearm in my neighborhood.

While there are always risks, pepper spray is intended to be a solution with a reduced chance of "final" consequences.

What Are Pepper Products?

Pepper spray, technically oleoresin capsicum, or "OC" in abbrevi-ated form, is a less-lethal irritant designed to incapacitate an attacker without causing permanent physical harm.

It irritates the skin, especially mucous areas like the inside of the nose, mouth, and eyes. When it contacts the eyes, it forces the recip-ient to close them involuntarily. If inhaled or ingested into the mouth and nose, it causes coughing and shortness of breath.

In short, a dose of pepper spray is intended to take the urge to fight out of the recipient. In a perfect scenario, it does that without causing lasting harm to the victim. Most of the effects will pass within an hour. Do be aware products like this are called "less" lethal for a reason. There is no guarantee against a bad or allergic reaction capable of causing more severe harm or even death. While rare, it can happen. So, as with any defensive tool, be sure you have to use it before committing to action.

Quality products in the OC category from companies like Pom and Saber have an excellent track record of performance in crowd control and defensive use relevant to this discussion. While not fail-safe, they've demonstrated the ability to end or at least temporarily disrupt a fight.

When buying pepper spray products, know there are no proper standards, so read the labels carefully. The easiest way to check the "potency" of your product is to look at the Major Capsaicinoid Content. You might see something like "MC" on the label of quality products. Ideally, look for a value of 1.33 percent—that's police-grade strength. Since the industry for "human" OC spray products is unregulated, ignore heat units and other marketing claims—there's no standard or performance guarantee behind them.

Gear Considerations

Pepper products can be packaged in various ways for different use scenarios. The different types we'll discuss aren't necessarily good or bad; each comes with benefits and drawbacks for different situations.

Be sure to read labels carefully so you know exactly what you're getting. Terms like "spray" are often used generically, and what's inside a package may be a stream or gel product.

The POM Original Pepper Spray unit is an excellent option and not much larger than a roll of mints.

Most good producers offer optional practice and training configurations. Filled with water or some other inert substance, the trainers allow you to experiment with the canister and release mechanism to see precisely how the spray, stream, ball, or gel operates. Spend the extra few bucks to get a couple. Before using the real thing, you'll want to know how it aims and its effective distance in varying conditions. For example, you'll want to know the impacts of distance and wind on the performance of your chosen product.

Sprays / Streams

The pepper compound will create a stream of liquid in the air, like a squirt gun, near-certain to get all over an assailant at close range. As a "spray," it also has an excellent chance of making its way into your attacker's nose and mouth to the point where they'll inhale the nasty stuff. That can certainly help you, as your opponent should be dealing with both visual and breathing impairment. Many products in this class will provide ten feet, give or take, of effective range unless it's windy. The liquid stream and spray effect means there's a chance you'll be exposed to the product as well.

Gels

Like a stream, a gel product gives you increased range and control, making you less likely to take yourself out of the fight. A gel is intended to make a sticky mess that stays on your attacker, which is good. On the other hand, even more than a stream, it's less likely to get in the mouth and nose. Many gel users report the time to incapacitate an attacker is longer.

Powder and Ball Launchers

A growing number of nifty products on the market can launch OC-filled "paintballs" from surprising distances. Configured vaguely like handguns or oversized flashlights, these products allow you to reliably hit human-sized targets from 20 or 30 yards away.

Some even come with integrated lasers for easier and more intuitive aiming. There are ultra-compact single-shot models and larger configurations capable of firing multiple shots. Models change frequently, so check with PepperBall or Umarex for the latest offerings.

While ball launchers give you fantastic range, you need to count on the product bursting on impact. Depending on what it strikes, it may or may not "explode" and release its charge. If you're using a single-shot product, that could leave you in a real bind.

On the other hand, when the projectile does burst as intended, you've created a cloud operating much like a spray product.

Many of the launcher products also contain an integrated flash-light. Hence, as a nighttime dog-walking tool, they are non-threat-ening to neighbors and provide visibility and standoff distance from two- and four-legged threats.

Usage Considerations

As with anything, dry runs and practice are essential, and therein lies the value of inert training products. Before you put a product into daily carry rotation, make darn sure you've thought through things like the following.

Which hand are you going to use? Dominant or weak hand?

What kind of grip will you use, and which finger (thumb or index) will you use to activate the product?

If the product has a safety device (yours does, right?), have you practiced disengaging it?

If the spray or stream isn't effective, what's your backup plan and next step? If you have to go to a firearm, have you practiced dropping the pepper spray container as you draw? It's surprising how hard it is for your panic brain to do something simple, like drop a now-useless tool when needed. The instinct to hold on to something can be surprisingly powerful.

If you carry a light, which hand will operate it? One benefit of using your strong hand for the spray is that you can continue to use your light if you need to fight or draw a firearm after the spray is gone.

One significant advantage of many compact pepper spray dispensers is that they look non-threatening. Have you programmed the idea of discreetly palming pepper spray in potentially risky situations into your response plan? Being "ready to go" dramatically improves your response time should you need to use it.

The bottom line is to plan and practice so your brain and muscles know exactly what to do.

Tasers and Stun Guns

For purposes of this discussion, we'll refer to two broad classes of electronic shock devices: Tasers and stun guns.

Think of Tasers as devices that launch wire-connected tiny barbs at a target. After they are stuck in clothing or skin, a high-voltage, low-current charge is sent through the wires by the battery-powered launcher, theoretically disabling the body by overwhelming the attacker's muscles with electrical impulses.

This Taser Pulse 2 unit launches barbs up to 15 feet and also features a contact stun feature.

The theory is the electric charge mimics the body's electrical system from the brain, amplifying it and causing muscles to contract violently. The attacker is rendered helpless by overriding the brain's control with more juice while the charge is active.

Law enforcement-grade Tasers can be effective, assuming all goes according to plan. However, be aware that there is a high percentage of cases in which a Taser fails to incapacitate an attacker. Maybe the probes didn't stick or make proper contact, or perhaps one of the probes missed the target altogether. Or maybe the attacker is so amped up that the effects are negligible.

Consider this. According to a study from APM Reports, over three years, from 2015 through 2017, 258 people were fatally shot after being tased by police. In other words, the Taser proved ineffective in stopping the behavior causing the police response. Of those cases, in 106 incidents, the subject became more physically violent after being tased.

In my opinion, while a Taser is an excellent tool for law enforcement professionals, who routinely pack a variety of gear for different situations, it's less than ideal for concealed carry defense. The units are large and, compared to pepper spray as a less-lethal deterrent, may be less effective overall.

Stun guns operate under a similar theory but require continuous contact between the device and the attacker. Contacts on the stun gun provide two points to complete a circuit with the body. With a "stun gun" device, you'll need to be within contact distance to even consider using it. While popular items at gun shows, most serious personal defense advocates won't advise relying on them to deter or stop an attack.

6

GUNS

I f you're buying a firearm for concealed carry, there are plenty of good reasons to choose a particular gun. There are also plenty of terrible reasons. For example...

"It's so small I can carry it anywhere!"
"My friend/husband/wife/second cousin twice removed told me this one will drop an elephant."
"It was in that movie..."

You get the idea.

When you boil down all the potential deciding factors, a concealed handgun has one job: saving your life. Everything else is secondary.

To use a handgun successfully in the worst moment of fear and stress, you have to have absolute confidence in its capability and your proficiency with it. That means it has to fit you. You have to be able to control it. You have to be able to hit your target. You have to be able to operate, load, unload, and clear malfunctions without stopping to think. It has to be powerful enough to do the job you're asking. Most of these factors rely on practice. If you choose a gun that's not right for you for whatever reason, you're not going to spend the time required to become naturally comfortable and proficient. As a result, your odds of using it successfully during an armed encounter will be significantly reduced.

So, how should you go about choosing a concealed-carry handgun?

A snubnose revolver like this Smith & Wesson 642 Performance Center model can be a great self-defense option, but it's arguably an expert gun, not always ideal for newer shooters.

Choosing the Right Handgun

The fact your friend or significant other loves the BB Blaster 12mm means nothing. That Tactical Beast Monster magazine pontificating that all the top Delta Ninja SEALS use it also means nothing. If a handgun doesn't work for you...it doesn't work for you. Don't buy a gun on anyone else's recommendation. Buy a gun you've tried and chosen because you like it and are comfortable with it.

When trying a new handgun, ask yourself the following questions.

Does it feel natural or even comfortable in my hand?

Can I reach the trigger properly without stretching or adjusting my grip?
With a proper grip, where I can reach the trigger comfortably, is the
handgun in line with my forearm?
After proper instruction, can I control the muzzle blast and recoil?
Is this a gun I'll enjoy practicing on the range, or is it painful to shoot?
Am I confident in its reliable operation?
Am I confident about loading, unloading, and checking its condition?
Would I feel comfortable resolving that situation if it doesn't go bang when I
expect?

Just as you wouldn't want to drive a car you didn't feel confident you could control; you wouldn't want to rely on a concealed carry gun you aren't confident using.

Be careful to hold off on these types of evaluations until you've had proper instruction on how to use them—some of the questions above require training and practice before you can determine a meaningful answer. For example, many people default to revolvers because they have trouble racking the slide of compact semi-automatic pistols. As we'll see later in this book, some techniques allow virtually anyone to rack the most challenging side easily—it's just a matter of knowing the proper technique.

Choosing a gun yourself presents a bit of a cart before the horse challenge, but never fear. Read on, and we'll tell you how to learn while deciding which handgun suits you.

Try Before You Buy

The best way to go about trying different models is to rent. No, you can't plunk down a credit card and take rentals out of the store. However, most shooting ranges keep various popular guns available for rent on-premises. Many will apply the rental fee towards the purchase price of a new model should you find one you like.

If you're new to shooting, there's a better way. Many ranges also offer instruction. Spend a little cash and hire an instructor to help you try different models. Tell them beforehand that you're considering getting concealed carry training and want help finding an appropriate handgun. Don't worry about this learning session duplicating what you may learn in the concealed carry class. Many concealed carry classes focus on legal issues and don't teach you how to shoot.

There's another benefit to getting some help picking out the right gun. A good instructor will show you the best and most efficient way to operate different models so you won't risk buying the wrong gun simply because you don't know the operational tricks.

Yes, it will cost you some money, but you'll come out ahead financially by buying the right gun the first time. I can't begin to tell you how many people I know who purchased a firearm based on recommendations and then had to sell it later to get the "right" one.

Bigger is Better

When we're talking about handguns, bigger is better. I'm not referring to caliber but the physical size and weight of the handgun.

This Sig Sauer P320 Compact Carry pistol has roughly the same "power" as a snubnose revolver but is much easier to shoot thanks to its larger overall size and semi-automatic action.

To use a handgun effectively, you have to control it. The easier you can handle it, the better you can shoot, especially when firing more than one shot. Two factors influence the ease of controlling your handgun.

First, we have to consider recoil. As Isaac Newton figured, every action has an equal and opposite reaction. When you fire a projectile forward, you will feel the equal force coming back the other way in the form of recoil. The heavier and faster the bullet, the more recoil energy you'll experience. However, the gun's weight stands between you and that force. The heavier the weapon, the less it moves and the less felt recoil you have to manage.

Ponder this example. Say you're firing a tank cannon. If you mount that cannon on a cardboard tank that weighs half a pound, what do you think will happen when you torch off the cannon? The cardboard tank underneath will self-destruct, and that barrel will fly backward. Now envision mounting that same cannon on 2,000,000 pounds of lead tank body and doing the same thing. If it moves at all, it will be very little.

The same thing applies to handguns. A 12-ounce polymer pocket pistol will kick like an ill-tempered mule every time you press the trigger, but if you shoot the same ammo out of a four-pound, all-steel handgun, it won't bounce and recoil nearly as much.

Physical size, specifically surface area, contributes to your ability to control a handgun. If you try to pick up a 20-pound weight using only the tips of your thumb and index finger, it will be tough to do. However, picking up the same weight with your entire hand gripping the object will be easier. Even though you were using the same hand and arm in both scenarios, the second one allowed you to grip the weight using more of the surface area of your hand.

If there is enough real estate for you to get your palm and all of your fingers on the gun, you can control it much better.

Buying a small and light pocket pistol is tempting because it's tiny and convenient to carry. They are much harder to shoot and control for the reasons stated above and a few others. A lightweight pocket pistol is rarely the best option for those new to handgun shooting. That tiny pistol that's oh-so-convenient to carry will inflict a pain penalty every time you press the trigger, so you'll be less likely to practice with it at the range. And the less you practice, the less effective it will be for you in a life-and-death situation.

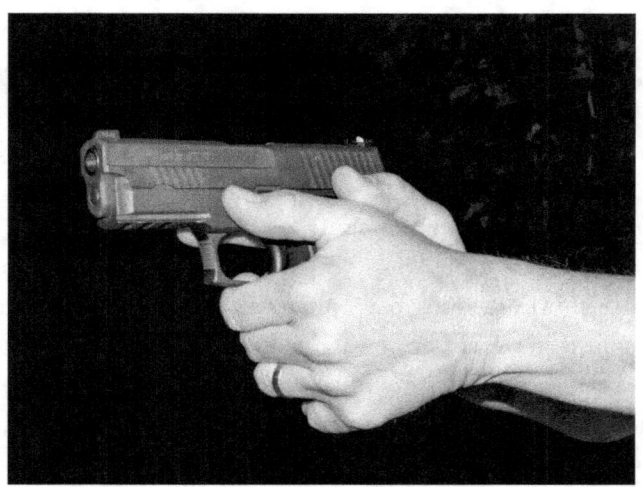

Notice how both hands can make good contact with this larger pistol, a Sig Sauer P229. The increased surface area contact aids with control.

There's nothing wrong with buying a tiny gun; they'll work fine if you're willing to persevere in training with it. Just know what you're getting into first.

What Caliber?

The "right" caliber for you depends on several different factors.

You'll hear that the "right" caliber is the largest one with which you can consistently hit your target. That's mostly true. You need to be able to hit your target consistently. You also don't want to use a "too small" caliber only because it's easy to control and get hits. Stated differently, you want to get as much power as possible without dramatically affecting your ability to use it accurately and confidently under stress.

Recoil and muzzle blast become factors when you get into harder-hitting calibers. For example, the 10mm and .357 Sig calibers are great but have significantly more blast and recoil than 9mm or even .45 ACP. As a result, some people may not be as proficient with these heavy-recoiling pistols as they are with a 9mm or .38 Special. A robust round does nothing for you if the recoil and blast cause you to miss your target. You're better off using that 9mm or .38 Special and getting hits than hoping for results with an overpowered concealed carry gun. Of course, good instruction and lots of practice will help you move up the caliber ladder as you build your handgun skills.

Small calibers like .22LR are excellent for developing accuracy and confidence. Almost every shooter can easily control those and hit their intended targets. However, it's not generally accepted as a dependable option for stopping violent attackers quickly. That's where the "largest with which you can consistently hit your target" part comes into play.

A significant size difference between 9mm (left) and .45 ACP (right) explains the capacity difference in similarly sized handguns.

When choosing the right caliber, you'll also want to consider potential capacity tradeoffs. For example, .45 ACP is an excellent caliber, but in "standard" pistol configurations, you'll only get about half as many rounds in a pistol with the same approximate size as a

9mm. Those .45 cartridges are larger and take up more space in the magazine. As a result, you have to carry fewer of them or use an even larger gun.

We won't favor a caliber here because it's an individual decision. However, 9mm seems to have become the sweet spot for most concealed carry users. For years, organizations like the FBI and state and local police agencies standardized on the .40 S&W. With modern ammunition advancements, many now find that 9mm is a better all-around option. The shift is caused by more capacity, less recoil, and better results across a vast community of shooters with varying skill levels. The .38 Special is analogous to 9mm thanks to its balance of power and controllability in revolvers.

That said, we're also seeing a resurgence of .380 ACP. While its ballistic numbers don't compare to those of 9mm or larger calibers, modern ammo is helping it become a reliable and effective option, especially for smaller guns.

Action Type and Handling

Earlier, we discussed handguns' different styles and various action types. It's time to apply those generalized features and benefits to your decision process.

The first decision to make is a revolver versus a semi-automatic pistol.

While a fine revolver can be a work of mechanical art, its mode of operation is utilitarian. Fill the chambers and press the trigger. That's about it. If you value simplicity, a revolver may be suitable for you. From a practical perspective, be aware that your capacity will be limited to five or six rounds due to the slower reloading speed. One can reload a revolver quickly, but it takes lots of practice.

Generally speaking, pistols require more understanding, practice, and training to operate. You'll need to learn and internalize concepts like magazine feeding, slide operation, cocked status, de-cocking and safety manipulation with a pistol. When a pistol doesn't go bang, you must understand its operations and practice malfunction drills to get it working again.

By no means should you take the above analysis to mean that you don't need to practice or train as much with revolvers. In fact, shooting a revolver well often requires more skill than a semi-automatic pistol. Instead, consider the differences more like a manual transmission car versus one with an automatic transmission. If you enjoy shifting gears and operating the systems, that's great; buy one. If you are more interested in getting from point A to point B without concern for how the gears work, buy a car with an automatic transmission. Both require the same driving skill and road awareness; they require different techniques to shift the gears and manage the engine's performance.

There are different action types for semi-automatic pistols. Above is a single action; below is a striker-fired model.

If you choose a pistol, you'll have more choices between single-action, double-action, and striker-fired. Think about what attributes are most important to you. Are you more concerned with the quality of the trigger press? Will the transitional trigger between a double-action's first and second shots bother you? Or are you more comfortable having that very intentional first trigger press because it adds another layer of intentionality?

Then, there is a second layer of options from which to choose. For example, many new models of striker-fired pistols have optional manual safeties. Consider the pros and cons of additional layers like this. If you go the manual safety route, you must train to disengage it at the right point during your draw stroke. You'll also need to train to re-engage it before reholstering your pistol. Test both models' triggers if your ideal gun comes in safety and no safety configurations. You'll often find that adding a manual safety changes the feel and even weight of the trigger press. That's not necessarily a drawback, but it's something to be aware of.

The best way to evaluate your decision factors is to spend some time on the range shooting various handgun types. Whether you rely on friends and their handguns or rent to try at the local range, there's nothing like some first-hand experience to help you find the right gun.

Ammunition Costs and Availability

The cost of defensive ammunition for any given firearm isn't a major consideration when choosing a handgun and associated caliber. Once you verify that your gun functions with a specific type of ammo, you won't need to buy lots of it. I generally rotate the expensive stuff out of my carry guns about once a year. That means I'm only using 50 rounds or less (what's in the gun plus a couple of spare magazines) once yearly.

A factor worthy of consideration is the cost and availability of practice ammo. If you've chosen the right carry gun, you'll want to practice with it throughout the year, and more expensive calibers can add up to a big dent in the wallet. For example, I like .357 Sig for recreational use and concealed carry. The per-round cost of premium self-defense ammo isn't all that different from that for 9mm, .40 S&W, or .45 ACP. However, the cost of practice ammo is significantly higher

—over double the per-round cost of 9mm. It's also much harder to find at the local sporting goods store.

Remember to do the ammo math if you run across a swinging deal on an oddball-caliber pistol. It's like the "printer and ink" business model. The long-term operating costs represent the actual expense.

How to Make Sure the Gun Fits You

Comfort is a factor when deciding what's best for you, but it's not the definitive method of fitting a handgun. Just because one grip or another "feels good" doesn't mean it's a proper fit. To be sure, you'll want to check a couple of other things to help you decide which gun or grip panel configuration is correct.

Trigger finger placement

Some experts will insist you should press the trigger with the pad of your index finger. Other equally credible experts insist that you should use the first joint in your index finger. I don't particularly care which trigger press placement you prefer. Settle on one, then check to see if your gun's grip size is too big or small.

Assume a regular firing grip with an unloaded gun and point at a safe backstop. Now, move your finger to the trigger as if you're going to fire. Hold that position.

I want you to look at the lower portion of your index finger—the section from where it plugs into your palm up to the first joint. When your trigger finger is ready to press, do you see daylight between the side of the handgun and your finger?

If so, you're good to go. If the bottom surface of your lower index finger is pressed against the side of the gun, that means you're having to reach for the trigger. This means that your grip is too large for your hand size. That matters because as you flex your finger to press the trigger, your index finger will contact the side of your gun and gently encourage it to move off target! The good news is that if you're a lousy shot, you can blame the fit of your gun. The other good news is that many newer pistols come with replaceable back straps that change the circumference of the grip itself. If you switch to a smaller size, your finger will be closer to the trigger, which may be enough adjustment to get a proper fit.

Alignment with your arm bone

This second test is a little less obvious. At the range, I see all sorts of shooters struggling with accuracy and the ability to control recoil due to a crooked arm/gun relationship.

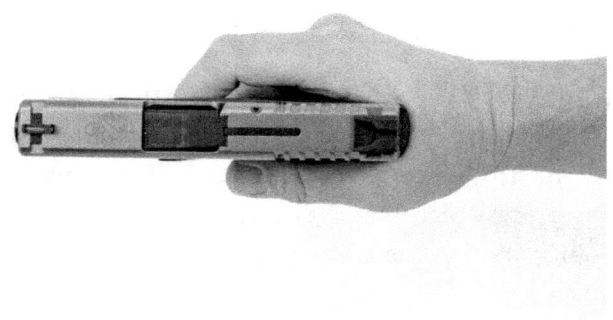

Note there is space between the trigger finger and the frame and the perfect alignment with the forearm. This "fit" is perfect.

When you hold your gun in a firing grip, with your trigger finger placed to pass the finger reach test, the gun barrel should perfectly align with the two bones in your forearm—the radius and ulna. You don't just want the gun barrel to parallel these two bones; you want it to be a direct linear extension of these bones.

If your gun grip is too large for you, you will tend to grasp the gun so that the web of your hand wraps around towards the trigger so your index finger can reach. This means your thumb moves around and is directly behind the gun. With a properly fitted grip, you won't need to reach around to get proper access to the trigger so that the handgun will be aligned as an extension of the bones in your forearm.

Why is this so important? If you have to compensate for a too-large grip by rotating your hand, the back of the handgun will press right against your thumb. There's not much body mass in your thumb to control recoil. You'll feel that recoil, and your gun will likely jump off target with each shot.

By aligning the bigger and heavier parts of your body directly behind the recoil impulse of the pistol, your body mass controls the recoil. Think of the recoil force pushing straight back through the handgun, into your forearm, then your upper arm, and finally into your body. Additionally, the gun benefits from your natural pointing direction. If you close your eyes and try to point your fist at something, you'll notice that your arm bones end up pointed directly at your target. Why not make the gun a simple extension of that natural process?

So, pick up your verified unloaded handgun and try these two tests. If you struggle with either, try a different gun. If yours has an adjustable grip, try a different size.

Grip Angle

Different handguns have different grip angles. The grip angle is the angle between the horizontal line of the barrel and the more "vertical" (give or take) line represented by the grip itself. Some pistols, like Glocks, have a more raked grip angle, while others, like the classic 1911, have grips that are closer to vertical.

You can learn to shoot a handgun with almost any reasonable grip angle, but there's a good chance that your body will point one type more naturally. Here's how to find out if a pistol points naturally for you.

Using an unloaded gun and facing a safe backstop with your finger off the trigger, assume your regular firing grip and start from a low ready position—the barrel pointed towards the ground at a 45-degree angle. Now, close your eyes. Keeping your eyes closed, raise the gun until you think it's pointed at a target of your choosing. Now, open your eyes.

If the sights are pointed high and the barrel angles slightly up, you may prefer a model with a more vertical grip angle. For example, I always point slightly above the target when I do this exercise with Glock-style pistols. I'm usually right on target when I do this with most Sig Sauer pistols, a 1911 or a Springfield Armory XD model. Those are a few examples of pistols with a more traditional grip angle. Other people have the exact opposite experience, so don't go by my findings; try it yourself.

The closed-eyes aiming test will help you find the right grip angle for your carry gun.

Try a few different models to see how they point for you when you're in the gun store. You might be surprised.

Types of Handguns

Just as there are manual transmission and automatic transmission cars with varying door configurations, there are multiple styles of handguns. Most any type or style of handgun can be appropriate for concealed carry, assuming that it's safe and reliable. As with anything else, different designs have pros and cons, so you'll need to weigh those to find the best option for your needs.

Let's review the different types of handguns available and discuss the benefits and disadvantages of each from a concealed carry perspective.

Semi-Automatic Pistols

A pistol is any handgun with the chamber (where the ammunition cartridge rests before firing) integral to the barrel. You might think of the chamber as the rearmost portion of the barrel. What makes a pistol different from a revolver is that ammunition is moved by other means to its single chamber in preparation for firing.

Semi-automatic pistols like this one have a single chamber. Fresh cartridges, stored in a magazine in the grip, are fed into it one by one.

A semi-automatic pistol partially automates the process of loading a cartridge into the chamber, firing it, removing the empty cartridge case, and loading a new one. Every time you press the trigger, the gun will fire. What makes semi-automatic pistols so popular for concealed carry is the use of magazines to store the cartridges. Magazines are easy to change, so reloading a semi-automatic pistol is as easy as inserting a new magazine after dropping the old one with a button press. Reloading is fast as all cartridges are loaded at once.

Pistols also tend to have larger capacities than revolvers. While a revolver may hold five to eight rounds, pistols often hold six to twenty, depending on the model. Common compact (mid-size) pistols typically pack 15 rounds, give or take, into a single magazine.

While the semi-automatic operation is a benefit in itself, there's another upside. With a semi-automatic pistol, some of the energy created by cartridge ignition is "bled off" to operate the ejection and reloading actions. As a result, the user generally feels less recoil than firing the same cartridge from a handgun with a rigid action like a revolver. For defensive use, reduced recoil can help the user get back on target quickly and control the gun more effectively.

Semi-Automatic Pistol Action Types

Because nothing is ever simple, we have to take a diversion to discuss the different types of semi-automatic pistols. We'll discuss the pros and cons of each action type, keeping in mind concealed carry use.

Single-Action

You can take the term "single-action" literally. When you press the trigger of a single-action pistol, one (single) thing happens. The cocked hammer (or internal striker) moves under spring pressure and drives the firing pin into the loaded cartridge.

Since a single action can only drop the cocked hammer, that action must be cocked somehow before the trigger press. Right after loading a single-action pistol, the user must cock the hammer, usually by racking the slide. Various safety mechanisms prevent the hammer from falling until you want it to. Since the pistol is semi-automatic, and the slide operates with each subsequent shot, the hammer gets cocked for the second through last shots until the magazine is empty.

This Smith & Wesson 1911 pistol is a classic example of a single action. Pressing the trigger does nothing unless the hammer is already cocked.

Since the spring-assisted hammer is already cocked, the trigger doesn't require much pressure to operate. That's an excellent bonus for accuracy. With less trigger force required, you're less likely to push the gun off target while operating the trigger.

Let's apply numbers to illustrate the point. Most handguns weigh two or three pounds when fully loaded. A single-action pistol might have a trigger that requires three or four pounds of pressure to operate. A double-action pistol might need 10 to 12, and a striker-fired pistol might require five to seven. What happens when you apply five to 12 pounds of pressure to a two-pound object? The object wants to move. It's up to the shooter and their skill to operate a heavier trigger without pushing the sights slightly off target during the trigger press. The net-net is that a single-action gun is "easier" to shoot accurately.

On the other hand, it's easier to fire an inadvertent shot because a single-action trigger is "light" compared to different styles. This is why most single-action pistols have one or more manual safeties. The operator must disengage the safety before that light trigger can be pressed. For example, the most popular single-action pistol design, the 1911, has two safeties the operator has to disengage. A grip safety is depressed when you hold the pistol properly. There's also a safety lever on the side of the frame that you must clear. Both actions are required before the pistol will fire.

It's up to you to train to disengage the safety every time just before you're ready to fire and not before. It's also up to you to prepare your body and mind to re-engage the safety before reholstering your pistol.

Double-Action

Double-action means that the trigger press motion can accomplish not one but two distinct actions. A double-action gun can use the trigger press to cock the hammer and release it to fire. So, with a double-action gun, you don't (necessarily) need to cock the hammer to fire the weapon. A trigger press can accomplish both functions.

By necessity and those pesky laws of physics, a double-action gun requires more force to operate the trigger when you are asking it to both cock the hammer and release it. It does more work, so it requires more energy on your part. There's no such thing as a free lunch.

Most double-action pistols use an exposed hammer. The first trigger press cocks and releases the hammer. The front lever (far left) decocks the hammer safely.

Here's the part where we start talking about complications and exceptions. You knew that was coming, right?

One of the benefits of most double-action guns is they can operate in either double-action or single-action mode. Technically, you could refer to these as DA/SA (double-action/single-action) pistols. For simplicity, we'll call them double-action—just be aware that some double-action pistols have no single-action mode.

To illustrate how it works, let's walk through a firing sequence for several shots using a double-action pistol.

- The normal resting position of a double-action pistol has the hammer down and un-cocked.
- To fire, that first trigger press requires extra pressure as the hammer gets cocked and released to fire the shot.
- Since we're talking about a semi-automatic pistol, the recoil action associated with the shot not only ejects the empty cartridge and loads a new one but also cocks the hammer.
- That means the second shot doesn't require a double-action operation. The trigger press must only release the hammer, so less pressure is needed to operate the trigger.

So, a double action has a longer and heavier initial trigger press requirement for the first shot. Most modern double-action pistols take 10 to 12 pounds of pressure. The second and subsequent shots require far less pull weight, usually about four pounds. The user experiences two different trigger press sensations for the first and second shots. Gun folks refer to this as a trigger transition.

The transition from a double-action first shot to a single-action second shot has pros and cons.

First, this transition is something to manage. Without practice, one will likely have difficulty placing first and second shots accurately due to the difference in trigger operation.

On the other hand, the heavier and longer initial trigger pull is considered by many to be a benefit that outweighs any transition-related disadvantage. The first shot requires deliberate and intentional effort. In a stressful defensive encounter, that's not a bad thing.

Double actions don't generally require manual safeties because that initial trigger pull acts as a layer of safety in its own right. Revolvers don't carry manual safeties for the same reason—their trigger press weight is also in the 10 to 12-pound range. That's not to say you won't see manual safety devices on double-action guns; they're just not always required. For example, most Sig Sauer double-action pistols don't have safeties—they rely on the heavy double-action trigger press. Many Beretta pistols have a safety device, adding another layer of protection against inadvertent discharge.

Even though a double-action pistol doesn't require a safety, it often has a de-cocking lever. This is a mechanical way to "un-cock" the hammer safely. If you don't fire all rounds in a magazine, you need a way to be sure that you're not reholstering or storing a cocked gun ready to fire in single-action mode, and that's what the decocking lever does. Training to always de-cock a double-action pistol when finished firing is as essential as training to re-apply a manual safety on a single-action pistol.

So, is double-action right for you? Maybe. It's certainly something to try. I like them and don't have an issue with the transition between double and single-action. After shooting them a lot, it's not something I ever notice. I also like that there are no mechanical safeties to worry about during the draw and fire sequence. As with most things, there is no right or wrong answer. Some people value extra peace of mind from a gun designed to use a manual safety. Others don't.

Striker-Fired

A striker-fired pistol is a compromise between a single-action and a double-action pistol. Its design creates a consistent trigger press like a single-action pistol but adds enough weight to make the handgun safe to use without a manual safety.

A striker-fired pistol uses a "striker bar" with a firing pin operated with internal spring tension. No external hammer bashes the striker forward into the cartridge base. The striker is pre-tensioned in its resting condition to get the trigger press weight in that middle zone between single-action and double-action. Think of it this way. There may be a spring between the firing pin and the cartridge with a hammer-fired gun. This spring prevents the striker or firing pin from hitting the cartridge until some external force, like the hammer, overcomes the pressure of the spring and forces the striker to hit the cartridge primer. The spring could be behind the striker or firing pin in a striker-fired gun. This means constant pressure is applied to the striker, encouraging it to move towards the cartridge primer and fire the gun. An internal part called a sear prevents this motion until the trigger is pressed. The sear is a piece of metal holding the hammer or striker in place until enough pressure is applied to the trigger. Most striker-fired guns maintain the striker in a "partially" ready position. The trigger pull applies the rest of the tension necessary to complete a strike on the cartridge base.

These Smith & Wesson M&P pistols are striker-fired designs.

Most striker-fired pistols offer a constant trigger pull from the first to the last shot. The gun is partially cocked with the initial act of chambering a cartridge for the first shot. Each subsequent shot also partially cocks the weapon. The trigger press completes the cocking process, then releases the firing pin. The result of all this striker science is the trigger pressure is usually between five and seven pounds for most pistols. For example, in its standard configuration, the Glock has a trigger press weight of 5.5 pounds. That extra pound and a half (or more) of pull weight is considered enough of a safety buffer that a separate manual safety is not required.

For the concealed carrier, the striker-fired approach has some benefits. There is no transition between the first and second shots. The trigger weight is not nearly as heavy as that of a double-action pistol or revolver, so they are easier to shoot accurately. Last, they are simple to operate—press the trigger, and it fires. For these reasons, most police officers are issued striker-fired pistols like Glocks, Smith & Wesson M&Ps, Sig Sauer P320s, and similar models.

Revolvers

As the name implies, revolvers operate with a revolving cylinder. That arrangement lines up fresh cartridges to the firing position with each double-action trigger press or manual cocking of the hammer. While a pistol has a single chamber and cartridges are fed into it from a magazine, all revolvers have multiple chambers arranged in this cylinder.

This Smith & Wesson 586 L-Comp revolver has seven chambers in its cylinder.

This design presents a technical limitation on ammunition capacity because you must make a larger cylinder to hold more cartridges. At some point, that becomes unwieldy. That's why most revolvers have a capacity of between five and eight rounds.

Like pistols, revolvers can be single-action or double-action.

Since a revolver has no semi-automatic capability, single-action revolvers (think cowboy guns) require the user to manually cock the hammer before each shot. There's no reason you can't use a single-action revolver for concealed carry, but it's rare due to the skill required to operate one proficiently at high speed.

A double-action revolver can be fired repeatedly by pressing the trigger. However, since there is no notion of semi-automatic operation, every shot will be double-action. If you want to take advantage of the single-action mode, you have to manually cock the hammer. For concealed carry, this is not recommended. The whole point of a double-action revolver for defensive use is to leverage the simplicity of just pressing the trigger, even though you will have that heavier weight for every shot. Many revolver models designed for concealed carry have their hammers shrouded or machined off so they can't be manually cocked. A good revolver can have a very light trigger weight in single-action mode, as little as two or three pounds, but that's not desirable for defensive use.

The significant benefit of a revolver for concealed carry is simplicity. There are no firing controls other than the trigger. There are no manual safeties. There are no magazines or slide lock levers. A revolver is as simple as it gets.

Revolvers are generally considered more reliable than semi-automatic pistols, but that's becoming less and less of a factor with modern pistol design and manufacturing quality. Besides, revolvers can malfunction, too. However, when using a revolver, if a cartridge doesn't go bang when you press the trigger, you can usually press the trigger again. A revolver will rotate the defective cartridge out of the way and bring a fresh one into place.

With a semi-automatic pistol, this scenario would require a quick malfunction drill to eject the bad round and insert a new one. Again, the quality of modern self-defense ammunition has largely made this a moot point. In the thousands of rounds of premium defensive ammo I've fired, I've had precisely one fail to ignite, and it was part of a pre-production test run for a new cartridge on the market.

Another simplicity-related benefit is that it's easy to see when a revolver is loaded or unloaded. You see whether cartridges are in the holes by swinging out the cylinder. With a semi-automatic pistol, you must remove the magazine and open the slide to check the chamber.

On the con side, a revolver has limited capacity—by design. Reloading a revolver is more complex and time-consuming than reloading a semi-automatic pistol. While there are speed loaders for revolvers, the operation requires more manual dexterity than simply inserting a new magazine in a pistol.

Derringers

You'll run across alternate handgun types in the concealed carry market. For example, Derringers are handguns that don't have an ammunition feeding mechanism like a revolver or pistol. Most have two barrels, and each is pre-loaded with a cartridge. When you fire those two shots, it's time to reload manually.

For concealed carry, we don't recommend them. When we talk about what handguns actually do and their relative "stopping power" in this book, you'll quickly see that in many real-world cases, two shots aren't enough to stop a violent attack.

7

HOLSTERS

There are few absolutes with concealed carry strategies and tactics, but here's one.

Never, ever, ever carry a handgun without using a proper holster.

That applies to any method of carrying. Don't stuff a handgun into your belt. Don't carry a handgun in a pocket without using a pocket holster. Don't toss your gun into a purse, backpack or briefcase without using an appropriate holster. Don't store a handgun loosely in your car's glove compartment or console. You get the idea. Always use a holster that's purpose-designed for your chosen type of carry.

If you don't use a holster, you risk a plethora of potentially harmful and possibly deadly consequences. Just ask former NFL star Plaxico Burress. While visiting a New York nightclub, Burress (illegally) carried a pistol jammed into the waist of his pants. And no, he wasn't using a holster. While walking up a flight of steps, he felt his handgun moving and instinctively reached to secure it. The resulting "don't let my pistol fall out of my pants" grab resulted in one of his fingers depressing the trigger, and he shot himself in the leg. Burress spent 20 months in jail for violating New York firearms law, but he should be thankful that was the least of his problems. While the leg wound wasn't fatal, it easily could have been. A hit in the femoral artery can lead to incapacity and death in less than a minute or two. Additionally, he was lucky that firing his out-of-control gun didn't hit any bystanders.

There are far too many stories like this one. Do you know what they all have in common? They're completely unnecessary and easily avoidable. Use a proper holster. Always.

Why the Right Holster is So Important

A proper concealed carry holster performs three vital functions.

1. Protects the trigger. A good holster will not only cover but protect the trigger from inadvertent movement during daily carry and even vigorous activity. The holster material should be rigid and durable enough to prevent foreign objects from applying enough pressure to operate the trigger.

2. Presents your handgun consistently. A holster secures your gun in a consistent position and orientation so it's ready for use regardless of physical activity. When you reach for your handgun, the holster should have it positioned in the expected location and oriented correctly so the grip is precisely where you expect it to be.

3. Secures your handgun. A proper holster keeps your firearm secured to your body and under your absolute control, regardless of what you're doing at the time. It won't allow your handgun to come loose under any reasonable circumstance. A great holster keeps your gun secure even when doing vigorous physical activity like running or fighting. I like to check holsters using an unloaded gun. Turn the rig upside down and see if the gun falls out easily. If it does, keep shopping.

There are other benefits to the use of a quality holster. The primary one is peace of mind. I can't speak for you, but I was sure it would show or even fall out at some inopportune moment when I started to carry a concealed handgun. I was constantly touching and verifying my gun to ensure it was secure and hadn't moved. That's bad because it's a visible clue you're carrying a concealed weapon.

A sound holster system, appropriately used, will provide you with plenty of confidence in short order. After a couple of weeks of use, getting in and out of chairs and cars, you'll find that the right holster is doing its job and keeping your handgun secure and concealed.

A good holster like this Galco Gunleather model provides security and stability while protecting the trigger.

A Word on Belts...

A race car with the best engine ever designed will stink if it sits on a poor suspension. The same concept applies to holsters and belts. A good holster can't shine if mounted on a lousy belt.

A proper gun belt might be made of leather, synthetic material, or a blend of both. Whatever the construction, its design goal is simple: It has to support a couple of pounds of handgun weight without stretching or flexing. Over time, a department store belt will soften and stretch. It's just not designed to support the weight, and it's also not designed to maintain rigidity when conditions are humid or sweaty.

By maintaining its structure over time, a quality gun belt will help manage the weight of your firearm. It's no different than the concept behind a good backpack. If you toss 50 pounds of bricks in a burlap sack, mount a couple of loose shoulder straps, and go on a hike, you'll immediately feel the burden of that load. However, a good backpack will mold to your body and hold the weight without allowing it to swing around as you walk. While the physical weight is the same, the load will feel lighter when mounted properly.

A good belt also helps with concealment. By not allowing the heavy pistol to twist or lean, the gun will remain tucked in tight to your body.

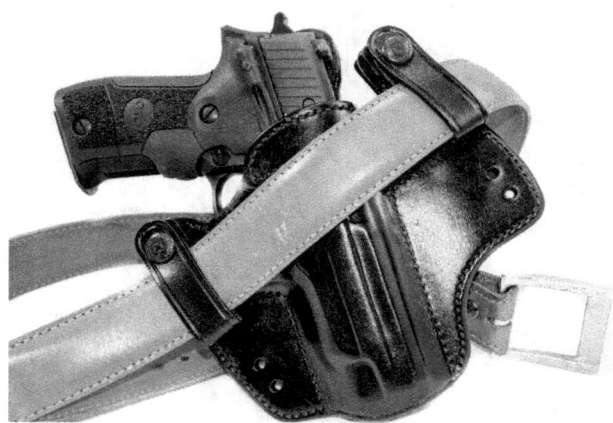

A proper gun belt has a structure appropriate to carry the weight of a holstered handgun without flexing or softening.

Buying a Good Holster

Choosing your defensive handgun is the fun part. Finding just the right one is a satisfying purchase, and most people can justify spending hundreds of dollars on a quality pistol. Whether you appreciate reliability, quality, and craftsmanship, or you recognize that it's worthwhile to invest in a tool that can quite literally save your life, the bite into the wallet isn't as painful when buying a handgun.

On the other hand, buying a holster is like spending money getting your air conditioner fixed. You know you need it, and the cash outlay will make a marked improvement in your life, but few people get excited about spending a bundle on a brand-new air handler.

Here's the thing to remember. Your ability to use that expensive firearm in a fight for your life depends largely on the quality and functionality of the holster you choose. The best defensive handgun on the planet, backed by thousands of hours of training on the range, won't mean diddly-squat if your gun falls out while running from danger or fighting off an attacker. The same applies when that bargain-basement holster belt clip breaks or the retention mechanism gets jammed up. Worse yet, an El Cheapo holster might even facilitate a negligent discharge leading to injury or death.

If you were getting heart bypass surgery, would you be comfortable with your Harvard Medical School surgeon using a budget pack of disposable scalpels from the *Our Prices Are So Cheap We're Insane!* medical supplies discount store? Of course not. So, consider your holster investment while deciding which handgun suits your needs. While not always a perfect indicator, you usually get what you pay for. Plan to spend between $50 and $150 on a quality holster. Yes, I know you can find holsters for less than $19.99. Trust me; it's not worth it. You can also put your old lawnmower gas in your new Aston Martin Vanquish. It'll probably run. More or less. But why would you?

The difference between quality and junk is usually only $25 or so. It's your life at stake, so buy a good one.

Carry Method Tradeoffs

There are four factors to consider when selecting a carry method and corresponding holster that's right for you.

1. Concealment

2. Speed and Ease of Access
3. Retention and Gun Security
4. Safety

The pros and cons of carry methods often contradict each other. For example, a deeper concealment method, like undershirt carry, might have the "cost" of slower and more difficult access. The more buried your handgun is, the more work (and time) it takes to retrieve it. On the other hand, depending on the specific design, that same method may offer a high level of concealment and outstanding gun retention.

You'll need to carefully evaluate how these tradeoffs apply to your lifestyle and daily routines. The important thing is to know what the tradeoffs are and make thoughtful decisions. Careful consideration in advance is the best way to avoid the dangers of a false sense of security.

For example, there may be excellent and unavoidable reasons you need to choose a deeper concealment carry method with the downside of slower access. Does that mean you have no chance of surviving a violent encounter? Not necessarily. It might mean you'll have a more challenging time with some types of defensive conflicts than others. If you use a deep concealment method, responding to the person behind you in line who suddenly pulls a gun and shouts, "Everybody down!" is going to be a challenge—just "having" a gun won't help you in that situation, especially when it's not instantly accessible. On the other hand, if you're at work or in the mall and hear gunshots from some other area, that same carry method may be less limiting to your response options. Just think long and hard about the tradeoffs before taking the easy way out and choosing a carry method for its convenience. While you're at it, ponder how well you might be able to draw your gun with the use of only one hand.

Concealment

Half of "concealed carry" is concealment. Your carry method should allow you to go about your day, doing whatever activities you usually do, without worrying about inadvertently displaying your gun.

In some states, allowing your concealed carry gun to show is a crime. While that may be considered an extreme interpretation of brandishing laws, that's the reality. Even if you live in a more permissive environment or a place where open carry is legal, displaying your concealed carry handgun can create a tactical disadvantage. Your role is to defend yourself and your family, not to be a walking billboard of deterrence. While visibly displaying a firearm may give someone second thoughts about attacking you, it also makes you the center of attention and a prime target. I prefer to keep the decision and timing of any potential engagement under my exclusive control. I only want anyone to know that I have a concealed weapon after I bring it into use.

As we'll discuss, some carry methods promise deep and discreet concealment benefits. Others require you to "dress around" the carry position for adequate concealment. So which is better? That depends. You'll almost always sacrifice something in return for deep concealment. As long as you know those tradeoffs, you'll be making an informed decision.

Speed and Ease of Access

As you evaluate the pros and cons of different holster types and carry methods, I want you to consider, and ideally test, your ability to access your defensive handgun quickly and without fumbling. Let's consider an extreme example to illustrate this point.

Suppose your work environment requires you to maintain deep concealment. You have to wear pants or a skirt with the shirt or top firmly tucked in. That rules out many forms of carrying on the waist. You could duct tape your handgun to your stomach, wrapping it around your body several times to press the pistol into your gut. When you dress normally, concealment will be perfect—nothing exposed or protruding will provide any hint that you're carrying. However, when you need to draw your handgun to fend off some violent attack, you'll need medical shears, three extra hands, and an uninterrupted half-hour to bring your firearm into the fight.

On the other end of the spectrum, you could use one of those action pistol competition race holsters perfectly positioned a couple of inches outside your hipbone. You can draw in less than a second but must wear a baggy trench coat to conceal your defensive rig.

While the comparisons sound extreme, that's the nature of the tradeoff you'll have to consider. If you need to wear tucked-in or more form-fitting clothing, you can use a deep concealment carry method like a carry undershirt or a belly band. Concealment is excellent, but drawing your handgun can require several steps and extra time. You'll need to move clothing out of the way and then extricate your firearm. There's a good chance these operations will require both hands, too.

That brings up a related consideration. Will your carry method allow you to draw and, ideally, reholster, only using your firing-side hand? On paper, you may think using two hands to retrieve your weapon quickly is not a problem. The assumption seems to make sense. "Hey, if I see trouble coming, I'll just quickly retrieve my firearm!" Here's the problem. *You don't get to decide whether you'll have two hands available.* You might be fighting off a surprise attack with one hand. You may be moving or shielding a child with one hand. You may be calling for help with one hand. You may be trying to open a door—or hold one shut. The list goes on. If you choose a carry method that requires two hands to draw your firearm, be aware of the potential consequences.

Carry Methods and Holster Types

In this section, we will explore some of the more common ways to carry a concealed handgun and present the pros and cons of each method. We're all different and have varying daily routines, so the best carry method for me may not work well for you. Consider various techniques, and when you narrow it down, test it out using a carefully unloaded and verified "safe" gun. Before making a final decision, remember a few things.

As the saying goes, concealed carry is intended to be comforting, not comfortable. No matter how you slice it, you add a pound or three of weight and some metal and plastic bulk to your wardrobe. This will carry a "comfort" price tag. Gear and technique can help minimize the impact; just be sure to have realistic expectations. Carrying a concealed handgun is a commitment.

Don't assume you have to carry a tiny handgun. There's a lot of "myth" around the "I can't carry a larger gun" claim, so don't fall for it. As we've discussed elsewhere in this book, a physically larger handgun is easier to shoot well, especially while under stress. Prioritize effectiveness over carry convenience. Many carry methods we'll discuss allow you to carry a mid to large-sized handgun.

With any carry method, always exercise extreme care when drawing and holstering. While you may need to draw quickly in an emergency, reholstering never requires speed. As the folks at Gunsite Academy say, "Reholster reluctantly." I love that advice.

Inside the Wasitband

There's a reason inside-the-waistband (IWB) is so popular.

It works.

IWB carry refers to mounting the holster and handgun on your belt but tucking the holster and the larger part of the handgun inside your pants or skirt. The classic IWB carry method has the handgun placed on your strong (firing hand) side, usually just behind the hip bone. When relaxed, your arm and hand are in a natural position to grasp your gun.

IWB holsters generally use loops or clips to attach the holster to your belt. These fasteners are attached to the outside of the holster body so that most of the body (and the gun inside) can ride inside your clothing. Imagine an upside-down "V" where one part goes inside the clothing and the other outside. You'll also find holster models that use loops outfitted with snaps. As long as the snaps are sturdy and won't come loose inadvertently, these can be handy as you can mount and remove the holster without unthreading your belt. You'll also see clip holsters. Instead of a complete loop, a clip wraps over the exterior of the belt surface and hooks underneath. This design prevents the holster from coming out of your clothes as you draw, thanks to the retention provided by that lower hook.

When your handgun is tucked inside your pants, shorts, or skirt, you get a couple of important carry benefits.

First, most of the gun is concealed by your natural clothing—no extra planning is required to cover the barrel and action. Sure, there's a bump, but few people inspect others' midsections. Of course, you'll need to plan to hide the gun's grip section that's exposed above the beltline using a shirt, blouse, or jacket. The grip must remain exposed above the beltline to get a proper firing grip as you draw.

IWB holsters keep most of the gun hidden inside the pants, so the user only has to conceal the part above the beltline. Different models are designed for different positions on the belt.

Second, IWB carry uses the natural pressure of your clothing and belt against your body to keep the gun tucked in close. Mounted correctly, it won't flop around as you move. So, you get both a concealment aid and better firearm retention. A quality holster makes your gun less likely to come out during vigorous physical activity. When I say "quality holster," I mean one that helps hold your gun securely. Those soft and mushy holsters feel comfortable but allow the handgun to slide right out. If you ever end up fighting for your life, the last thing you want is your gun slipping out at some inopportune moment.

There is a downside to IWB carry. Unless you already wear slightly oversized clothing, you'll have to plan for the extra space required on the inside of your pants or skirt. You're sticking relatively large objects (a holster and gun) inside of your pants, so plan on an extra wearing a size larger than usual—as much as two inches. Yes, this is inconvenient. Depending on your waist size and clothing preferences, you may find you can do with a smaller size, so experiment a bit. Hey, look on the bright side. That extra size penalty will incentivize you to lay off the donuts!

One more thing. Even though you're getting an assist from your clothes to support the weight and bulk of your handgun, you'll still want to use a proper gun belt. The difference between comfortable and secure carry almost always comes back to the quality of your belt. While some department store belts may look wide and sturdy, authentic gun belts are purpose-built to resist softening and flexing over time. That sturdy platform on which you mount a gun and holster keeps things from moving around, making your rig feel lighter and more secure.

Here are some tips to make your inside-the-waistband carry easier.

Use Layers

Here's a trivia fact for you. Ever wonder how they sand the rust off old container ships? They use inside the waistband holster rigs. OK,

I'm just kidding, but if the holster body against your bare skin doesn't cause a raw spot, the textured grip on a handgun will.

Many folks swear by a cotton undershirt's comfort properties, even in hot weather. You'll get additional benefits if you carry a handgun inside the waistband. A t-shirt between the holster and gun and your body will certainly help protect your sensitive areas from abrasion. In addition to the padding benefit, a t-shirt will help stabilize the whole rig. The friction between the gun, holster and undershirt will keep your gun from moving around as you go about your day and help distribute the gun's weight. You'll be surprised at the difference.

Be Careful with Tuckables

Holster company marketing teams promote the ability to wear tucked-in shirts or blouses with their tuckable clip features. These holsters (the clips) are made so that the belt clips attach to the holster somewhat lower than the belt line. This creates a hinge effect that leaves some space between the inside surface of your IWB holster and the clip mounts. Your shirt drapes down over the handgun grip and tucks between the holster clip mounts and the outside surface of the holster body. In the previous photo, the two holsters on the left are "tuckable." You can see how your shirt can fit between the belt and holster body.

In theory, the only thing visible is whatever portion of the clip is on the outside of your belt and perhaps a bit of metal or plastic hooking over your pants or skirt and looping back inside your clothing. With some models, the color of the exposed portion of the clip is designed to match the color of your belt. With other designs, the clips may hook on the bottom and top of the belt, limiting what is exposed on the outside surface of the belt.

This might be a viable option if you work in an office environment where tucked-in shirts are required. But there's a catch, and we're getting into opinion territory here. I'll share mine, but I will readily admit your mileage may vary.

The tuckable design relies on minimal exposure of parts and the hope that people generally don't pay attention to others' midsections. Both are typically true statements—the average man or woman on the street is usually so immersed in their smartphone that they pay attention to little else, and even with a face-to-face encounter, few are likely to be inspecting the more awkward zones on the human body.

I notice. And I know many other habitual concealed carriers who notice, too. I guess it comes with paying closer attention to one's surroundings than the average bear. And in this case, there are two things to see: a significant bulge created by the handgun and holster and the belt clips. Do professional criminals pay attention to such things? It beats me, but I'll bet the average law enforcement officer notices such details. Assuming you're adhering to concealed carry laws in your state, you're probably OK whether or not someone else knows you're carrying, at least from a legal perspective. After all, none of your firearm is showing, so you're not technically "brandishing" a gun.

I do like tuckable IWB carry when wearing a jacket or sportcoat as it offers "layers" of concealment. With most of the gun and holster tucked under clothes, I don't worry too much about a blazer or jacket swinging open and exposing my handgun.

Location, Location, Location

Traditional IWB holsters are designed to be worn just behind the hip bone. This placement takes advantage of a natural pocket in your body contour that helps hide and protect the handgun. Not only is the gun slightly hidden behind the bulge of your hip bone, but the placement allows the gun's grip to wrap around the back of your body rather than sticking out straight backward. If it's placed right on the hip bone, you add bulk to the broadest part of your midsection, which can hinder concealment and result in more "gun bumps" against doors, chairs, and other people.

If you carry some extra weight, this placement helps avoid the areas in the front and sides that tend to collect the spare tire. Do experiment with specific placement, as small location shifts forward and back can significantly improve comfort and concealment.

Cover Garments... For Concealment

IWB carry relies on a cover garment—a shirt, blouse, blazer, or jacket that is untucked and covers the exposed grip area of the gun.

I've always had the best concealment success with materials with structure. The softer and silkier the cover material, the more likely it is to wrap around the contour of your handgun rather than drape freely over it. Shirts like those nylon polos or t-shirts can work, but be sure they're not too form-fitting. I have much better luck with "stiffer" materials like cotton, linen or more rigid synthetic materials. Fake stuff can also cause problems with static electricity, causing your shirt to cling.

Also, consider the color and pattern. Busy patterns tend to hide printing lines, so it's less likely to show even if your cover is draping around your firearm. I lean towards darker colors for solids as they do a better job of hiding shadows.

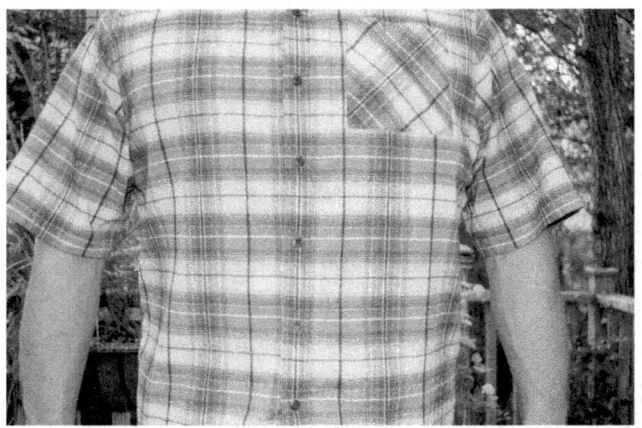

This Blackhawk shirt is designed for concealed carry. It's made from a sturdier material, and the design helps hide printing. There's a full-sized gun under here somewhere. Can you spot it?

Cover Garments... For Access

While hiding your firearm is essential, making sure it's accessible and fumble-free can be a life—or—death matter. When you go to draw in a hurry, those thin, silky shirts are more likely to get tangled up.

The heavier and more structured the cover material is, the more likely you can lift it completely out of the way until you withdraw your firearm. While shirts and jackets require different motions, the underlying principle is the same. Think about swinging a heavy coat out of the way. The weight and structure provide enough "inertia" to help it remain clear for a fraction of a second while you draw the gun. Materials with no weight must be held in a cleared position while you complete your business. The more a fabric type wants to flop back into place, the more trouble you'll have moving it out of the way to draw your gun.

Companies like 5.11 Tactical and Blackhawk make excellent concealed carry shirts with both concealment and access features included. Many of these have a bonus feature: faux buttons that are snaps. You can tear the shirt open in a jam to access your defensive weapon. While it looks cool in the movies, ripping actual buttons rarely works—they're surprisingly hard to tear off. This is especially handy for alternate carry methods like those undershirts with gun pockets. You'll need to clear a lot of material out of the way to reach our gun.

Move Like You're Old

You should break your habit of bending forward at the waist to pick things up. With a gun on your side, that motion will cause the grip to poke backward past your body's profile. Even with a long enough cover garment, this motion will likely set off alarm bells if bystanders are paying attention.

So, take a grace lesson from the Queen of England and bend at the knees to lower your body.

Experiment!

Don't get discouraged. Success with carrying inside the waistband is a game of trial and error. Fractions of an inch with holster placement, up, down, higher or lower, can make a big difference in comfort and concealment. Remember you are carrying an extra pound or two, so it may never be "comfortable."

Appendix Carry

Appendix carry isn't new; the tactical cool kids have been doing it for years, but it is becoming more mainstream. There are some significant benefits to appendix carry but also some potential disadvantages. There's plenty of hearsay on the topic, so as a committed strong-side IWB daily carrier, I embarked on a multi-month trial and training regimen to find out for myself.

We'll present both benefits and concerns here, and like any other commentary in this book, it's up to you to evaluate and make your own decisions.

Security

With appendix carry, your rig rides in the most protected area of your body. Not only are we naturally protective of our "guts" area, but our hands are, by definition, always in the nearby vicinity, so it's relatively easy and natural to protect that zone. If you are in a struggle, you have good leverage to protect your handgun.

The positioning also uses your body as a natural protective backstop. With traditional "on the hip" carry, your gun protrudes outward from the side of your body. It's not unusual to bump against chairs, doorframes or people as you go about your day. With appendix carry, these impacts are very unlikely.

Put all this together, and this carry position makes it easy to keep your gun under your control.

Concealment

Like traditional IWB carry, the gun's muzzle is hidden under clothing, so concealment is kind of "built-in." You are left with hiding the handgun grip. When carried on the hip, a handgun grip can easily extend past the body. With appendix carry, since we are usually wider sideways than front to back, your body naturally covers the entire grip area. If you need to bend over or lean forward, nothing sticks out the side to tent your cover garment.

For me, concealing any gun is almost always easier with appendix carry. I also find I can more easily carry a full-sized gun. For example, I often carry a full-size, double-stack, 9mm 1911, while wearing shorts and a T-shirt.

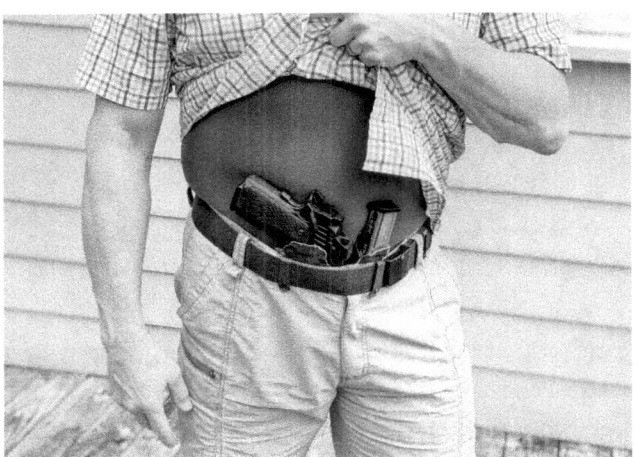

One big advantage of appendix carry is the ease of concealment for both a larger gun and a spare magazine. They're both easy to secure in this position too.

Speed of Draw

Drawing from an appendix position can be exceptionally fast. If you think about the draw motions in terms of economy of movement, you're arguably removing some movement compared to a traditional strong-side hip position. Rather than moving your shoulder to get the firing hand back near the hip position, appendix draws only require raising your firing hand by bending your elbow. Likewise, clearing the cover garment requires less movement by the support-side hand. With a similar elbow bend, the support hand is perfectly positioned to raise your shirt or other cover garment. The bottom line is that both hands have to make shorter and more natural movements to access the handgun when it's in the forward location.

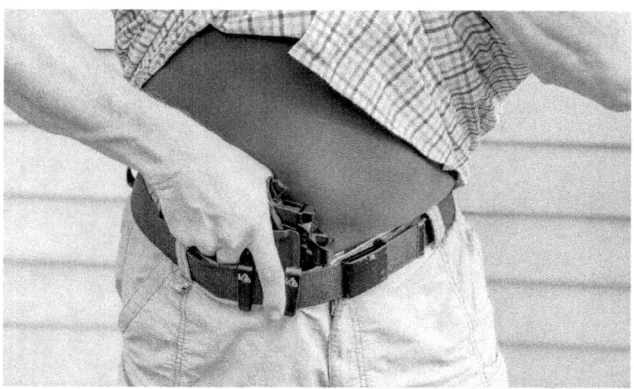

One advantage of appendix carry is the efficiency of clearing the cover garment and accessing your handgun.

As a side note, you might also find that appendix carry allows improved gun access from a seated position. With an unloaded and checked gun, you may want to experiment with draws from different positions: standing, seated, in a car, etc.

Error Rate

For the same reasons that draw speed can be noticeably faster, the "error rate" of an appendix draw is lower, at least in my experience. The farther back your handgun is placed (think behind the hipbone), the farther both hands have to reach away from their natural working area to move the cover garment out of the way and access the gun. More awkward reach and movement can translate to snagging and tangling your gun and clothing. This scenario was a contributing factor leading to a security volunteer's murder in the West Freeway Church of Christ 2019 shooting incident. While he was fighting to extricate his handgun from under his clothing, he was shot and killed by the attacker.

Any drawing method relies on variables like position, cover garment fabric qualities and more. Still, reducing the reach and travel required for both draw and support hands can minimize the "error rate."

Muzzling Sensitive Areas

The wisecracks about appendix carry refer to the risk of shooting your private parts. Other folks raise concerns about the handgun's muzzle pointing toward the femoral artery. Please make no mistake; it is possible to muzzle both areas. Depending on your precise carry position (12 o'clock, two o'clock or somewhere in between), the muzzling scenario is more likely while drawing or reholstering your pistol.

While your body shape may vary, with most appendix placements, the muzzle is pointed more between your legs than toward the deep interior of the upper leg where the femoral artery resides. The gun size and length have a say on whether the muzzle, when holstered, is directed toward sensitive body parts. For those of us with extra baggage around the waist area, the belly can apply pressure to the gun's grip, levering the muzzle back toward the body. Hold this thought until we get recommended tips in the next section.

As with any carry method, the gun is "inert" while safely holstered, so the genuine concern over muzzling boils down to removing and reinstalling the gun into the holster. When people manage to shoot themselves, and they do with virtually any carry position, it's almost exclusively during holstering and drawing operations. When evaluating your preferred carry method, consider not just where the gun points when holstered but how the muzzle moves when drawing and holstering your gun.

The Net-Net

Appendix carry offers several benefits and one big potential draw-back—a negligent discharge aimed at higher-risk parts of the body than with other carry positions. While you can shoot yourself with any carry method, the more traditional placements might result in injuries to your outer leg rather than sensitive body parts of your inner thigh areas. If you're going to evaluate appendix carry seriously, don't play around. Get quality training. Practice and train with inert or carefully unloaded firearms. Develop perfect trigger discipline. Develop extremely reluctant reholstering procedures.

Here are a few tips for more successful appendix carry.

Padding!

If your holster pivots around the beltline, driving the muzzle toward your body, try adding a foam pad to the back of the holster body. The foam will press the muzzle away from your body and the grip closer to your body. If you envision your belt as the fulcrum, adding pressure to the part below tilts the whole rig in a favorable direction for both concealment and comfort.

These are commercial wedges made with sturdy, closed-cell foam and attached with Velcro.

Many holster companies sell pads with hook and loop fasteners for just this purpose, but you can easily fashion your own. If you go that route, use closed-cell foam, which will hold up to daily wear and tear. You also might want to experiment with different thicknesses and shapes. Many commercial versions are shaped like a wedge, with the thicker part of the foam lower on the holster body.

I use wedges on all my appendix holsters, and they make a big difference. If you're struggling with this carry choice, give it a try!

Larger Guns Can Be Better

There is a counter-intuitive tip for appendix carry, especially if you're not as fit and trim as one of those fragrance models you see on TV. A longer handgun, usually full size with a four-inch or more barrel, can be more comfortable and concealable.

I know this makes no sense but bear with me. With the proper appendix position placement, the gun's muzzle is kinda-sorta between your legs, so the extra handgun and holster length have a place to go. Now, think of your belt as a fulcrum, with the grip on one side (above) and the muzzle on the other (below). When combined with a bit of "spare tire around the waist," a short pistol can often apply pressure on the grip, rotating the muzzle back toward your body. A more extended setup applies pressure from clothes and body against the muzzle, pressing the grip above that belt fulcrum back towards the body.

This is one of those "your mileage may vary" things, and you'll want to experiment. Just be aware that shorter and smaller handguns don't always work better in the appendix position. I always carry a full-size gun this way because it conceals and rides more predictably. Smaller handguns seem to flop around more for me when carried in the appendix position.

Concealment Wings

A concealment wing extends from the holster body away from the centerline toward your hip. Its purpose is to exert pressure against the rear of the belt, pushing the grip side of the holster and gun toward your body. This causes the gun grip to ride closer to the contour of your body.

Note the concealment wing on the far left. It presses against the inside of the belt, forcing the gun grip closer to the body to aid concealment.

Position Matters

A slight adjustment closer to or farther from the centerline can make a big difference in comfort and concealment. I find the most comfortable position at about one o'clock, just to the right of my belt buckle. I rotate my belt a touch counter-clockwise to move the buckle to the left, keeping it out of the way from the holster mounts. I'm right-handed, so reverse these positions if you're a left-handed shooter.

Adjusting your holster position will alter the tradeoffs between the holster riding between your legs or on top of your strong-side thigh. You'll feel the results of your tradeoffs when you sit. More toward two o'clock, you'll feel more pressure against your leg.

Reholstering

While you should always reholster your handgun reluctantly, slowly, and with great care, making sure your finger is off the trigger, safeties or decockers activated, and no other obstructions are present, there are things you can do to add additional layers of protection.

You can remove the holster, insert your gun, and then reinstall the holster. Or, if you want to reholster with the holster mounted to your belt, you can shove your midsection forward. In this position, as you lower your handgun into your holster, the muzzle is pointed at the ground, forward of your body.

Outside the Waistband

Lots of gun folks claim outside-the-waistband (OWB) carry is the only way to go. Lots of gun folks also live on prairies in cowboy land, where it's perfectly normal to dress like Clint Eastwood in one of those old spaghetti westerns. All kidding aside, OWB is a great way to carry a gun. It may not work in your locale, especially if you live in New York or Chicago. It can also be challenging when you go about your daily business sans jackets or coats in warmer climates.

The primary benefits of OWB carry are comfort and accessibility. With nothing jammed inside of your beltline, your midsection will thank you. That same lack of pressure provides a bit more room during the draw to obtain a proper firing grip when you reach for your gun.

Outside-the-waistband holsters require a cover garment long enough to hide the gun vertically and wrap around the body sufficiently to hide the gun horizontally. Remember, with OWB carry, no part of the gun is inside your pants or skirt, so you have to plan for full coverage. That means a longer shirt or jacket.

Many gun folks use photographer vests as a cover garment because they are bulky and long—perfect for hiding a gun and holster on the belt. Lots of other gun folks refer to these as 'shoot me first' vests. That's because they believe the only people who wear them are either carrying guns (pretty likely) or professional photographers (pretty unlikely.) As with most things, the reality is probably somewhere in the middle.

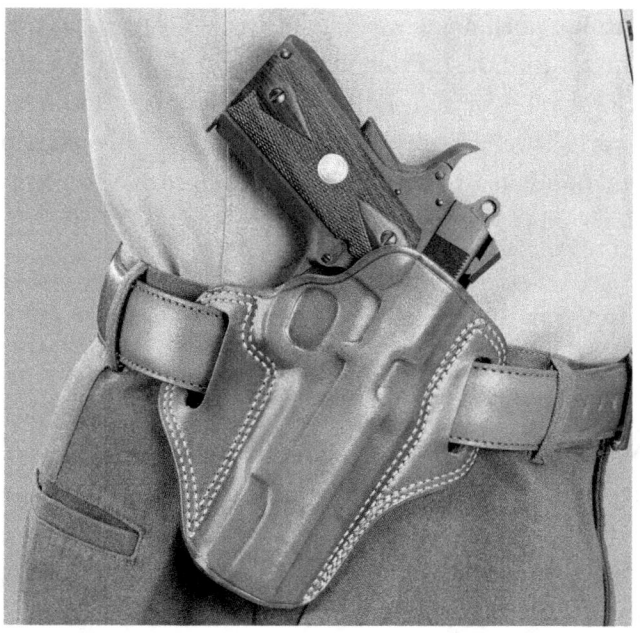

This Galco Gunleather Combat Master is a perfect example of a quality outside-the-waistband holster. Photo: Galco Gunleather.

I prefer getting more creative with cover garments and using untucked button-down shirts. Heavier weights of fabric work best to hide the print of your gun. I also like to use a blazer to dress things up a little, and the weight of a blazer does a pretty good job of concealment as long as you mount your gun behind the hip bone. Be careful of how you move, though, to avoid flashing! Windy days will drive you nuts, blowing your coattails backward, so check the weather before you leave the house. Be sure to maintain constant awareness of your jacket position.

Consider these tips for outside-the-waistband carry.

Dress Heavy

Heavier cover garments are always better. Yes, we know it gets hot in the summer, and you have to compromise, so do the best you can. Here's why. Not only does heavier material show less of an outline of a gun, but the weight helps prevent it from moving or blowing out of the way and exposing your gun.

Use Angles to Your Advantage

Consider using a holster with a forward cant. In plain English, the grip is angled forward while the muzzle is positioned more to the rear if you envision the holster pivoting at the beltline.

Not only does the forward angle make for a smoother draw motion, it brings the muzzle of your gun closer to the belt, which means you don't need as long of a cover garment.

A forward cant angle also reduces the distance the handgun grip protrudes backward, minimizing visible tenting when you lean forward. Note the effect of the cant angle in the previous picture.

Use Weights

If your cover garment is a sports coat or jacket, put something heavy in the pocket on the gun side. Consider things like a roll of dimes, a fishing weight, or car keys. Be resourceful! If you want to do it right, sew a fishing weight in place for a more permanent solution. A little weight will help keep your cover garment from moving around as much. Another benefit is that when you sweep the garment out of the way to draw, the weight will help it stay clear while removing the handgun. I also like to put something in the opposite pocket so one doesn't hang lower than the other.

Retention Features

Pay attention to retention—those features of a holster that secure the gun. People assume that law enforcement officers are the only ones who need a retention holster. That's because law enforcement types are more likely to get into a scuffle with someone who's trying to take their gun. But positive retention is also a great feature, even if you're just moderately active. Do a lot of walking, climbing, running, motorcycle riding, or Samba dancing? A retention feature might be helpful to make sure you and your gun stay together throughout your daily travels.

Most concealed carry holsters rely on a tight and perfectly molded fit to keep the handgun in place via friction alone. Others have a retention adjustment screw, which allows you to tighten the pressure of the holster body against the gun. You find your preferred tradeoff between retention and ease of draw. Other holster designs have "positive" retention—some lock or lever system that keeps the gun in place until you manually release the mechanism with a finger or thumb.

As OWB holsters don't have the extra benefit of your belt squeezing the holster and gun between your belt and body like IWB holsters, you need to make sure your holster is up to the task. I like to insert my unloaded gun into the holster, turn it upside down, and shake it to ensure it doesn't easily fall out. Remember, the gun will be a lot heavier when loaded.

Save the Back

Hollywood loves to show heroes and villains alike tucking guns into the back of their belts, usually sans holsters.

Even with a holster, there are some potential downsides to this location.

While under stress, the draw itself can be problematic—it's a long way to reach, and you can't use your other hand easily to move clothes out of the way. This increases the odds of a snag and results in a slower draw. Then there's the issue of pointing your muzzle in undesirable directions as you bring the gun to the front.

The real risk is the potential for injury. In a self-defense encounter, you may very well find yourself in a physical confrontation, and if you hit the ground on your backside, you've got a hunk of steel jamming into the base of your spine. Even without a direct injury, should you find yourself on your back, that gun will be hard to access.

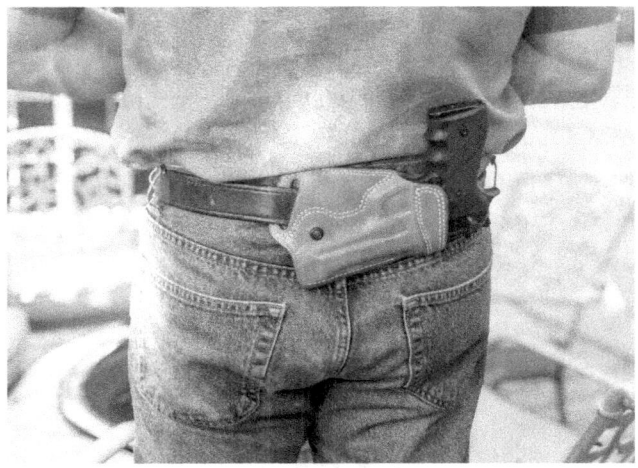

I worry about security and ease of reach with this position.
Another problem is you have a hunk of steel behind your spine. If
you hit the ground during a fight, it may cause serious injury.

Body Carry: Shirts and Belly Bands

The most common form of "body" carry is concealment undershirts. Usually made of tight, stretchy Spandex material, these undershirts have special pockets under the support side arm to hold a handgun. To draw, you reach across your body with your firing hand, drawing your gun from underneath your opposite side arm. It's a reach. Now remember that all of this is underneath your regular shirt. Hold that thought...

A similar alternative is a belly band. Made of a thick elastic band with sewn-in holster pockets, a belly band is worn under a shirt or similar clothing. You can position it wherever you like—closer to your waist or higher on your torso. Many belly bands have multiple holster pockets, so you can adjust your carry position to draw from your firing side, like IWB or the opposite side, as with an undershirt holster. You can even position it similarly to appendix carry placement.

The level of concealment with body carry would make a tax-evading Congressperson proud. Folks will find your Swiss bank accounts and campaign staffer romances long before they find your concealed gun with this carry method. Your gun is entirely covered by everyday clothing, and you can even wear tucked-in shirts.

With most body carry methods, gun security is fantastic. You feel it. You know it's there. There's very little chance that your gun will tumble out of your control without you noticing.

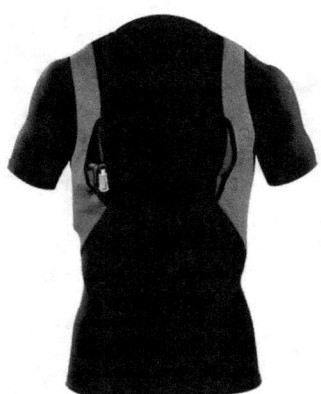

This 5.11 Tactical undershirt holster features pockets on both sides.
Photo: 5.11 Tactical.

As for practical considerations, hugging Aunt Martha can be weird if you're not careful. If you carry the gun on one side of your body or the other, you can adjust your hugging style to be more angular. If you carry a gun on one side and spare magazines on the other, then I suppose you have to quickly develop a case of Aphenphosm-phobia. That's fear of being touched, which should cover the bases for most hugging encounters.

On the other hand, drawing your gun is like removing your underwear while keeping your pants on. The reach is long and awkward, but you must also reach under or through whatever shirt or garment is over the holster undershirt. This is the big drawback of body carry methods—the relatively slow speed at which you can draw your gun.

Consider these tips for interior carry methods.

Custom Carry Shirts

In Hollywood, if you need to get your shirt out of the way quickly, you rip, and buttons fly everywhere, resulting in instant clothing removal. In real life, buttons are more stubborn than a toddler candy shopping in the checkout lane. Using an old shirt, try it sometime. You'll be shocked at how hard it is to clear a path through a buttoned-up shirt to access an undershirt or belly band holster.

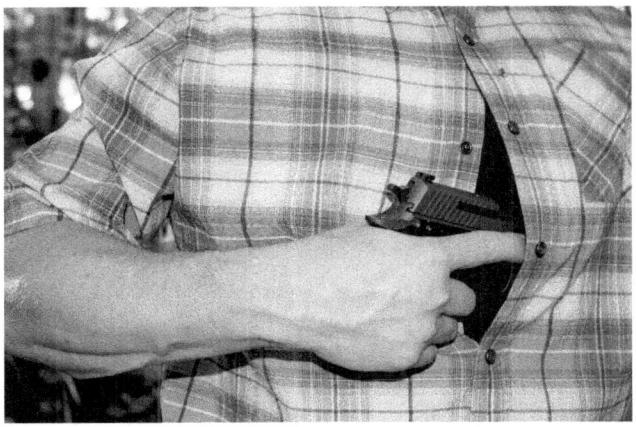

If you're carrying using an undershirt "holster" snaps instead of buttons are a must for easy access. Shirts like this one use snaps disguised as normal buttons.

Enter an ingenious solution. Enterprising companies have developed "normal looking" shirts with a secret twist: snaps disguised as buttons. If you need to reach through your shirt to access an undershirt or belly band-mounted gun, jam your hand between any fake buttons, and the snaps instantly pop, clearing plenty of space.

Companies constantly change their product lines, so check with 5.11 Tactical and Blackhawk for starters. Some enterprising concealed carriers make their own clothing.

Holster Pocket Retention and Access

Undershirt holsters rely on two methods for gun retention. One method is to place the gun pocket high and directly under your arm. This achieves good retention from your arm covering the gun's grip, although some models still have a velcro retention strap. Retention is usually good, thanks to your arm helping keep the gun in place and protected. Practice frequently for models with extra retention straps, as clearing that strap with one hand can be tricky.

Other designs use a pocket mounted lower on the shirt and rely on a Velcro closure to keep the gun in the pocket. These models are a bit easier on the draw as you don't have to reach as far around the body. However, as the gun isn't directly under your arm, you need to be sure the closures are strong enough to keep your gun in place. The stretchy material of the shirt is slippery, and I've seen guns slide right out if not properly secured.

Be sure to order your undershirt on the tighter side: this will help with gun retention.

Belly Band Placement

Experiment, experiment, experiment! Try it higher and lower on your body. There are lots of ways to use a belly band holster.

If your belly band holster has any angled pockets, try wearing it inside-out to achieve a different gun position. This will reverse the cant angle of holster pockets. Doing this may allow you to use your belly band holster in a completely different setup. Use your imagination!

Undershirts are your friend with belly band holsters. While they are wearable against bare skin, the elastic materials used in their construction are not necessarily comfortable.

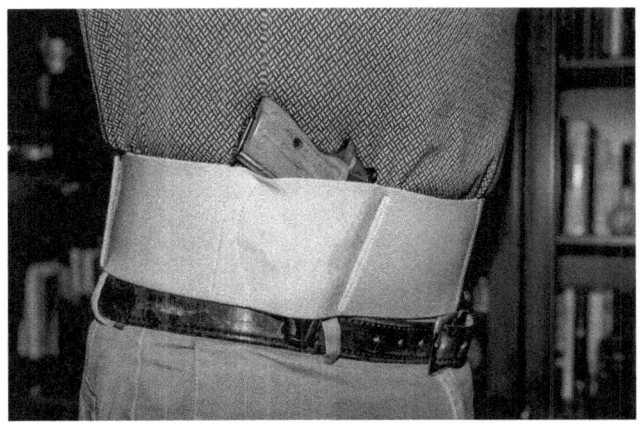

This Galco Belly Band features multiple holster pockets. By reversing it, you can create many carry configurations. It's shown here outside the shirt for clarity.

Pocket Holsters

It's hard to beat a properly sized pocket holster for convenience. Headed out to the local Stop and Rob for a gallon of milk? Grab your pocket pistol and go. Skip the hassle of mounting and dismounting belt or other holster rigs.

Another benefit: if you find your "evil dude" radar going off, you can casually stick your hand in your pocket to be ready if things go sideways.

Do you spend much time in an environment where concealment is paramount? With the advent of smartphones, folks are accustomed to seeing others with lots of junk in their pockets. With the right gun and pocket holster, no one will ever know you're carrying a gun instead of other daily necessities.

The pocket limits the size of the gun you carry, but weight is also a consideration. Of course, a cargo pants pocket can allow you to carry even a mid-sized gun discreetly, but traditional pants pockets will limit you to a small revolver or pocket-sized auto pistol.

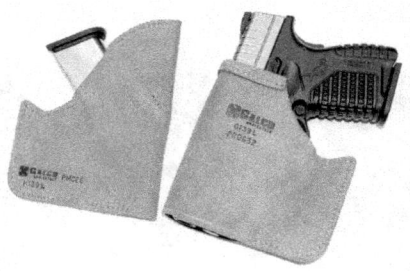

This matched pair of Galco pocket holsters is designed for your gun and spare ammo. Insert them in opposite pockets.

With today's handgun offerings, you should have little problem finding a pocket-suitable gun that works for you in 9mm, .380 ACP, .38 Special, or .357 Magnum. There are even some .40 S&W and .45 ACP models available that are pocket-holster-friendly. However, they might be a little less friendly in terms of recoil!

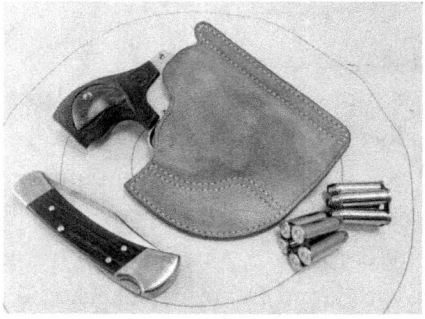

The snubnose revolver is the classic pocket-carry handgun. Note the "hook" designed to catch on the insider of the pocket to keep the holster in place while you draw the gun.

Here's the main thing to watch out for when choosing and using a pocket holster—the monkey trap gotcha. According to the story, the way to catch a monkey is to place a piece of fruit on the far side of a hole just big enough for the monkey's hand. When the hungry monkey grabs the fruit, its hand is too big to withdraw from the hole. Monkeys, greedy like humans, are unwilling to relinquish the fruit to regain their freedom. True? Got me, but it's an excellent analogy for trying to draw too large of a gun from too small of a pocket.

Consider the circumference of your pocket opening. Now, figure the approximate circumference of your gun in its pocket holster, with your hand wrapped around it in a proper firing grip. And herein lies the key: with any drawing technique, the idea is to get a firing grip the first time your hand contacts the gun—you don't want to be shifting it around as you draw. When you grasp the gun, is the pocket circumference larger than your gun-filled hand? This sounds a bit silly, but ensuring your pants and pocket holster choices are compatible is critical. Try it on with the pants you'll most likely wear before you buy. Make sure you can draw easily and without hangups. If you're not able to draw already having a firing grip, it's not a viable solution.

Here are a few tips for pocket holster carry.

Reholstering

The safest way to secure your gun in almost all pocket holsters is to place the gun in the holster first. Only then do you put the holster into your pants pocket with the gun inserted. Shoving a gun with an unprotected trigger into a pocket is asking for trouble. Be sure to check the manufacturer recommendations for your specific model.

Pants Testing

I can't over-emphasize the importance of careful pocket size consideration. Pants with more horizontal pocket openings, like those on many blue jeans, tend to have a smaller opening than dress pants. Wear the pants you intend to use most frequently when you shop for pocket holsters. And do test, with an unloaded gun, all of the pants you plan to use with your pocket holster. Pocket sizes and geometry vary.

Travel Clean

Never carry anything else in the same pocket as your gun and holster. This is asking for trouble! The last thing you want is a set of keys or loose breath mints to get jammed up in the trigger guard. And you certainly don't want to fight through a pocket scrapyard to reach your gun.

Don't Draw Your Holster

Good pocket holsters are designed to separate from the handgun during the draw. Some use a sticky exterior material to "grab" the inside of your pocket. Others have shaped hooks or wings designed to catch on the edges of the pocket so the gun comes out, but the holster remains trapped inside. As you might guess, quality matters with pocket holsters, too. It's not only embarrassing to draw a gun with a holster still attached; the consequences can be tragic.

Look for Stability

One of the primary purposes of a good holster is to keep your handgun oriented precisely as you expect, so when you reach for it under stress, everything is as you anticipate from prior practice repetitions. Many pocket holsters use some kind of base shape to keep the gun oriented upright in the pocket.

The holster design is only part of the solution. You must ensure that your pocket is shaped and sized to be compatible with your holster. For example, if you carry a standard pocket holster in a cargo or large coat pocket, you might find your gun upside down or sideways when you reach for it.

Ankle Carry

While I wouldn't recommend ankle holsters for a primary carry gun in most situations, they are an excellent option for a backup gun They also have a place for situations where you may be seated for much of your day. For example, an ankle holster might be easier to access if you spend all day driving or sitting at a desk.

Ankle holsters can offer excellent concealment. Most people don't tend to stare at your ankles, so a little forgiveness is built into ankle holster concealment.

Sitting in an open environment (think chairs, not at a desk) can present a concealment problem, especially if you tend to cross your legs. This raises your pants higher on the leg, exposing your well-armed ankle to your guests.

This Galco Gunleather model is first-rate. The shaped leather pouch combined with retention strap ensures your gun remains in place.

The other disadvantage is the draw itself. While speed and fluidity can be achieved with practice, you must learn amateur-level inversion yoga poses to draw smoothly from an ankle holster. It almost always requires body movement and two hands. You're also forced to move into an unstable and possibly more vulnerable position with reduced visibility while you draw. Then, of course, you may have to stand back up.

Many law enforcement officers use an ankle holster for a second backup gun. If you're involved in a tussle, and things are going badly enough that you may require resorting to your backup, an ankle-holstered handgun might even present an advantage. It's in a completely different location, so the attacker may be focused on what he can see around the midsection. An ankle holster is also relatively accessible if you've been forced to the ground.

Here are a few tips to get you started if ankle carry is right for you.

Position

Generally speaking, ankle holsters are intended to be worn low around the ankle. This makes the holster more accessible for a draw and helps keep it in place—if it's at the bottom, it can't slip down! It also makes it easier to clear pants out of the way while performing the draw.

The Extra Sock

Try wearing a larger sock that can go outside the bottom part of your ankle holster and cover it. While there will be a bulge, most people won't see a holster and gun if your pants ride up.

Boot Up

The right pair of boots can be wonderfully compatible with an ankle holster. I use a pair of Dustin Ropers that are not too high and have a wide opening. The grip of my handgun is perfectly accessible over the top of the boots, and concealment is excellent. If your pants ride up a bit, all one sees is boot leather.

Easier Reach?

If your mobility isn't quite what it used to be, try this technique. Instead of trying to bend down from a "normal" standing position, take a step forward with your ankle holster leg, almost like a lunge performed by weightlifters and cross-fitters. This movement brings your torso (and arms) closer to your ankle, making your gun somewhat easier to reach. The technique also tends to maintain your forward line of sight so you can keep tabs on what's happening in front of you while drawing.

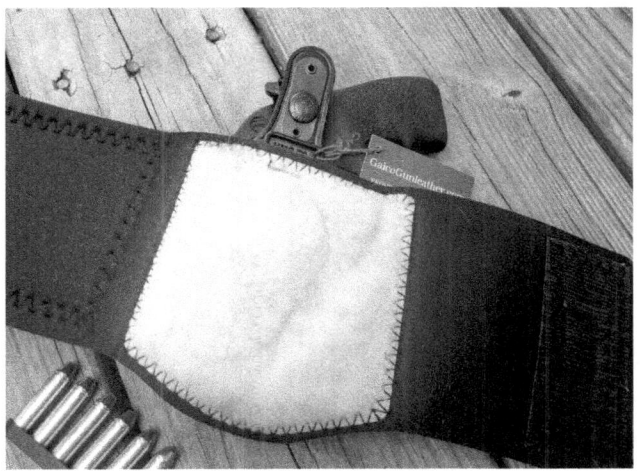

The interior wool padding of the Galco Ankle Holster makes a big difference in comfort and stability.

Off Body Carry

There are many ways to carry a gun that is not directly affixed to your body or clothing. As with other methods, there are advantages and disadvantages to consider.

Generally speaking, 'off-premises' carry offers great comfort and convenience as you are not attempting to stuff a large metal or polymer gun into your pants, shirt or underwear. Additionally, like pocket carry, if your Spidey-sense goes off and you have the opportunity, you can casually place your hand on your gun while it's inside your pack or purse without setting off alarms.

The trade-off is accessibility and firearm security. If your gun is in a purse, briefcase, portfolio, or other container not affixed to your body, it is probably not always under your direct control. It can be left unattended by mistake, lost or worse yet, stolen. A surprise purse snatching or briefcase/backpack theft is even more tragic when your gun is in it! Likewise, a gun in your briefcase will not do much good if it's sitting across the room or elsewhere in the car.

Ideally, a carry pack or purse will have a dedicated carry compartment with an internal holster to secure your handgun.

Tips for off-body carry options.

Reality Check

Assume that every time you set down your purse or bag, even for a second, you've created a potentially dangerous situation. Are there children nearby? Could it be grabbed? If something happens, can you get to it in time? How many times per day is the purse or pack more than three feet from you?

Before defaulting to this carry method because it's convenient, think long and hard about the use case scenarios. You might feel more secure having a gun nearby, but will it be usable and realistically accessible in a surprise encounter? Especially if you have to go through a zipper or other enclosure to reach your gun. Is this bag or purse always attached to your body? Many defensive encounters begin and end within seconds. Will your hidden-away firearm be a factor?

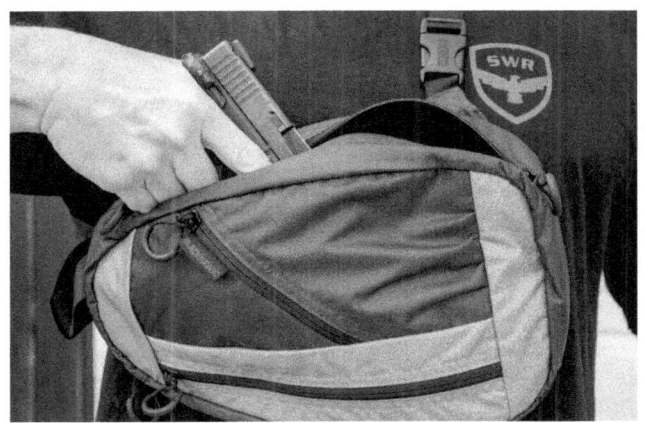

Many companies make slingpacks that rotate to the front, presenting a dedicated gun pocket.

Habits

When you plant yourself somewhere, either store your purse within arm's reach or remove your gun and secure it somewhere else. If you have kids at home, be sure to remove your gun from your purse or pack and place it under lock and key the minute you arrive.

Holster Up!

As with pocket carry, always use a "holster" device to orient the firearm in the purse or pack. Many models built for concealed carry have holster pockets built-in. You may need to rig your own if you're using an off-the-shelf bag. Ensure your gun can't move around with all the other stuff in your purse or pack, that it remains oriented correctly and that the trigger area is protected.

Most concealment purses are designed to be carried on the opposite side of your drawing hand. Many purses, but not all, have gun compartment openings on both sides so that they will work for righties and lefties. Check before you buy, especially if you are left-handed!

Spare Magazine Carriers

Clint Smith, one of the nation's premier self-defense trainers, likes to say, "Two is one, and one is none." No, this isn't the new math your kids learn in school. It says redundancy and backup are good things —especially when it comes to potentially life-saving decisions.

Magazine carriers are available in many configurations: inside the belt, outside, single, double and more.

The most common failure point of semi-automatic handguns is the magazine. Perhaps the magazine is jammed or bent, and the rounds are not feeding correctly. Dumping the magazine and inserting another might be the best and quickest resolution to the problem.

Another consideration is capacity. If you're ever in a situation where you need to use your gun to protect yourself or others, who's to say that one magazine of bullets will stop whatever situation caused you to draw your gun in the first place? Ask any law enforcement officer how many shots it can take to hit and, more importantly, stop an attacker. Now consider scenarios with more than one adversary.

So, suitable magazine carriers are a necessity. When we refer to 'good' magazine carriers, we mean those designs that make it as easy and comfortable as possible to carry extras when you go out. If the carrier is effective and comfortable, you're more likely to carry spare magazines. And that's a good thing.

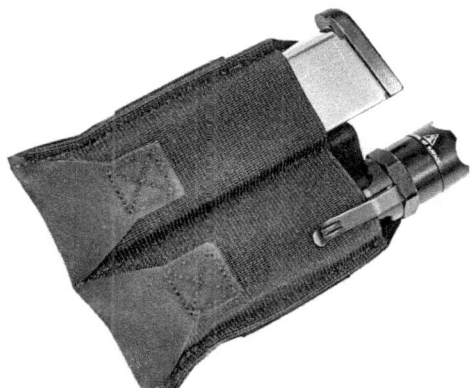

This flexible model from Blue Force Gear allows carry of other items, too, like a flashlight, knife or multitool.

8

AMMUNITION

For self-defense use, it's essential to use the correct ammunition. The goal in a self-defense shooting isn't lethality; it's to stop the attacker from doing whatever they're doing as quickly as possible. If that can be done without a lethal outcome, that's a good thing.

An example of quality defensive ammunition. These Sig Sauer V-Crown bullets were fired into ballistic gelatin for testing. Note how they expand beyond their original diameter.

Defensive Ammunition

As discussed earlier in the book, handguns are far less than ideal for reliably stopping a determined attacker. Sure, they can be lethal, but compared to other options like rifles and shotguns, they are comparatively lacking. As a result, ammunition manufacturers have gone to great lengths to develop premium self-defense ammunition designed to produce maximum effectiveness from handguns.

Additionally, modern defensive ammunition is designed for maximum reliability. Whether it goes bang or not in adverse conditions may be a matter of life and death. Other reasons defensive ammo is so expensive include its corrosion resistance, precision, testing and, in many cases, moisture resistance.

Performance Characteristics

While some specialty ammunition uses other technologies to maximize fight-stopping characteristics, most defensive ammunition is designed to do two things: expand and penetrate. The expansion part is to increase the diameter of the wound channel to cause more immediate damage, thereby stopping an aggressor more quickly. It also helps keep the projectile inside the target as the expanding projectile slows more rapidly. The penetration objective is to make sure that the bullet goes in deeply enough to reach vital organs to cause fight-stopping damage.

Here's the catch. These two factors represent a zero-sum situation. The more aggressively a bullet expands, the faster it loses velocity and the less it penetrates. All else being equal, more of one will mean less of the other. As a result, manufacturers invest lots of money to develop ammunition that will walk that fine line across various shooting scenarios. They'll test it in ballistic gelatin. They'll test it by passing through clothing layers. They'll test it by passing through wood. They'll test its performance by passing through steel as found in an automobile. They even test it through automotive safety glass. If everything goes according to plan, they'll produce a bullet and cartridge to offer the proper expansion and penetration performance in all these scenarios.

While most modern self-defense ammunition lives up to its marketing claims, there are still variables to consider. For example, barrel length is one of the variables that wreaks havoc on ammunition performance because the shorter the barrel, the lower the bullet's velocity—all else being equal. In my testing, I've found (for handguns) that every inch of barrel length reduction results in a velocity loss of about 30 feet per second, give or take. The velocity difference between the same self-defense cartridge in a two-inch barrel gun and a five-inch barrel gun can be 100 feet per second! As the expansion performance of self-defense ammunition is correlated with velocity, that difference might determine whether your bullet expands appropriately.

Modern defensive ammunition is usually designed to expand like this in organic targets to increase its effectiveness.

When choosing self-defense ammunition, make sure it is appropriate for your firearm. For example, opt for the "Short Barrel" versions of defensive ammunition if you use a subcompact pistol or revolver. These loads are optimized to perform at the lower velocities expected from smaller handguns.

Choose Wisely

Don't fall for the marketing gimmick of "ultra-lethal" ammunition with exotic or scary names. Before buying that box of "Instant Vaporization +P+" ammo, think about how you would answer a question about why you chose to use that in your self-defense handgun from the witness stand.

Traditional hollow point ammunition is used by virtually every law enforcement officer in the country for a reason. It works, and its performance has been documented for decades. If you ever find yourself defending your choice of ammunition, wouldn't it be nice to say you chose the same ammunition that the local police force uses?

Practice and Match Ammunition

It's important to understand the difference between practice or match ammunition and self-defense ammunition and under what circumstances each type should be used.

Practice ammo is for precisely what the descriptor implies—practice. It's designed to be safe, "reliable enough," and to make holes in paper. That's about it.

This Federal American Eagle ammo is designed for volume shooting. It's plenty accurate and reliable but not designed for self-defense.

Match ammunition is usually practice ammo that uses premium components and has received extra care in the manufacturing process. The goals are precision and repeatability. For example, match pistol ammunition uses precisely weighed and shaped projectiles and is loaded to have consistent velocities. Those attributes make it accurate on targets where scores and bullseyes depend on fractions of an inch.

Practice and match ammunition are not appropriate for self-defense use for several reasons.

The projectiles in practice and match ammo are not designed to do anything special except fly straight. Practice ammo is usually constructed using full metal jacket (FMJ) bullets. This means that a copper or similar metal covers the lead core of the projectile (bullet) to contain the lead and prevent it from gunking up the inside of gun barrels. When FMJ bullets hit something, they make a hole similar to their original diameter.

When using FMJ practice or match ammo in self-defense situations, the tendency to make small holes can present problems. Making holes in a determined attacker doesn't necessarily slow them down. It might or might not, depending on the strike's location and the aggressor's determination. Worse yet, FMJ bullets tend to go right through soft targets. So whoever is behind that attacker is now also potentially in danger.

Strangely enough, some studies have shown that FMJ ammunition is actually more lethal to the person being shot than expanding hollow-point ammunition because more shots (on average) are required to stop the attack. While not immediately deadly, the after-effect of more shots and more holes include increased lethality.

The bottom line is this: you should only use practice ammunition for practice. Yes, it can be dangerous or lethal to an attacker, but it may be less effective as a defensive tool and potentially more hazardous to bystanders.

Reloaded Ammunition

If you reload your ammo or buy reloaded ammunition, that's great! Use it for practice. Use it for hunting. Use it for competition. But don't use it for concealed carry.

I'm a reloader and can make pretty good ammunition. It's a great hobby that I enjoy. Yet, I don't have the millions of dollars of test equipment that large manufacturers have. My man cave lacks laser measuring devices to ensure primers are seated within a ten-thousandth inch of spec. I don't have precision scales to detect if a completed cartridge is out of tolerance by a tiny fraction of a grain. While I can optimize ammo for a gun, I can't duplicate the absolute consistency that millions of dollars of custom equipment can produce.

If you ever have to use your gun in self-defense, everything you did will be analyzed after the fact. Nothing is off the table, including your choice of gun and ammunition. You want unknown variables in your legal case like a hole in the head.

For starters, in a complex case where facts are blurry, a crime lab may try to replicate factors in your shooting incident. To do so, they'll typically find the ammo you used, acquire some, and test it. That's a no-can-do with custom-reloaded ammo.

Adversarial attorneys may question your decision to use reloaded ammo. Was the factory stuff not powerful or lethal enough for you? What exactly did you do to that ammunition to make it more lethal? Are you testifying that you can make better ammunition than the factories that produce millions of rounds per month? You get the idea. While I am unaware of a case where this strategy was used, why allow it to be an option?

It's much easier to make the ammunition choice a non-issue by simply testifying that you "use the same ammunition as that deputy over there and police departments all over the country. They chose it because it's reliable and safe, so I did, too."

The bottom line is this. The benefits don't outweigh the risks. Sure, you may make super-accurate ammo. You may want to save money on defensive ammo by loading it yourself. Whatever the reason, resist the temptation and buy name-brand premium self-defense ammunition for use in your carry gun. Once you verify the functional reliability of your gun, you won't purchase self-defense ammunition regularly. You may only spend $20 to $50 annually if you rotate fresh cartridges into your carry gun once a year. Is saving a couple of dollars (literally) worth the risk? You can probably figure out how to make your own fire extinguisher flame retardant, too. But why?

9

SIGHTS, LIGHTS AND LASERS

C hoosing the correct type of sights for a concealed carry handgun is a different exercise than for a target or recreational pistol. While many modern handguns come equipped with standard sights that will work for concealed carry, it's essential to recognize what attributes matter for defensive use. That knowledge might impact your choice of handgun or encourage you to upgrade the sights on a gun you already own. Of course, if you find a new gun with less-than-ideal sights, there's nothing wrong with buying it, knowing that you intend to replace them. It's an easy and affordable upgrade in the scope of things.

You also might consider red dot optical sights or even laser sighting aids. We'll take a look at the options, considering the pros and cons of each.

"Iron" Sights

For concealed carry use, consider these attributes when selecting sights.

Precision

As strange as it may sound, extreme precision isn't a critical requirement for self-defense handgun sights. Precision often comes at the expense of speed and visibility, and that tends to work adversely towards the goal of getting shots on target quickly. In a self-defense situation, shooting will be fast, chaotic, and likely done at close range. Ideally, you will be moving. Your attacker will also be moving and trying very hard not to get shot. Lining up precise bullseye shots isn't a realistic requirement for self-defense sights.

"Iron" sights require lining up the notch in the rear with the front post. Then, all of that has to line up with the target.

Target sights built for precision are often all back, usually made of steel, have sharp and well-defined edges and typically feature a narrow front sight blade or post. That narrow blade allows precise side-to-side alignment with a small target. A target pistol with a narrow front sight blade will allow one to shoot bullseye competitions at 25 or 50 yards. However, that narrow target sight is not only fragile, it's hard to see, especially when in low light conditions or when you're moving. Blackened, narrow sights may not show up well against different or busy backgrounds.

Speed

Hand-in-hand with precision goes speed, meaning the time it takes for your eye to see the sight and line it up with the desired target. Good combat sights will leap into view as you raise the handgun into your sight picture. You want features that trick your eyeballs and brain into seeing nothing but the front sight as it comes into view. Manufacturers leverage all sorts of optical science to make sights faster to use.

You'll find that color is a key component that helps improve the speed of sight acquisition. Combat sights are available with white, green, yellow, and orange paint on the front and rear sights. Sometimes, manufacturers use a combination of colors. For example, some sights will have lower-intensity yellow dots on the rear but higher visibility orange or green colors on the front sight. That's to help the eye quickly identify the front sight.

These XS sights have a Tritium vial in the center for use in the dark. The photoluminescent paint glows in partially lighted conditions, and the orange shows well in daylight.

Other tricks include using shapes, rounded edges, and corners to help guide your eye to the relevant areas. For example, the F8 Sights from XS Sights feature a rear sight groove with rounded corners at the bottom but sharply squared edges at the top. Your eye naturally gravitates to the hard corners and, in this case, to the top edges of the sight. That's the rear sight area that needs to line up with the front sight blade. It's a subtle design element, but every benefit counts.

You'll also see different sight shapes. Most pistol and revolver sights use some form of a rectangular notch in the rear sight that frames a squared-off post front sight. But you'll also find sights with an open and shallow "V" notch in the back and a giant round dot for the front sight. The idea is to rest the round "ball" in the "V," and there's your sight picture.

There's no right or wrong answer for the "fastest" sights. That depends on how your eyes and brain work together and the quality of your eyesight. Be sure to experiment with a variety of sight types. When you're at the gun store, raise different types into your line of sight as if you were drawing the gun and see which ones "leap" out at you. Also, check to see which ones get lost when facing different colors or patterned backgrounds. Finding a sight against an unusual background is one of the most significant "speed" issues you'll face.

Front Sight Emphasis

When shooting, it's essential to precisely line up rear sight, front sight, and target. Your eye can't keep all three of those things in perfect focus at the same time, so you have to pick one. The sight that should get your absolute focus is the front. The rear may be a bit blurry, and that's OK. The target may appear a bit blurry, and that's OK, too.

When choosing combat sights, embrace this front-sight emphasis. Many premium defensive sight designs deliberately emphasize the front sight using shape and color while simplifying the rear sight to help your eye avoid focusing there. For example, many defensive sights will have colored dots or glow-in-the-dark inserts on the front sight but nothing on the rear sight besides black steel. That's not necessarily a cost-saving measure; it's intended to simplify the picture for your eyes and brain.

Low-Light Visibility

While the urban legend states that most crime happens at night, statistics don't support that, at least not to the degree we assume. Even if you assume that half of violent encounters happen in daylight, that leaves the other half for low-light conditions.

Don't just consider daylight and pitch-black conditions. Every day, we experience a broad range of lighting situations. Early mornings and evenings are characterized by dusky, in-between outdoor light. More importantly, indoor environments can instantly change between bright light, pure darkness, or anywhere in between. Then there's the challenge of moving from inside to outside or vice versa.

Before getting all carried away about the need to have sights that will work in pitch-black conditions, consider whether or not it's wise to shoot in total darkness. You're responsible for everything at which you shoot, so you're not going to be sending bullets into conditions so dark that you can't see your target. I mention this because there's an assumption that a self-defense gun has to have Tritium sights that glow in the dark. Don't get me wrong; it's a great feature to have. I'm just asking you to think through scenarios before settling on your requirements for combat sights. We'll return to this topic when we talk about Tritium night sights.

The takeaway here is to test your sights in a wide variety of conditions, both indoors and outdoors. Be sure to "transition" from outside to inside and vice versa—that can be eye-opening. For example, sights that rely on Tritium alone for dark conditions can be almost invisible in transitional light conditions. Be sure to experiment.

Durability

A self-defense handgun, by definition, carries life and death consequences. Again, by definition, if you ever have to use it, you will be in a lethal confrontation, so your handgun and any parts on it won't be babied like at the range. It may get dropped, kicked or otherwise abused.

Please pay attention to the material construction of your handgun sights and ensure they are mounted solidly. If a sight starts sliding to one side at the range, it's not a big deal. However, if that happens during a self-defense confrontation, you've got serious problems.

Alternate Functionality

When things go wrong, you may need to resort to unconventional measures to perform simple actions. When shopping for sights, you may see features advertised that refer to a "hard front edge" on the rear sight. This is because you can use the rear sight housing to operate a pistol with one hand if necessary. By hooking the front edge of a rear sight on a belt, boot, wall, or any other surface, you can rack the slide to clear a malfunction or complete a reload with one hand.

It would be very unusual to have to do that, but it's worth mentioning so you know what that sight feature is for.

Standard Target Sights

The majority of new pistols come with standard three-dot sights. The rear sight offers a rectangular notch flanked by two (usually) white dots. The front sight is a thick post with a (usually) white dot in the center. You can simply line the three dots up in a horizontal row, align that with your target, and shoot. For greater precision, you can ignore the dots and line up the sights by shape, keeping the top of the front sight post perfectly aligned with the top edge of the rear sight notch and the post in the center of that same rear notch.

You'll find variations on the "three dot theme in the pistol market, but those are the most common. Most self-defense revolvers have a similar arrangement, but usually without the white dots. Maybe it's just a traditional thing, but revolvers tend to rely on sight shapes alone, although some will use white or color inserts in the front sight blade.

There's nothing wrong with standard target sights. It's just a matter of getting what you pay for. Of course, they won't help you much in dark conditions, but more importantly, you might find they wash out against drab target backgrounds. Be sure to test against different colors and patterns.

Fiber-Optic Sights

Fiber optic sights use colored translucent tubing housed in a sight body. The top of the fiber optic tube gathers available light, so when you look at the end facing the rear of the handgun, it appears as a brightly glowing dot.

Fiber optic sights work great in daylight conditions but also surprisingly well in lower light. Since they "amplify" what light is present, they show up better than a painted-on color. Of course, they won't glow on their own accord in pure dark conditions; however, some manufacturers have developed fiber optic sights that house a Tritium source at the far end of the tubes. In daylight, you see the fiber optic effect; in the dark, you see the Tritium lamp glowing through the tube. You'll find fiber optic configurations for front and front and rear sights. Usually, the tubes in the rear housing use a different color, so it's clear which glowing dot is the front sight.

This fiber optic front sight also features an internal Tritium vial for nighttime use.

The other benefit to fiber optic sights is that you can easily swap colors to use the one your eye sees best. Most sights come with yellow, orange, green, and red replacement tubes.

Tritium Sights

Tritium sights use the radioactive element of the same name to provide a light source. That radio-active magic will operate for seven years before it starts to dim significantly. Since most Tritium night sight sets cost between $100 and $150, there's your once-every-seven-years sight budget.

Tritium sights allow visibility of the dots in which the Tritium vials are contained in pure dark conditions. That sounds great on paper, and it's certainly a benefit. Just be aware that we're not talking LED flashlight power here. Tritium vials provide a relatively dim light source, so they are not nearly as visible in transitional or dusk conditions. You might be disappointed if you rely on Tritium sights to appear brightly in an indoor room.

To solve that problem, manufacturers have started to use a combination of light technologies in the same sight body. By surrounding a centered Tritium vial with other materials, you can design a sight where elements are highly visible in different conditions. Those XS F8 sights we referenced before offer three layers of visibility. In very dark conditions, you'll see the center Tritium lamp. Surrounding is a photoluminescent ring that collects light and glows for a while. This covers transitional light, as when moving from outdoors to indoors or from a lit room to a darker one. Last, the color of the ring material itself is optimized for daylight conditions.

Red Dot Sights

Putting optical or red dot sights on handguns isn't a new thing. Competitors have been doing it for years and with great success. What is new is how they're moving onto mainstream guns like those for recreation, home defense, and even concealed carry. The inevitable march of technology has made them small, amazingly durable, and affordable.

To be more specific, a red dot sight (usually) operates by using a holographic approach. The unit projects a red dot (sometimes other patterns) onto a small window mounted on a handgun. The shooter looks through the window at the target. Unlike traditional iron sights, there is nothing to line up. Just place the dot on the target and shoot. It's simple and fast.

This pistol features a Trijicon RMR HD red dot sight. It's reliable, and the battery lasts for years.

Advantages

- Aiming with a red dot is intuitive. You don't have to worry about coordinating the rear sight, front sight, and target. Just place the dot where you want to shoot.
- Red dot sights facilitate our natural tendency to focus on the target. Our brains want to do that anyway, so this sighting system allows us to follow our instincts.
- Those with older eyes will likely find red dots a great visual aid. There are no tiny sights on which to focus. That red dot is bright and easy to see for almost anyone.
- Red dot sights work equally well in daylight, low light, and dark conditions.

- Red dot sights are easy for first-time shooters. Since sighting is so intuitive, they can focus on technique rather than lining up iron sights.
- Many brands are available with green dots and patterns too.

Disadvantages

- Optical sights are electronic, and like anything else, they can break. Modern options are shockingly durable, however, so it's unlikely you'll have trouble with a quality model. Since the dot is projected, you can continue to use an optical sight with a cracked lens.
- Learning how to "find the dot" takes some adjustment. We'll get to this in a minute, but the trick is to not look for the dot.
- You have to remember to change the batteries, especially if you rely on a handgun with optical sights for defensive purposes.

There is no downside if you're considering using optical sights on a recreational handgun. They're fun and make hitting small targets at longer ranges easier. If you're thinking about getting into competitive shooting, most types of competitions have divisions where optical sight usage is fine. If you want to use optical sights on a home or carry gun, then be sure to dedicate time to practice and training so their use becomes instinctive.

Tips

The most important tip is to forget about trying to "find the dot." With a red dot sight mounted low on a handgun, the sight position is hardly different than when using iron sights. As you raise your gun to target, let your brain look for the front sight as usual. The dot will appear on its own. The more you focus on the proper mechanics of grip, stance, and looking for the front "iron" sight, the less of an issue "finding the dot" will be.

If you're still struggling, apply pressure with your pinkies to the bottom of the grip. This will rotate the muzzle down just a hair, often dropping the red dot right into view. More often than not, when people struggle with a lost dot when the pistol is at eye level and on target, the "dot" is above the red dot sight body. Lowering the muzzle brings it into view.

The best way to consistently achieve foolproof sighting is to practice your motion where you raise your gun to the target. Building consistency in how your sights come into view will ensure the red dot appears on its own every time. As you do this, think in terms of raising the sight into view rather than extending the gun fully and then beginning to look for the sights. Sighting "after the fact" is inefficient and slows you down. Why not be ready to break a shot the instant the gun comes into position?

Laser Sights

Like weapon-mounted lights, laser sights are one of those things you don't fully appreciate until you try them.

Some instructors will scoff at laser sights because they insist that shooters should learn to use the iron sights on the gun. I couldn't agree more. All shooters should become proficient at shooting with iron sights. Those don't break or run out of battery juice, so you can count on them to work forever or until you break them.

Having a laser on your handgun won't make you a better shooter. However, when appropriately used in practice, it can help you become a better shooter. More importantly for the concealed carrier, lasers can add advantages to defense shooting situations.

These Crimson Trace LaserGrips replace the pistol's factory grips, adding hardly any bulk. Note the laser emitter at the top of the wooden grip panel.

One more thing about lasers in general. They're for low-light conditions. While you can see some of them, especially green ones, in daylight conditions, that's not where they shine, if you'll excuse the pun. Indoors and in low light, lasers can dramatically increase your speed of getting shots on target. If you're at the range in broad daylight, struggling to find the laser dot on target, you're missing the point. Those conditions are what iron sights are for!

Types of Laser Sights

Laser sights are available for many, if not most, modern self-defense handguns. Modern technology has brought them to the mass market as reliable, small, light, and affordable accessory add-ons.

Several different styles offer various pros and cons. Let's take a look.

Lasergrips

Given the shockingly small size of laser diodes these days, companies like Crimson Trace have been able to integrate laser sights into replacement handgun grips.

For self-defense guns having replaceable grips like 1911s, many Sig Sauer P-series models, Beretta 92 / M9 pistols, and others, you buy Lasergrips, remove the original grips on your pistol or revolver, and replace them with the laser-enabled grips. Usually, the left grip panel houses a battery. The right grip panel may house a second battery and the laser circuitry. Riding at the top of the grip is the laser. This positioning projects the beam alongside the handgun's frame towards the target. Nothing gets in the way since it's above the position of your firing finger. Even if the beam is parallel to the bullet's flight path, it's only offset by a fraction of an inch down and to the side.

Of course, you can adjust the positioning of the beam to zero it in any way you like. For example, I prefer to adjust mine so that the point of impact and laser dot coincide at 25 yards. The impact point and beam are at most one inch apart at the muzzle. As the range approaches 25 yards, the impact point and laser beam dot get closer and closer together until they finally meet at 25 yards.

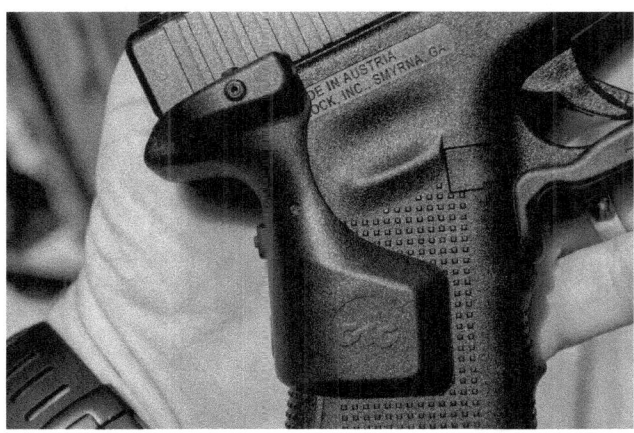

These Crimson Trace LaserGrips are designed for pistols without replaceable grip panels, like this Glock.

There are two important benefits to the Lasergrip design.

First, you rarely, if ever, need a special holster to accommodate the laser. Even though the grips are slightly usually wider than factory grips, the grip itself isn't contained in the holster body, so that's a non-issue. The laser body at the top of the grip rarely interferes with the holster fit.

Second, Lasergrips offer instinctive activation. The two grip halves have to be connected anyway so batter power can flow between them, and this is usually done by a rubberized strap that goes across the front of the handgun grip. That strap contains a pressure button. When you grip your gun, your fingers activate the pressure pad, and the laser turns on. There are no switches to remember in the heat of the moment—it's just there. If you want to deactivate the laser, loosen your grip, and it'll shut off. Most models offer a positive power switch to disable the laser for daylight conditions practice. That's a nice feature that saves battery life.

You will find some models of lasers that offer the same benefits as laser grips but are designed for guns without removable grip panels. For example, some models for Glocks have a wrap-around body that rests on top of the factory grips. Usually, with these models, the pressure pad is located on the back of the pistol grip and activated by your hand's web.

Rail-Mounted Lasers

Some guns, like Springfield XD-family, Glocks, Smith & Wesson M&Ps and others with solid polymer frames, don't have removable grip panels that can be replaced with lasers. For those, companies like Streamlight, Crimson Trace, LaserMax, and Viridian produce rail-mounted laser models that mount under the barrel forward of the trigger guard. For these models, there are two modes of activation.

Some will have paddle switches that the user toggles on and off with the trigger finger or support hand finger. That approach provides ultimate control over when you want the laser on and off but relies on the operator to remember to activate the laser during a self-defense encounter. That's a real issue. I vividly remember one training run in a shoot house equipped with such a laser when the instructor asked me a slightly embarrassing question at the end of my drill. "I wonder if you might have done better if you remembered to turn the laser on?"

Other rail-mounted lasers feature extensions that travel along the trigger guard back to the front of the grip. These configurations offer the same instinctive activation benefits as Lasergrips. Just pick up the handgun, and the laser is on. Reduce grip pressure to turn it off temporarily.

These Streamlight light and laser combo units are rail-mounted. You operate them with levers accessible by the trigger finger or support hand.

Rail-mounted lasers offer flexibility as they can fit almost any gun. The drawback of concealed carry is finding a holster that fits your specific configuration. There are hundreds of guns on the market and dozens of lasers (and lights), so holster makers can't account for every combination. You'll have to search the holster websites for a combination that works for you.

Guide-Rod Lasers

The folks at LaserMax developed a zero-footprint solution for laser sighting. By replacing the recoil guide rod with a custom one that contains a small laser inside of the rod itself, you can have a pistol with laser capability that doesn't add one millimeter of size or bulk to the gun's exterior. The laser is activated by the gun's takedown lever, which is replaced with a special Lasermax version during installation.

Guide rod lasers are available for popular Glock, Beretta, Sig Sauer, Springfield Armory, and H&K pistols.

Red and Green Lasers

Red lasers on handguns date back a couple of decades, although they've certainly gotten smaller, more durable, and less expensive. The industry started with red because red diodes are easier to make, less costly, and require less power. Original green lasers required conversion steps to output green light, so more parts were needed. More recently, companies have been manufacturing native green lasers, so you'll find plenty of red and green models on the market.

Here's how the two net out. Red (usually) continues to be less expensive and requires less power. So, as a rule of thumb, a green laser might get half the operating time with the same batteries, or your setup might require more battery power to get similar run times. On the other hand, green is (generally and to most people) more visible in various conditions. I've found that it doesn't matter in low light, practically speaking. Both red and green laser dots leap into view. In lighter conditions, the green ones will be more visible. Before you rush out and buy green, test out the demo units in the store. While it sounds good on paper, green lasers still aren't all that good in daylight conditions. We'll talk about ideal conditions for laser use and how they can coexist with iron sights in just a bit.

Laser Sight Myths

Lasers have been standard handgun accessories for a decade, give or take, yet myths still morph and self-replicate all over the internet. You may have heard or seen comments like the following.

A laser will give away your position!
What are you going to do when the batteries run out?
It's another piece of gear that will break at the most inopportune time.

And so on...

Like most myths that circulate through gun counter and online forum discussions, they tend to stick because there is a little bit of truth to them. Whether that "bit 'o truth" is significant or even relevant is another topic of discussion.

Let's look at the most common laser sight myths from a concealed carry point of view. As you'll see, context is everything.

A Laser Will Give Away Your Position

This is one of those myths that can contain some truth, but it usually occurs in unrealistic situations or in a completely different context.

Before we get into it, let's talk about how a laser would work in concealed carry. By definition, we're talking about self-defense—reacting to an offensive action that someone else has taken. If the event has escalated to the point of grave bodily harm or death and you have been forced to draw your handgun, you have one mission: to get shots on target as quickly and effectively as you can to stop the attack and save your life. That's it.

Concealed carry does not involve sneaking around dark areas looking for bad guys in some ninja cat-and-mouse game. It does not involve bursting through doors in the middle of the night to capture a meth-dealing kingpin. It does not involve sneaking through a village and up to a terrorist safe house so you can apprehend him. Fair enough?

So, in terms of "giving away your position," let's consider counterarguments to the myth.

First, remember that lasers are mostly invisible except for the dot projected onto the surface at which you're aiming. In normal environmental conditions, you won't see the beam at all. You might sometimes see a faint beam when using a green laser. Of course, if it's smoky or foggy, those beams will reflect off airborne particles and show the laser's beam. Next time you're in a gun store, try this with one of the demo units, and you'll see what I mean. The dot will shine on a surface, but you most likely won't see any beam. That leaves two things for an attacker to see: the dot on their chest or the red glow on your firearm itself. That leads us to the second counterargument.

If you're drawing your gun in self-defense, your position is already well-known in most cases. If you're the intended victim, your presence is no secret to the attacker. If you're a bystander and, for whatever reason, make a decision to intervene, it's possible that your presence is not known, but then again, in the heat of the moment, it's not going to be a tiny little red or green glow on your handgun that gives you away. It'll be your actions. Again, your number one priority is to...get shots on target as quickly and effectively as possible.

Here's the bottom line. If you're sneaking around playing hide-and-seek to find the bad guy, you're almost certainly no longer in the self-defense business—you're playing offense. Are there potential scenarios where you might need to do that? Sure. Just think through the pros and cons of using lasers in terms of the most likely realistic scenarios. Then, rather than succumbing to hearsay, make your own informed decision.

The Batteries Will Run Out at the Worst Time

Do you fill up your car before or after it runs out of gas? How about your electric bill? Do you remember only to pay it when the power company shuts off your lights? I suppose if you usually wait until the engine grinds to a halt on the I-95 entrance ramp or your X-Box stops working, then this battery myth might apply to you.

For most people, and especially those of us who voluntarily assume the responsibility of carrying a concealed firearm, it's not too much to ask to schedule battery changes as needed. Just as we do every week when putting gas in our cars, it's easy enough to change batteries proactively before they die. Most lasers last for two to four hours of continuous use. That doesn't sound like much, but the key is the "continuous use" part. If you're practicing with it frequently, then change the batteries often. If you turn your laser off for practice sessions, set a monthly, quarterly, or annual reminder in your calendar to change the batteries. They're cheap and easy to find at almost any store for most laser models.

They're Unreliable and Likely to Break

Twenty years ago, the reliability myth was probably true. Just as we trust mature and tested electronics to operate our cars and the heart and lung machines used during transplant operations, lasers have evolved to the point where they're as reliable as your gun and its ammunition.

As long as you buy quality gear from a reputable manufacturer, your laser gear will almost certainly work when you most need it. But guess what? If it doesn't, remember this. Adding those Lasergrips didn't take away any of your handgun's existing capabilities—like using the iron sights.

They're Slow

I hear this argument against lasers often. Almost always, the assertion is based on a faulty premise.

Consider this scenario. You buy a laser for your handgun. After mounting it, you go galavanting off to the range to try it out. Who wouldn't? Whether your range of choice is indoors or outdoors, it's well-lit. After sending the target downrange, you assume a firing position and start looking for the laser dot. Guess what? It's hard to see because it's light in your current environment.

And here is the faulty logic. You shouldn't have to look for a laser dot. If you have to look for a laser dot on target, it will be slower because that's not how it's designed to be used. *Lasers are not designed to be used in daylight conditions.* The laser should be the most obvious thing you see in its proper context and intended environment—the dark. You literally cannot miss it—there is no "looking for the dot" in its intended usage (dark) scenario.

Let's flip this upside down. If you continue to embrace your existing sighting habits and focus on raising your gun into view until the sights are on target, the process is automatic, whether you're using a laser or not. You'll see the traditional iron sights if you're in a well-lit environment. Use them. If it's dark, that laser will literally leap into view on the target. Use it. That's it. Just because you have a laser on your handgun doesn't mean it becomes the primary sighting system in all conditions.

I encourage you to make your own decision through trial and error. Using a carefully unloaded gun, try activating your laser in darker conditions, say, somewhere in your home after it gets dark. Raise your gun, just as you usually would, and see what your eyes pick up first: the laser or the sights.

Laser Sighting Benefits

Laser sights add new options and capabilities to your defensive repertoire. They don't replace iron sights. They don't make up for poor skills and techniques. They're just a tool like any other. It just so happens that lasers create more options without taking away any you already had.

Low-Light Aiming

Lasers generate light. Therefore, it's no surprise that one of the most significant benefits of laser use is that it provides a low-light aiming solution.

Regardless of how dark it is, a laser will project a bright and highly visible dot about the size of a coin on your target. The dot size will vary with distance, but we're talking handgun self-defense ranges here, so the "coin" estimate holds.

Keep in mind that while a laser allows you to aim in low-light conditions, you are still responsible for positively identifying your target before you shoot.

Focus on the Threat

When you're attacked, and in a high-stress situation, your lizard brain will scream at your eyes to focus on the threat. It takes conscious practice and training to pull the focus back to the sights of a handgun. The desire (and self-preservation need) to focus on a pending threat has served us well for a long time. Unfortunately, it's not ideal for accurately shooting a handgun.

In dark conditions like this, a laser leaps into view and supports shooting from virtually any position, allowing the user to focus on the target. The only reason this beam is so visible is because this cave is full of gun smoke from a lot of shooting by a lot of people!

If you ever have the opportunity to shoot in a shoot house or virtual simulator where your instructions are simply to "deal with any threats," you might find that many hits tend to be right around the hand and gun area on those bad guy targets. Your brain is evaluating for a threat, sees the gun, and directs you to shoot there.

One of the benefits of laser sighting is that it supports the natural tendency of your brain to focus on the threat. A laser superimposes an aiming point on the threat itself, so there is no need to pull your eyes back to the standard sights to make an accurate shot. If your hold and trigger techniques are solid, your shot will hit right where the laser's dot sits.

Non-Traditional Shooting Positions

When you use traditional iron sights, you must line up four distinct objects: your eye(s), the rear sight, the front sight, and the target. For that to work, the handgun sights must be up high in your direct line of vision. That means you'll have to fire from some semblance of a traditional shooting stance with the gun extended in front of your face and eyes.

Lasers don't require alignment of the handgun sights with your eyes because the laser dot sits on the target. So, when using a laser, the gun can be anywhere. It can be up high in front of your face as with a traditional shooting stance. It can be in a low-ready position. It can be off to the side. It can be down low at waist level. As long as the dot is on target, you can see it, and you exercise proper trigger technique, you can place accurate shots from unusual positions.

Keep in mind shooting from non-traditional positions isn't something one does to be cool. However, it just might be a necessity. You may have your handgun in a lower position to avoid obscuring your vision when identifying a threat. You may be on the ground and having to shoot from an awkward position. You may be forced to shoot from behind cover, where it's difficult to assume a standard shooting position without exposing yourself. The list goes on, but the point is the alternate sighting system offered by a laser may present more options to get shots on target reliably.

Practice and Training

A laser is a great training tool at the live-fire range and at home when practicing dry-fire. Since the dot shines on your intended target, you'll get a real-time picture of what your muzzle (and associated accuracy) is doing before, during, and after the shot. If you tend to flinch just as you fire a shot, you'll see that laser dot move just as you press the trigger. If your hold is unsteady, you'll see the laser dot wobble all over the target areas.

Try having a buddy load some snap cap rounds in your magazine. As you fire and encounter a "dud" round, that laser dot on target will be brutally honest about whether you flinched and moved the muzzle as you pressed the trigger because you were anticipating recoil. While errant shots on target will show you that you did something wrong and maybe offer a hint at the specific problem, a laser shows you in real-time exactly how and when you moved the gun.

Lights

Two types of light accessories can help the concealed carrier.

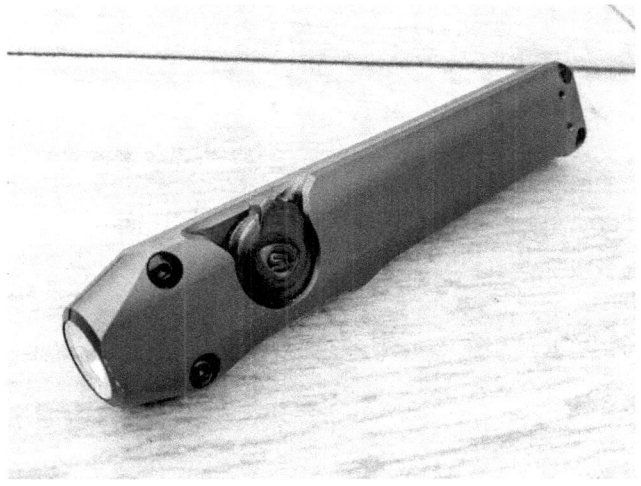

A tactical light like this Streamlight Wedge is a must-have carry tool. It complements a light mounted on your handgun.

Hand-held lights are valuable tools for a wide variety of everyday life situations. Power out? Lost your keys in the dark? Can't see where to put your key in the lock? You get the idea. The beauty of adding a hand-held light to your carry gear is that you can do all of these things without drawing your gun. As we'll see later in the book, some techniques allow you to use a hand-held light while shooting, so a flashlight can also serve as a "temporary" weapon light.

Weapon lights are mounted to your handgun itself. They are intended to aid in shooting and not for looking around for things. Remember safety rule three: never point your gun at anything you're unwilling to destroy. By definition, if you're using a weapon light to look for someone or something, you're pointing your muzzle at people and things at which you may not want to shoot.

In a perfect world, we'd all have access to both types of lights all the time.

Hand-held Lights

Just as pocket knives are used far more frequently for mundane daily tasks rather than self-defense, flashlights are used chiefly for non-tactical tasks.

A simple keychain or penlight can be infinitely helpful not just to avoid tripping in the dark but also to find the car lock, get through a power outage, and many other things. Additionally, as an alert and aware citizen, a flashlight can be a deterrent tool. If you often leave the office after dark, it's a great tool to help you make your way safely to the car while checking that no one is lurking in that dark parking lot. While there is no guarantee of safety, a potential victim "armed" with a flashlight shows a higher level of vigilance and awareness than the average citizen, so you just might avoid being identified as the "easy" target. As the old saying goes, when being chased by a bear, you don't need to be the fastest—just faster than the other guy. A similar principle applies to making sure you're not the easiest target.

Also, light can be a helpful tool to distract a potential attacker in dark conditions. Modern LED penlights can crank out lots of lumens —enough to temporarily blind or distract someone when shined at the face. A quality flashlight is a perfectly innocuous tool that just might buy you a couple of extra seconds in a bad situation.

Many "tactical" flashlights are built from rugged aircraft

aluminum or steel and can be used as impact weapons, too. They're still light and portable but tough enough to withstand blows and keep on lighting your way. If you travel in gun-unfriendly places like airports and government buildings, you might consider carrying a good hand-held light.

Quality matters, as with any other tool, and you get what you pay for. For small keychain lights that get knocked around in pockets and purses, stick to quality brands like Surefire, Streamlight, and Fenix. Many solid brands are on the market; check the reviews carefully to find a model that works for you.

Weapon Lights

A weapon light attaches to a pistol (and sometimes revolver) to illuminate whatever it is that you're about to shoot. Most lights attach to the rail segments under the muzzle and forward of the trigger guard, but some are custom fit for specific pistol models.

A weapon-mounted light similar to this Streamlight model is a valuable home-defense or concealed-carry handgun accessory.

The new crop of lights delivers astounding amounts of white light with modern LED light technology. Even compact handgun models generally crank out 100 to 500 lumens. Versions for full-size guns can provide 1,000. That's far more than the 60-lumen tactical hand-held lights in vogue just a few years ago.

As technology has advanced, footprints have gotten smaller. In addition to small "light-only" models, there are equally concealable lights with integrated laser sights.

We mention these lights because they've now gotten to the point where they are perfectly feasible for concealed carry. They're light, durable, and compact enough to add no appreciable bulk to a carry pistol. As long as you find a compatible holster, you'll have no trouble with concealment.

We'll return to this topic later, but know that weapon-mounted lights are not for searching. They're for shooting. Remember Rule Three—never point a gun at something you're not willing to destroy. If you're pointing one of these weapon-mounted flashlights, you're also pointing the handgun in the same direction.

Case Study: The Importance of Light

 A St. Cloud, Florida, woman will spend the rest of her life lamenting a split-second decision to fire at an "intruder" in the dark. The woman was in bed, as was her husband, asleep late on a Tuesday evening. The woman awoke to see a dark figure headed toward her bed. Assuming it was an intruder, she fired a single shot.

Sadly, the woman quickly determined that the "shadowy figure" was her 27-year-old daughter. Immediately calling 911, the husband and wife attempted CPR while emergency response personnel made their way to the scene. The daughter died at the hospital.

Lessons

While crimes happen 24x7, the law of averages mandates that many will occur at night or in other dark or low light conditions. As a responsible armed citizen, it is up to you, and only you, to be absolutely sure of your target before pulling the trigger. As this tragic story illustrates, the consequences of a split-second decision can forever change your life, not to mention taking someone else's.

You have two options if it's too dark to identify your target clearly. First, don't shoot. Second, use a hand-held or weapon-mounted light to ensure you can see what you're shooting in all conditions.

10

BASIC SHOOTING SKILLS

Much like playing quarterback in the NFL, you need to know the fundamentals of footwork, movement, handoffs and passing before going into a game.

When using a firearm for self-defense, you won't have the luxury of time and space to think and physically prepare to put shots on target. There's an excellent chance you'll need to shoot while moving from awkward positions, with little time to concentrate on your shots and under extreme stress. All this is to say you need to master the fundamentals of "relaxed" shooting before even thinking about relying on a firearm as part of your overall defensive strategy.

You'll want to not only put shots on target every time, but you'll also want to be able to do that without thinking through the fundamentals for each shot. Obtaining a proper sight picture should be instinctive. Operating the trigger without moving the gun should be automatic. Removing your finger from the trigger when not actively shooting should be a subconscious reflex. You get the idea.

Case Study: Gun Safety Always Matters

A DEA agent was speaking to a group of adults and students at an Orlando Minority Youth Golf Association event. At one point in his gun safety lecture, the agent displayed his pistol, a .40 S&W-caliber Glock, to demonstrate "safe" gun handling. After stating, "I'm the only one in this room professional enough that I know of to carry this Glock 40," the man promptly shot himself in the leg. After hobbling around trying to regain his composure, the agent stated, "See how that accident happened; that could happen to you, and you could be blown away."

This was not a case of mechanical malfunction but rather one of poor gun handling. Waving a gun around with a finger on the trigger is bound to end badly, and in this case, it did. Fortunately, the man was not seriously injured and returned to work after medical treatment.

Lessons

The rules of gun safety exist to prevent situations like this. As they overlap, it's virtually impossible for such a negligent discharge to occur if they are followed at all times. The rules of gun safety aren't just for beginners—they're for everyone, always.

Gun Safety Rules

Before picking up a handgun for the first time, and every time thereafter, one must know and relentlessly adhere to the rules of firearm safety. If you do, no one will ever get hurt unless you intend that outcome. It's that simple.

The four rules of gun safety are brilliant in their construction and how they overlap. If you think through them, you'll note that one has to break multiple rules before someone can get hurt via careless gun handling.

These rules aren't legal disclaimers or standard boilerplate text. Any responsible shooter will take them seriously every single time they handle a firearm. Having attended dozens of shooting training events across the country, I can relay what every single event, without fail, had in common. Every class began with a thorough overview of the rules of gun safety, even though all attendees were experienced shooters.

Let's explain them.

Rule 1: A Gun Is Always Loaded

How many times have you heard a story about someone shot with an "unloaded" gun?

"I thought it was unloaded!"
"I'm sure I unloaded it the last time I put it away!"
"It wasn't loaded before!"

Obviously, a gun is not "technically" always loaded. However, the intent of Rule 1 is to treat a firearm as if it is. If you treat a gun like it's loaded, you tend to change your behavior regarding how you handle it.

- You won't check out the sights by aiming it at someone.
- You won't pull the trigger unless ready to fire the gun at a safe target.
- And indeed, you won't do anything else careless with it.

Rule 1 is first on the priority list because it covers a lot of safety territory. Treating a gun like it is loaded and ready to fire has a fantastic ripple effect that makes everyone around safer.

So take it seriously. Pretend that a gun is loaded every single time you look at it or touch it. Pretty soon, you'll start believing that it is actually loaded. Even when you look and verify that it's not, you'll want to look again to make sure. This is a good thing. Never ignore a gut feeling to check the status of a gun just one more time to be sure.

Rule 2: Keep Your Finger Off the Trigger Until Ready to Fire

Modern guns are incredibly safe, and their safety devices are reliable. While you should never rely on any mechanical device for safety—as anything can fail—it's exceptionally unlikely, bordering on impossible, that a modern gun will fire without someone or something moving its trigger. Most guns can be dropped or even thrown with no risk of firing. Don't try that at home—we're just making a point. Others require one or more safety devices to be deactivated before even a trigger press will allow the gun to fire. So, more than likely, when you hear a story about a "gun just going off," you can assume that someone or something, somehow moved that trigger.

The correct placement for your trigger finger anytime you're not actively shooting.

All of these are reasons why Rule 2 is so important. It's nearly impossible for a modern gun to fire without someone or something pressing its trigger. If your finger is not on the trigger, it sure is hard to press it inadvertently!

Rule 2 might be the most problematic habit for new shooters to adopt. The shape and placement of a trigger make it a perfect finger rest, kind of by design. All your available fingers prefer to move together in the same direction, so when the middle, ring and pinky finger close around a gun grip, the index finger also wants to close. When picking up a gun, the natural and instinctive motion is to grasp it with your finger on the trigger.

It's a massive temptation yet a terribly unsafe habit that can only be broken through practice and repetition. Scientists say it takes 1,000 to 2,000 repetitions of an action to establish an automatic reflex in the brain. The same concept applies to learning to keep your finger off the trigger.

Safe trigger discipline has to become an ingrained reflex regardless of the scenario. Immediately after your last shot, does that finger come off the trigger? When changing magazines, does your finger come off the trigger? Does your finger come off between the last shot and setting the gun back down on the table or putting it back in a holster? What if you have to move during the middle of shooting? Will your finger automatically come off the trigger? What about if you are interrupted or startled while shooting? Will your brain still remember to tell your finger to back off?

These scenarios may sound impossible, but repetition really does ingrain trigger finger discipline into the subconscious brain. I can't tell you how many times I've seen a competitive shooter trip or stumble during aggressive movement on the range, and ... guess what? The finger is off the trigger. One shooter tumbled head over heels into a complete forward roll, yet even in that moment of panic, his reptile brain remembered to keep his finger off the trigger. Ah, the benefits of ingrained habits...

So training yourself, or others, to keep the finger off the trigger until ready to fire is a chore. Reminding someone repeatedly to get their finger off the trigger can ruffle some feathers. But you can make the training process respectful, un-intimidating and even fun. When taking new shooters to the range, I tell them (with a smile, of course) that I will have to remind them frequently to remove their trigger finger. With some discussion beforehand, no one gets defensive when you nudge them at the range. You can also have your family and friends train you. Just ask them to watch you shoot.

Rule 3: Never Point a Gun at Anything You're Not Willing to Destroy

The key part of Rule 3 is that it doesn't just refer to aiming. Of course, you should never aim a gun at something you are not intending to shoot. It's far less obvious to think about "pointing" as allowing the muzzle to face someone or something for the briefest instant. It's still considered "pointing" if that muzzle moves across something you don't intend to shoot.

I like to tell shooters to envision the muzzle of a gun as a laser beam. The beam continues straight from the gun muzzle to infinity—and beyond. So if the muzzle "points" at something, even for a microsecond, that certain something is destroyed by the laser.

The concept of not "muzzling" anything you don't want to shoot applies whenever you touch a gun. It doesn't matter if it's in a gun store, a show, at the range or in your home. When you touch it, the beam turns on, and you have to watch every single movement every single instant. As you move the gun around, what does that beam cross? Or, if you set a gun on the shooting bench, where is it pointing? I see this scenario at the range all the time. If there is a malfunction, people will set the gun down to work on it, not realizing it's pointed at the shooter next to them.

It may sound obvious as you read this, but Rule 3 includes your own body and extremities—not just those of others. Consider where the muzzle points as you pick up a gun, inspect it, put it away, draw it from a holster or whatever. Be especially cautious of muzzling your arm or leg.

Rule 4: Be Sure of Your Target and What's Behind It

Bullets tend to go through things. That's one of the reasons they are so good at being bullets.

So, the key part of Rule 4 is the "what's behind it" part. There are two reasons that you need to consider what's behind the target.

First, your bullet may go through the target and continue out the back, still traveling at high velocity. If it's still moving after passing through the first target, it's still dangerous.

Second, you might miss your primary target. That endangers whatever is beside or behind your target.

Rule 4 uses the words "be sure" for a very good reason. Unless you are positive about what's behind your target, don't shoot. Being "pretty sure" isn't good enough when it comes to gun safety. If your view is obscured, don't shoot. Be positive.

Gun Handling Etiquette

Statistically, gun-related accidents are rare, but even one is too many. Preventing a gun-related incident requires a little knowledge and a lot of diligence. If you invest in both, you'll never have a problem.

Whenever picking up a firearm, first verify magazines and chambers are empty.

This section will discuss some standard best practices for gun handling. However, there are thousands of guns on the market, each with a slightly different mode of operation. Always refer to the owner's manual for manufacturer-recommended safety procedures.

If you bought your gun used, no worries. Gun manufacturers almost always post owner's manuals online, so check their website for proper documentation for your specific firearm.

First, let's review some safety procedures for all guns.

General Handling Tips

- Every single time you pick up a handgun, verify its loaded or unloaded status. (Remember, a gun is always loaded!) Even if you just saw a salesperson or your range buddy check it, do it again. Any safe gun person won't be the least bit offended that you're double-checking. They'll appreciate your commitment to safety procedures.
- Remember to keep your finger off the trigger while inspecting a gun.
- If you're handling a gun, keep ammo separate and distant. Whether cleaning, practicing dry fire (more on that later) or whatever, you won't want ammunition nearby unless you're preparing to shoot.
- Avoid handling guns without reason. The more you handle a gun, the more opportunity for something to go wrong. If you don't need to...don't.
- Especially avoid handling loaded guns. If you carry a loaded gun, keep it in its holster when you take it off. The more you can minimize handling a loaded gun, the better.
- When you pick up a semi-automatic pistol, always do two things immediately. First, while pointing the gun in a safe direction, eject the magazine and verify it is empty. Second, and even more importantly, open the slide and check the chamber to ensure no cartridge is inside. On a related note, whenever you remove a magazine from a semi-automatic pistol, remember to check the chamber, too. *Removing the source of new cartridges doesn't guarantee there's not already one in the chamber!*

Due to the wide variety of action types, we can't cover every procedure here. But we don't need to. Gun manufacturers do an excellent job of documenting safe practices for loading, unloading and checking their specific models. Read that manual! If you don't read the manual for your new TV, it's no big deal. You might have trouble changing the channel. If you don't read the manual for your handgun, the consequences are potentially much worse.

Modern guns are designed with layers of safety features. For example, most new guns are drop-safe, meaning they can't discharge simply from falling onto the floor. You're far more likely to inadvertently press the trigger trying to catch a dropped gun. So, as hard and unnatural as it seems, if you lose control of your gun, let it fall. Any potential scratches or dings are far better than the possible consequences of a negligent discharge with the muzzle pointed in an unknown direction.

Case Study: Range Safety and Etiquette

A number of shooters were at the Knight's Trail Park gun range in Nokomis, Florida. It's an outdoor facility with permanent shooting benches, but no barriers between shooting positions as used by many indoor facilities.

Leslie Koren, age 64, allegedly racked the slide of their gun with a finger on the trigger, and the gun fired. Koren did not have the gun pointed down range while loading, and the bullet went sideways right down the shooting line until it struck Walter Perkowski, age 56.

Perkowski immediately fell to the ground, wounded, and subsequently spent several days in the hospital recovering.

Lessons

First, the gun didn't "fire." Koren fired the gun. That's an important distinction. While nothing is impossible in this universe, guns don't just "fire." When someone or something presses the trigger, they fire.

This is a lesson about the four rules of gun safety. When followed religiously, this type of thing simply can't happen. A finger should never be on the trigger until ready to shoot. You should always assume a gun is loaded. The gun should never be pointed at anything that you don't want to destroy. In this case, the shooter violated all three of those rules, and someone was shot as a result.

Range officers were on site, but that's irrelevant to this story. Koren's action was completed in a split second, and even a nearby safety officer could not have prevented it, nor should they have had to. That's what the rules of gun safety are for.

The Foundation: Stance

There's endless online squabble about which stance is correct. To listen to the arguments, you might believe that choosing the "wrong" one will get you and everyone within three square miles killed. That's not likely. Nor is there one "correct" stance for everyone.

I would encourage you to consider a few questions when developing a good shooting stance.

Does the stance facilitate your ability to control the gun? Does it help you manage recoil and muzzle flip? Does it help you get accurate shots on target at the rate of fire needed to solve your problem?

Does the stance in question help you maintain possession of your handgun?

Is your stance "relaxed" enough to allow the various muscles of your body to act as intended? How often do you see professional athletes contorted into a ball of maximum-strain musclebound flesh?

What are the odds of you being able to use a proper shooting stance in a defensive encounter? The odds are pretty good that you'll be moving, fighting or running rather than planting yourself in a bullseye competition shooting stance.

Regardless of which stance variant you choose, it's important to be aggressively forward with your upper body to better control the gun.

You might think of an analogy to a football quarterback. In basic skills practice, the quarterback will step forward, rotate the shoulders, and follow through as they make a pass. In a game with a 300-pound defensive end chasing him, that quarterback may need to complete a pass while on a dead run. Even though the scenario isn't identical to basic skills practice, knowing these "perfect pass technique" fundamentals will help them land a ball on target under adverse conditions.

In this section, we're going to talk about basic shooting stances and techniques to build a solid shooting foundation. That will help you develop core shooting and gun handling skills. Later, we'll talk about shooting in a defensive scenario when you rely on those basic skills while improvising your way out of trouble.

Fighting Position

Since we're talking about concealed carry, we won't concern ourselves with competition shooting stances. Instead, we're going to speak more to a fighting position approach. If you want to put a name to this approach, a realistic one might be the "Point the damn gun downrange and try not to get hurt" stance. Fair enough?

With that said, let's consider a couple of principles.

First, if a bully is about to shove you, you will naturally assume a "fighting stance." Your feet will be spread apart with one (usually your support or weaker side) foot placed forward. With that slight diagonal foot placement, you've got stability in all directions. It's harder for someone to knock you over backward or pull you forward. You've also got good lateral stability since your feet are spread apart. Better yet, this is a good position to move in any direction. You can push forward with your back foot, backward with your front foot, or to either side easily. Simply put, it's a stance that gives you stability and lots of options.

Second, this stance is (not coincidentally) similar to what law enforcement officers call the "interview" stance. With that slight diagonal position, the officer's firearm is bladed away from the suspect, so there is some positional protection if that suspect becomes aggressive.

Here's the bottom line: When shooting a handgun, be stable. Make sure your position gives you good front-to-back and side-to-side stability.

Forward Lean—with Balance

Let's do something weird to illustrate a proper forward lean—with balance. I know that sounds like a contradiction, but stick with me here.

I want you to pretend to hold a pistol in a standard two-handed grip. Now, imagine holding a quarter against your collarbone. Now, if that quarter would fall to the floor, magically passing through any body parts in the chest or midsection, would it hit the floor somewhere around your toes? Or would it land near or behind your heels?

When a new shooter steps up to the firing line and is instructed to "lean forward," they inevitably thrust their hips forward while tilting their shoulders backward from the waist. I think it's a subconscious effort by the brain to force the gun as far away from the body as possible. After all, there's about to be a big explosion out there at the end of their arms, and no one wants that happening right in their face.

Yes, this shooting position looks awkward. More importantly, it hurts your ability to put shots on target quickly. When the "strong" and "heavy" parts of the body, including the torso and shoulders, are already thrust back, there is no leverage with which to drive the gun and control recoil. You're already pushed as far back as you go. In this position, you can think of each shot tilting you back farther as the muzzle rises. It's just not a good way to drive the muzzle down and keep it on target.

On the other hand, by "leaning forward" with the shoulders, as you would before wrestling with someone, you're leaning into the recoil that's coming and can easily control your gun. All that body weight is working productively for you. If done right with a proper grip, you can effectively prevent the muzzle from flipping up between shots.

Weaver and Isosceles

While there are other named shooting stances, the Weaver and Isosceles methods are the two most popular. As this is a book about concealed carry, we won't get all wrapped up in the nitty-gritty differences between the two. As with anything, there are pros and cons to each, so give them a try and see what works for you, again, knowing you may not be using either in a dynamic self-defense situation.

Weaver Stance

The Weaver Stance dates back to the 1950s. As you might guess, it's named after a guy named...Weaver. Deputy Jack Weaver developed this technique to use both hands to get aimed shots on target effectively—fast—while controlling recoil. As you might know from watching old films, in those days, many folks shot one-handed using a heavily bladed bullseye stance and even from the hip in that crouched-down tough guy position.

Here's how it works for a right-handed shooter. Just reverse the steps if you're a lefty. Start with a boxing stance with your support side foot slightly forward. Your left foot will be in front. Apply some knee flex to your right leg. This will cause your left leg to be straighter and less bent.

A Weaver stance looks something like this. Note the bend in the elbows.

Assume a two-handed grip as described in the previous section. Now, slightly bend your firing arm at the elbow instead of locking it straight out. If you've done everything right, your left elbow must be even more bent. That's because your left shoulder is farther forward (with your left foot), and your left arm has to be shorter to grip the handgun in the same place as your firing hand. OK so far?

The last step is what makes the Weaver Stance unique. With your firing arm, push forward toward the target. At the same time, pull back on the gun with your support arm. This opposing tension is part of what gives the Weaver Stance its stability.

Isosceles Stance

The Isosceles Stance takes a different approach. As you might guess from the name, it creates a triangular position when done correctly. Instead of using the push-pull technique of Weaver, the

Isosceles stance has you pushing the gun forward with both arms. Some people lock their elbows, but most seem to naturally allow a bit of bend in both elbows for control and shock absorption.

Technically, foot position is side by side, but most people who shoot with this general style assume a boxer stance with the support side foot slightly forward.

This is an example of the Isosceles stance technique.

There are a couple of benefits to this general style. First, it's very natural. Most new shooters tend to fall into something similar before instruction. Second, it facilitates side-to-side movement, much like a pendulum. Last, if you adapt the support foot forward variation, you have stability and easy movement in any direction.

Grip

Arguably, no shooting fundamental is more important than a proper grip.

A proper grip sets the foundation for aiming, allowing proper trigger finger movement, helping you control recoil, and keeping shots on target during slow and steady and rapid fire. While some of the building blocks are the same, techniques vary depending on whether you're shooting a semi-automatic pistol or a revolver.

Oh, one more thing. Since we're talking about defensive shooting in this book, we will assume all shooting is done using both hands. Yes, you might be called upon to shoot with one hand, but the firing hand grip fundamentals are similar. Let's begin with proper grip fundamentals for a semi-automatic pistol.

Establish Your Firing Hand's Position

The first step is to get your firing hand in the correct position, as that sets the stage for placing your support hand. If you remember that Vulcan greeting hand gesture from Star Trek, you'll be off to a good start. With your four fingers together (more or less), extend your thumb away from the fingers to expose the web of your firing hand.

Next, jam that web between your thumb and fingers onto the backstrap of your pistol grip as high as it will go. Imagine pushing up as you do this so the web of your hand is jammed against the beavertail area of the grip. You are trying to locate your firing hand as high as possible on the pistol.

First, jam the firing hand up against the upper limit of the grip to position your hand as high as possible.

There is a good reason for the high grip. Think about the position of your pistol's barrel. Now, imagine that barrel moving straight backward each time you take a shot. The closer your hand is to that line, the less the gun can torque or rotate during recoil. Due to the design of semi-automatic pistols, where the slide moves back to eject spent cartridges and load new ones, you can't place your hand directly behind the barrel, but you want to get as close as you safely can.

It's simple biomechanics. The closer your hand, and by extension, your body, is to the line of recoil movement, the better job you can do controlling that recoil.

Position Your Firing Hand Fingers

Now wrap your firing hand fingers around the pistol's grip, allowing your trigger finger to rest along the slide. Your middle, ring, and pinkie fingers will wrap around the grip.

Be sure to place your middle finger as high as possible on the grip, preferably so that it pushes up against the bottom of the trigger guard. The logic of positioning your fingers as high as possible on the gun is the same as we just discussed.

Next, wrap your firing hand fingers around the front of the grip, positioning the middle finger high and tight against the base of the trigger guard.

Support Hand Position

If you've placed your firing hand correctly, you should see some space on the grip on the side opposite your trigger finger. It'll be more or less underneath the meaty area at the base of your firing hand thumb. Depending on the size of your hand and your pistol, it might be a large or small area on the grip.

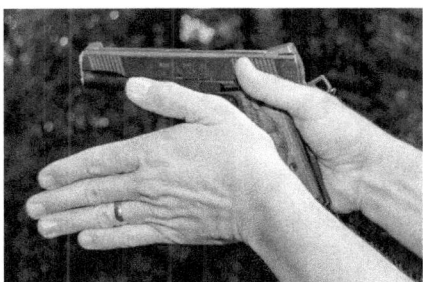

There may not be adequate space, and that's OK. Place the support hand's lower palm against the exposed area of the grip.

Regardless of the space available, I want you to imagine planting the base of your support hand thumb right on that space. Try to establish contact between the base of your palm and the grip surface. You probably won't be able to fit much skin on there, and that's OK. We're going for position here.

Last, wrap your support hand fingers around the front of the grip, on top of your firing hand fingers, placing your support hand index finger as high as possible against the trigger guard base. Note the thumbs pointed at the target.

If done correctly, the base of your support hand palm should nestle between the meat under your firing hand thumb and the tips of your firing hand fingers. Refer to the pictures for a clearer understanding.

Now, wrap your support hand fingers around the front of the

handgun. They will overlap your firing hand fingers. As with the firing hand, place your support hand fingers as high as possible on the gun, right up to the point your support hand index finger is pressing against the bottom of the trigger guard.

Firing and Support Hand Grip Pressure

We're headed back into unintuitive territory, so hold on to your shorts. I'll share the method I've chosen here, but be aware that there are other valid approaches.

Once a proper grip is established, accuracy depends on a perfect sight picture and pressing the trigger without moving the gun. Your body generally does better with fine motor movements, like pressing a trigger perfectly with your finger, when the muscles aren't under tension and stress. For this reason, I've settled on the 60/40 or perhaps even 70/30 grip pressure method. This means I apply 60 or 70 percent of total pressure with my support hand and far less pressure with my firing hand. This keeps my firing hand loose and more flexible, offering improved control over the trigger finger. The other consideration is the sympathetic movement of all your fingers. If you crush grip something with your pinky, ring, and middle fingers, the index (trigger) finger will want to do the same thing. See what's happening here?

So, I prefer to apply lots of grip pressure using my support hand, freeing up my firing hand to do its job. Again, feel free to experiment; there's rarely a single correct answer to anything except political debates. Just kidding...

One more thing. Also, using the support hand, try the mental trick of focusing on tight pressure with your pinky. If you think about the leverage, your pinky is the finger that exerts the most control to counter muzzle flip when you fire a shot. Try it. I guarantee you'll be amazed at how well you control recoil with a proper grip and a side order of pinky focus.

Remember, you may find conflicting advice on this topic, so experiment and choose your method based on your best judgment.

Contradictory recommendations about proper grip pressure are just living proof of that old axiom—there's more than one way to skin a cat.

What About Your Thumbs?

You might have noticed I "skipped" the discussion on what to do with your thumbs. That was on purpose. Here's a shocker for you. Your thumbs are not a required element of a good shooting grip. In fact, they're kind of in the way.

The most common thumb placement for a two-handed semi-auto pistol grip.

We must take a quick diversion here because you'll get contradictory information from the various experts. And guess what, they're all right—in a sense. There are multiple viable thumb placement techniques, so you're going to have to try them out and see what works for you. I'll share the method I've settled on and briefly mention other approaches.

I allow my firing and support hand thumbs to point toward the target. However, your thumbs aren't positioned or angled to help you control the gun or shoot accurately—your fingers perform all that work.

Some prefer the method of allowing the thumbs to point straight up in the air. I used this for a time but found the "thumbs forward" more natural for me. One advantage of "thumbs up" is they stay out of the way of safety or slide lock levers.

Suppose you try to crush the support side of your pistol with your thumbs. In that case, you're working against the natural biomechanical operation of your fingers to the point of encouraging your muzzle to shift towards the firing-hand side.

Your mileage may vary!

What Not to Do

When shooting a semi-automatic pistol, there are two big no-nos to remember. One will make you shoot poorly and subject you to heckling at the range. The other will make you bleed profusely.

Avoid this seemingly intuitive grip technique. While it seems like it might help stabilize the handgun, the "cup and saucer" hold offers no useful control over the gun.

First, under no circumstances should you place your support hand as a "rest" underneath the pistol's grip. This technique, often called "cup and saucer," feels natural but doesn't help you control the gun at all. You'll see it plenty on TV and...shocker...all those actors are doing it wrong. This position offers no physiological advantage in either stabilizing the gun or controlling recoil shot to shot. In fact, it'll ensure it takes you longer to get on target for your second shot.

Second, and to prevent bleeding, pay close attention to the position of your support hand thumbs. Under no circumstance should you cross that thumb behind the back of a semi-auto pistol.

Here's why. When you fire a shot with a semi-automatic, the slide will zoom backward at warp factor nine to eject the newly spent cartridge. That means it'll ride right across the meaty area at the base of your support hand thumb. The base of a pistol slide is sharply machined steel, and it will cut you like a razor blade from hell. Ask me how I know.

When shooting a semi-automatic pistol, do not cross your thumbs like this. When the slide operates, the result will be a large cut in the web of your hand.

So, pay close attention to the fundamentals when building your habits of a proper grip, and always make sure both thumbs are safely on the support-hand side of your pistol. Don't worry; it'll quickly become a subconscious habit.

Revolvers

Most of the basic principles of the semi-automatic grip technique apply to revolvers, but there are some differences.

First, pay close attention to thumb placement with a revolver. Extending thumbs forward might cause you to get burned. When a revolver fires, hot, fiery stuff shoots out of the cylinder gap—that thin space between the front of the cylinder and the rear of the barrel. While you probably won't see it in daylight, it's there and will burn your thumb tip quite handily.

Second, follow the "grip the revolver as high as possible" advice. That applies to any handgun. Recoil doesn't know or care if it's generated by a semi-auto or a wheelgun, so get your hands and, by extension, the rest of your body up high and as close to the bore line as possible.

For medium and large revolvers, you'll want first to try to curl both thumbs into the support side grip of the revolver. The bent thumbs keep them away from the cylinder gap, and the position allows the thumbs to apply some back and downward pressure on the gun.

When shooting a revolver, crossing the support hand thumb is OK and possibly preferable. Try curling it down on the same side to see what works best for you.

For smaller revolvers, if you don't have room to curl both thumbs into the support side grip, try crossing your support hand thumb over the backstrap. Since there is no moving slide to slice your support side thumb clean off, you can wrap your support hand around the back of the grip, effectively crossing your thumbs.

Sight Picture

Traditional handgun sights require one to line up the front and rear sights with each other, then combine those with the target. However, your eyes can only focus at one distance at a time. When shooting a handgun, there are three distinct objects at different distances.

1. Rear sight
2. Front sight

3. Target

When you line up to shoot, there's a chance that all three of these may appear to be in focus to you. That's because the human brain is an awesome thing. It's processing all three and switching back and forth to create the appearance of simultaneous focus. On the other hand, if you're like most people, two of those three objects will be at least partially out of focus.

A perfect sight picture looks something like this. Note the front sight is the only thing in focus.

You'll need to learn to focus on just one of these objects: the front sight. It's OK if the target is a bit blurry—your brain figures it out, and you can see it well enough to get a hit. It's the same with the rear sights. They are an aid to getting on target, but it's the front sight that's most important.

Front-sight focus gets tricky when dealing with moving targets or high-stress situations. Your brain naturally wants to zero in on the target. But you'll have a greater chance of missing if you're not focused on the front sight.

So when you dry-fire practice (discussed later in the book), focus on that front sight. Like finding your natural point of aim, it's a habit you want to build, so you don't have to think about it.

One more thought on the front sight. Like a golf or baseball swing, you want to follow through. Following through on your shot means keeping your eyes on the front sight until after the shot has left the gun. If your front sight stays on target before, during and after the shot, it's impossible to miss. So, for each successful shot, you really see two pictures—one before and another after.

Trigger Press

So far, we've covered grip, stance and sight pictures. The fourth and final component of handgun accuracy is your trigger press technique. It's the number one cause of missed shots.

When you consider the underlying math, the problem is entirely understandable. Depending on the style and model, handguns require between 3 1/2 and 12 pounds of pressure on the trigger to fire a shot. While some handguns weigh over two pounds, most modern defensive guns weigh a pound and change. And therein lies the issue. The gun tends to move when applying "more pounds" of pressure to "fewer pounds" of handgun weight. The slightest movement of the gun during the trigger press will cause a missed shot.

The learned skill is applying enough pressure to break the trigger without moving the gun. The second part of that skill is learning to move your trigger finger without the natural sympathetic response of moving the other fingers on the same hand.

You'll hear experienced shooters refer to "jerking" the trigger. As the formal definition of a "spasmodic muscular movement" implies, that refers to a shooter making a rapid and uncontrolled trigger press that moves the gun, causing a missed shot.

In theory, a perfect trigger press is not difficult. Slowly move the trigger while keeping the gun as still as possible. Interestingly, the "slowly" part gives everyone so much trouble. Invariably, when teaching new shooters, I ask them to press the trigger s-l-o-w-l-y, and the result is still almost always a rapid, jerky press, often leading to a missed shot.

This tendency stems from our natural temptation to "time the shot" and press the trigger quickly at the precise instant the sights are perfectly aligned with the target. Timing the shot and jerking the trigger go hand in hand. Trying to "time the shot" just doesn't work. So, what does?

Try the opposite approach. Hold the gun as still as possible, but allow the sights to wander or wobble as they always will. We're not statues, after all, so there will always be some movement. As you become more skilled, that movement zone will shrink, so your "wobble" zone will get smaller. Now, while accepting whatever level of movement you have, focus on s-l-o-w-l-y pressing the trigger. Slowly, I mean, take two or three full seconds to move the trigger from the start to firing the shot. Do the one-one-thousand type of count while you operate the trigger.

Again, while doing this, forget how the sights move around on target. If you follow this technique faithfully, you'll be surprised at your resulting accuracy on target. If you do your part, all your shots will land somewhere in your sight wobble zone. Your wobble zone and group sizes will get smaller as you practice. I promise.

There's no secret other than focus and deliberate practice. While at the range, tune everything else out except making a smooth, motionless trigger press. Don't worry about accuracy—yet. Later, we'll discuss an at-home practice technique to help you develop a perfect trigger press.

Natural Point of Aim

Competitive rifle shooters rely on the "natural point of aim" concept to wring maximum accuracy out of their technique. Simply put, the concept takes advantage of your body's natural "default" positions so you don't have to exert deliberate muscle control to fight the body's desired status quo.

Imagine standing in the yard, facing a tree. If your objective is to see the tree, the "natural" position of facing the tree requires the least amount of work by you to accomplish that goal. If you face the opposite direction from the tree, you have to contort your shoulders, neck and head to achieve the goal of looking at the tree. This is a silly example, but it illustrates the value of natural point of aim when shooting.

By taking advantage of how your body wants to position itself relative to the target, you can reduce the muscle strain required to aim the gun at the target and, therefore, avoid accuracy-robbing fatigue. If you have to move any body part against its will to get the gun pointed at the target, you'll create muscle strain, which robs stability. When you relax those muscles, your handgun will fall off target.

Shooting from a naturally relaxed position where body parts are "pre-aligned" with the target will reduce the work required and facilitate more accurate and consistent shooting. As you consciously learn the position of your body, arms, hands, and head associated with your natural point of aim, you'll build the habit and "fall into" that perfect position without thinking about it.

Here's how to learn your natural point of aim position.

A shooting range is the best place to tinker with your natural point of aim. The benefit of the range is you have a built-in safe backstop, and you can test the results of your efforts.

- First, ensure your firearm is safe and unloaded.
- Next, assume your normal shooting stance with your gun aimed carefully at a precise aiming point on your target.
- Close your eyes and take a deep breath. Don't try to keep your gun aimed at your aiming point—that's cheating, and your goal here is to help yourself, not "win" the exercise.
- Now, open your eyes. Are your sights still lined up on the original aiming point?
- If you are pointing the gun to one side or the other or your aiming point, that's easy to adjust. Move your feet slightly so your body rotates into a position where the gun is pointed at your target.
- If you find your sights pointed a bit high after opening your eyes, try moving your foot on your firing-hand side a

bit forward. That can help lower your sights. The opposite works if your aim point is low—move that same foot back just a touch.

- To ensure you've found your natural point of aim, briefly close your eyes again. When you open them, are you still pointing the gun directly at your chosen aiming point?
- Repeat this exercise until you start to assume a stance and position that is "naturally" consistent with the target you want to shoot. You'll find that when you assume a shooting position, your body will find its natural point of aim.

Obviously, this isn't something you would ever do in a self-defense situation. Like a quarterback carefully setting up to throw a perfect spiral in practice, the motions involved will become ingrained, so during the chaos of a game, the ball will still fly true without all the careful planning.

Ready to Shoot!

Earlier in this book, we covered the different types of handguns and how they operate. Handguns vary in operation details, so the safe approach is to familiarize yourself with the information outlined in the owners' manual. If your gun was purchased used, no worries; manuals are readily available online or by calling the manufacturer.

We'll cover some operational basics here.

Loading/Unloading Semi-Automatic Handguns

A semi-automatic pistol with a detachable magazine, almost always located in the handgun grip, uses a two-stage loading and unloading approach.

Think of the magazine as the "source" of extra bullets that feed the handgun. But it's not ready to fire until a cartridge is moved from the "source" supply into the chamber. So, the process of loading requires two distinct steps: inserting a loaded or partially loaded magazine and racking the slide to strip a cartridge from the top of the magazine and load it into the chamber itself. At that point, the handgun is ready to fire, assuming any applicable safety devices are in the ready position.

Removing a magazine from a semi-auto pistol doesn't mean it's unloaded. There still may be a cartridge in the chamber.

Unloading a semi-automatic handgun is also a two-step operation. Sadly, too many careless gun users forget this critical fact. Removing the magazine only cuts off the supply of new "incoming" cartridges. **It does not remove a cartridge that already might be in the chamber.**

To fully unload a semi-automatic, first remove the magazine so no "new" cartridges can enter the chamber. Then, rack the slide according to the specific procedures outlined in the owner's manual. Rack the slide a couple extra times to ensure the chamber is clear.

When these two operations are complete, check the magazine well and the chamber to make sure no cartridges are present. During these operations, follow all four primary safety rules, ensuring no fingers are on the trigger and the gun is pointed in a safe direction.

Loading/Unloading Revolvers

Revolvers offer a distinct safety advantage over semi-automatic pistols. There is no extra "chamber" where a cartridge might remain hidden away from the magazine. Each "chamber" is its own magazine in a revolver, so if all the chambers are empty, the revolver is easily verified as unloaded.

With revolvers, it's easier to quickly check the loaded/unloaded status as you can see all cylinders at once.

There are a couple of details that may come into play. Most modern double-action revolvers use a transfer bar safety system, so unless the trigger is stroked, it is mechanically impossible for the firing pin to come in contact with a chambered cartridge.

Many vintage (or modern replicas of vintage) single-action revolvers use a fixed firing pin on the hammer itself, so if the hammer is resting in the uncocked position, the firing pin can contact a cartridge underneath. A blow against the revolver or a drop might cause unintended firing. For these types of revolvers, you always leave the chamber underneath the hammer unloaded to prevent such a mishap.

Racking the Slide

Racking the slide can be challenging with many semiautomatic pistols, especially small, compact guns with strong springs. I constantly hear of new shooters turning down certain guns because they can't easily operate the slide to load and unload the pistol.

Simply put, racking refers to cycling the slide of a semi-automatic gun with enough vigor to remove a spent (or live) cartridge from the chamber, reset the hammer and allow the recoil spring to draw the slide back into position. Then, a new cartridge is stripped from the magazine and loaded into the chamber.

In addition to preparing a pistol to fire, racking the slide can also complete the process of unloading a pistol after removing the magazine. Racking the slide is also used to clear jams or malfunctions. The most important element of a successful slide rack is not to be gentle or timid. Ejecting a chambered round takes some force, and you want to withdraw the slide as far rearward as it can travel. If you don't, there's a great chance of causing a jam or malfunction.

OK, I'm exaggerating slightly for the camera, but most people try to rack the slide using a "pinching" technique with the thumb and index finger. If you can do this easily, great! If not, a better way is to use the larger hand and arm muscles.

Likewise, when the slide is fully retracted, never ease it forward with your hand. Always let go and allow the powerful recoil spring to slam that slide forward with enough pressure to load the chamber and return the pistol to its ready-to-fire position. Gently easing the slide forward is a great way to induce a malfunction. The gun is designed to operate faster and more vigorously than you'll ever accomplish by hand, so let it work as intended.

In several circumstances, a command to rack the slide may be used on the range or in a competition. When a semi-automatic gun is first loaded, the slide must be racked to load a cartridge into the chamber to prepare the gun to fire. Second, a range officer may issue a "rack the slide" command to verify that your gun is empty when shooting is finished. After removing the magazine, several rapid racks will help ensure the chamber is empty. Always confirm by sight and sticking a finger in the chamber to make sure it is, in fact, clear.

Let us assure you, with very few exceptions, that almost all people are stronger than a pistol's springs. Successfully racking the slide on a semi-automatic handgun is a matter of technique.

I'm using all large muscles here, and rather than pulling the slide back, I'm pushing the gun forward with my whole arm while holding the slide still with my other hand.

The idea is to use natural leverage and larger muscles rather than relying on the small and weak ones in the fingers and thumbs. Without instruction, most folks will hold the gun with their firing hand and pinch the back of the slide with their support hand thumb and index finger to pull back the side. While the strong hand is perfectly capable of keeping the frame still against the spring pressure of the slide, those thumb and finger muscles are not exactly ideal for the job. You've got much larger arm and body muscles right nearby doing nothing, so why not use them? If you're having difficulty racking the slide of your pistol, try following these steps instead.

- First, take a firing grip with your strong hand, ensuring your finger is off the trigger.
- Bring it close to your body, making sure the pistol is pointed safely downrange.
- Next, flatten your support hand and turn it so your palm faces the ground.
- Move your whole flat support hand over the back half of the slide of your gun, taking care not to cover the ejection port in case you desire to remove a spent or full cartridge from the chamber.
- Close your hand over the top of the slide so that your palm is on one side of the slide and your fingers on the other. Now you're grasping that slide with your larger hand and arm muscles instead of thumb and finger mini-muscles. Squeeze!
- Keeping your support arm in the same position up close against your body, push the gun's bottom half (frame) forward with your entire firing arm like you're going to jab the target with the muzzle.
- If you did this right, you held the pistol slide still, close to your body, using your whole hand and the strength of your support arm while using the powerful muscles of your firing arm to move the gun against the stationary slide. You have completely reversed the instinctive way to do this, and now you're using large muscles to overcome spring tension.

- When you have pushed the gun as far forward as the slide will allow it to go, quickly release the slide with your support hand. Let the springs snap the slide closed.

Be careful to keep the pistol pointed safely downrange while doing this. If you blade the support side of your entire body toward the backstop, the muzzle will remain pointed in a safe direction throughout the operation.

Malfunctions

The loudest sound in the known universe is the sound of a "click" when your gun is supposed to fire. We'll refer to that sound as a malfunction. Sometimes, there's no warning click, and the gun still won't fire. We'll call that a malfunction, too.

While malfunctions are rare in recreational shooting conditions, they're more likely to happen during a fight. You may be shooting from a non-traditional (and less supported) position. You may be fighting up close and personal, and your gun may get pushed out of battery. The magazine button may get depressed in the chaos, causing a temporary jam. Whatever the reason, understanding and knowing how to address malfunctions is a vital skill to learn.

Revolver Malfunctions

If you shoot a revolver, you have the easiest "first thing to try" when encountering a malfunction. If you hear a "click," just press the trigger again. Perhaps you just encountered a dud cartridge that didn't ignite. While rare with quality factory ammunition, it does happen in rare instances. Pulling the trigger again advances the revolver cylinder, cocks the hammer and brings a fresh cartridge into position. If pulling the trigger a second time does not clear up the problem, you might consider changing your plan, as two consecutive duds are highly unlikely—there's probably something wrong with the gun.

If the trigger won't work or the cylinder won't turn, there's no simple and immediate way to rectify the situation if muscling the cylinder past the jam doesn't help. It's possible that a primer has backed out of a cartridge and jammed up the works, a bullet has crept forward and prevented the cylinder from turning, or maybe there's a mechanical breakage. If you can't open the cylinder, empty the cartridges, and start over, it's time to go to a new plan.

Semi-Automatic Pistol Malfunctions

Not counting a catastrophic pistol breakage, two categories of failures may require your intervention. It's important to recognize them, as the rectification procedures are slightly different.

Failure to Feed / Failure to Eject

A semi-automatic pistol is a nifty invention. The "auto" part of semi-automatic refers to how the gun is designed to automatically eject a spent cartridge casing and load a new one after each shot. Sometimes, things go wrong, and the cartridge scheduled for forcible ejection doesn't want to leave.

More often than not, a failure to eject is caused by the shooter. Semi-automatic pistols rely on the user holding the gun frame with forward pressure during ejection so that the slide and springs have something to work against. If you use a weak grip, the gun moves backward with the slide, and that whole bit of fancy recoil mechanism engineering may fail. This may cause an empty cartridge case to get stuck in the ejection port. This prevents a new cartridge from loading and prevents the slide from closing fully. In case it's not already obvious, a gun in this condition won't fire again until things are cleared up. Most modern pistols are designed not to operate unless the slide is fully closed.

Sometimes, the failure to eject or feed malfunction is caused by a magazine not being fully inserted into the gun. It may stay in place but not be fully locked into position. As a result, the cartridges in the magazine aren't lined up with the chamber properly and won't feed reliably as the slide moves forward. Guns are designed to be operated with authority, not kid gloves, so whenever you insert a new magazine into a semi-automatic pistol, smack it in there like you mean it.

Whatever the cause, to make the gun work again, you must remove the spent cartridge casing, allow the slide to grab a fresh cartridge from the magazine and load it into the chamber.

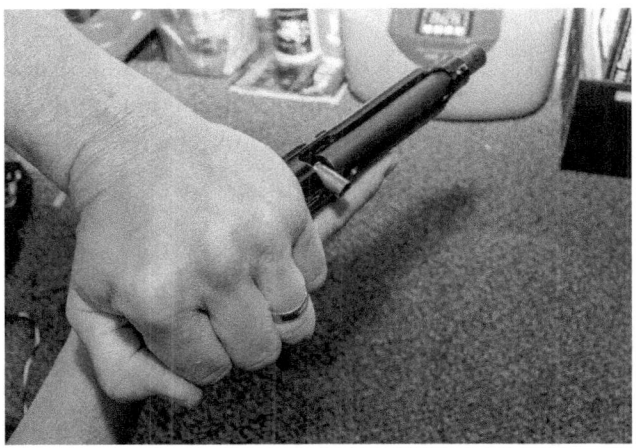

The failure to feed malfunction often looks something like this. Called a "stovepipe," the spent case hasn't fully ejected. I'm rotating the ejection port toward the ground while racking the slide to clear it.

Here's the solution: It's commonly called the Tap, Rack, Bang drill, but I prefer to call it Tap, Rack, and Reassess. After you "tap" and "rack," it may be appropriate to reassess whether you still want or need to fire before pressing the trigger again. It works like this:

1. Keeping the gun pointed safely down range, enthusiastically smack the bottom of the magazine to ensure it's seated properly. That's the "tap" part. Smack is probably more descriptive, as you don't want to be gentle. The goal is to ensure the magazine is firmly locked in place. You won't break it.

2. Rotate your pistol clockwise so the ejection port faces the ground. Gravity helps here, and most pistols have the ejection port on the right side, hence the suggested rotation to the right. Now rack the slide vigorously once. This will (hopefully) clear any spent cartridge casings stuck in the ejection port and load a new round in the chamber. If you rack the slide more than once, you might be flinging perfectly good ammo from the magazine onto the ground each time you rack.

3. Here's the "bang" part. But we prefer "reassess" because you may not always want or need to shoot. Do things look normal again? Is the slide fully closed (in battery)?

If this drill does not solve the problem, it's time to move to the following method of malfunction clearance: You might very well have a double-feed malfunction.

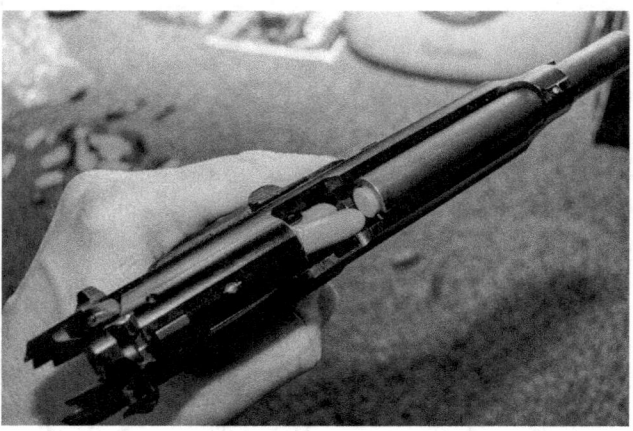

A double-feed malfunction looks like this. The magazine will have to be removed to clear it. I'm using dummy cartridges for safety.

The Double-Feed

This malfunction scenario is nasty. It's called a double feed, and it's double trouble because you have to perform some fancy hand manipulation to clear it.

1. The first step assumes you've already done the Tap, Rack, Bang/Reassess drill with no success.
2. Using the slide lock on your pistol, lock the slide to the rear, keeping the muzzle pointed down range.
3. Remove the magazine. If you have a double-feed, you must exert some serious force to remove it. Don't be afraid to use some muscle to tear it out of the magazine well while pressing the magazine release button.
4. Save the magazine. You can tuck it under your shooting hand arm, stuff it in a pocket, or, if you have the coordination of a mature spider monkey, hold it between a couple of fingers. You may need this magazine when the jam is cleared, especially if it's your only one!
5. Now, rack the slide several times vigorously. The magazine has been removed, so you don't have to worry about ejecting perfectly good ammo. You're trying to clear out anything in the chamber area that might be jamming your gun.
6. Now replace the magazine and smack it into place.
7. Rack the slide one more time to chamber a round.
8. Unless your gun malfunctioned for some other reason, you should be good to go.

If these methods don't clear the problem, then there is more going on than can be solved on the spot.

Drawing from a Holster

Before you practice drawing from your holster, be sure your gun is completely empty. If you have a semi-automatic pistol, be sure to empty the magazine first and then remove the round that might be in the chamber. Put all the ammunition far away, preferably in another room. You won't want any ammunition nearby when learning and practicing drawing from a holster.

Consider the following before we get into the step-by-step components of a safe draw from your holster.

We'll present the complete sequence as a series of steps. However, once you master the motions, the process will be smooth and continuous.

Practicing your holster draws should be a safe "how slow can you go" process. Safety is paramount. If you go for speed, you're more likely to point the muzzle of your gun at one of your body parts or someone else nearby. Take your time.

You'll get faster the slower you practice. Here's why. If you go slow and focus on performing the draw steps precisely the same way every time, you'll "burn" the routine into your brain and muscles. The concept informally called "muscle memory" is a real thing. How much do you have to think about stepping on your car's brake pedal? It's the same idea. You've done that motion thousands of times, so it's now fast, efficient, and completely automatic. If you do your holster draw identically and perfectly in practice, the speed will take care of itself. Trust me on this; you can't practice drawing from a holster too slowly.

There is never a need to "speed reholster." Whether on the range, at a competition, or after a self-defense encounter, take your time. Depending on the type of handgun you have, you may need to decock it first, and you want to be positive that your finger is out of the trigger area. If you try to holster a gun that's still cocked (for double-action pistols), not on safe, or if you have a finger inside the trigger guard, there is an excellent chance you'll shoot yourself. The trigger finger is the most significant hazard because the lip of the holster will drive your finger and the trigger backward.

Holster Draw Steps

Here, we will enumerate the standard non-defensive draw method from an open (not concealed) holster. It's a vital base skill one should master before drawing from concealment, which we'll cover later in the book. For this section, we'll assume you're using a standard outside-the-waistband holster positioned on your strong-side hip.

Step 1: Clear your support hand; Establish a firing grip

Move your support hand straight to the base of your sternum until your hand is touching your chest. This gets your support hand in close to the body to eliminate the risk of it ending up in front of the muzzle as you draw your gun from the holster. It also positions your support hand in the perfect place to grip the handgun as you bring it up into a firing position.

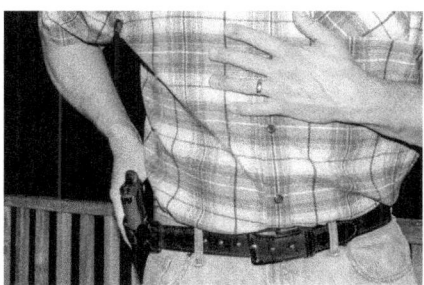

Note how my support hand is planted against my chest, safely out of the way, while I assume a firing grip on the pistol.

As your support hand moves to your chest, establish a proper firing grip, nice and high on the gun with your shooting hand. Your trigger finger should ride outside of the holster alongside your gun. Do not curl your trigger finger, allowing it to move inside the trigger guard as the gun clears the holster.

Try to grasp the gun grip perfectly on the first try so you don't have to adjust or reposition it later. Keep your elbow tucked in close beside your body; it should extend straight backward.

Step 2: Raise your gun from the holster

As you lift your handgun from the holster, your finger should remain outside the trigger guard. Only raise the gun as high as required for the muzzle to clear the holster. Any excess movement is wasted motion and time. Your support hand should remain right where you placed it in step one, planted against your chest.

Step 3: Rotate your firing arm

Rather than lifting the muzzle and shoving the gun forward, I prefer to think and move in terms of simply dropping my firing arm elbow. The muzzle has already cleared the holster, so driving (rotating) your elbow straight toward the ground will orient the gun toward the target most efficiently.

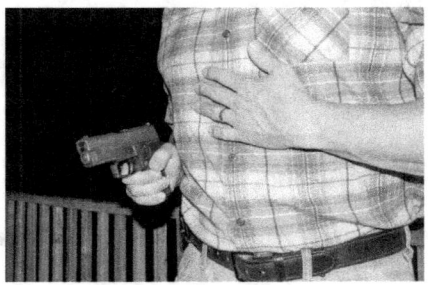

Here, I have cleared the holster and driven my elbow down to rotate the gun toward the target. If necessary, I could shoot from this position.

If you were in a defensive situation at this stage, you could technically shoot if necessary. Your gun would be pointed down range, and your support hand would be out of the way. If you've done everything right, your muzzle would be forward of any part of your body.

Step 4: Join firing and support hands

As you extend your firing hand with the gun (finger still off the trigger!) forward, bring your support hand into the picture. Marry your support hand with your firing hand as the gun comes in front of your body. As with step one, you'll want to establish the perfect support hand grip on the initial movement so you don't have to adjust or reposition. This is yet another reason for slow, slow, slow practice. Get the movement right!

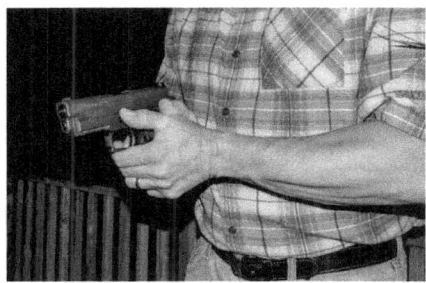

As you raise the gun to a normal shooting position, you can bring your support hand into a proper two-handed grip.

Step 5: Extend to the target

With a proper two-handed grip, all that's left is pressing forward and raising the sights to eye level. Resist the temptation to scrunch your head down to gun level—that creates a violation of natural body position.

Last, extend and raise the sights into view.

As the gun travels forward to normal arm extension, the sights will rise into view. Keep the muzzle at or below the line of the target.

What you don't want to do is raise the muzzle above the target so that you have to lower the sight back down when your arms are fully extended—that's wasted motion.

Also, at this stage, depending on the specific type of handgun you use, you can consider disabling any manual safety levers, such as on a 1911-type pistol. As always, keep your finger off the trigger until you decide to shoot.

Reholstering

When it's time to reholster your gun, take your time! Ensure the safety is engaged and the firearm is decocked if applicable. Make sure your finger is out of the trigger. Make sure all clothing is out of the way. While all the draw steps aren't necessary to reverse, pay particular attention to the muzzle orientation as you slowly and carefully return the gun to the holster.

Remember, there is never a reason to "speed reholster." As the folks at Gunsite Academy say, "Reholster reluctantly." I like to place my firing-hand thumb on the rear of the slide as a tactile reminder to check the position of any safeties or decocker levers. I do this because I shoot different guns regularly, so the mini-procedure serves as a reminder to check the overall condition. If you focus on one gun, develop your own routine to check the status as warranted.

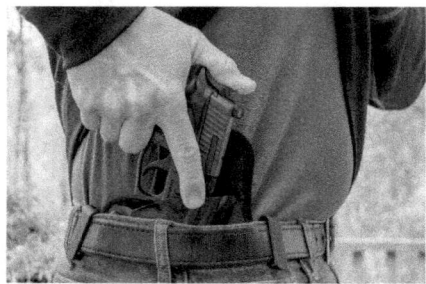

I like to place my thumb on the hammer or back of the slide when reholstering as a tactile reminder to ensure the handgun is decocked or on safe as appropriate.

Ongoing Practice

Like golf or any other activity involving fine motor skills, shooting is a perishable skill. As you've likely picked up by now, effectively controlling and operating a handgun is somewhat of an unnatural proposition. Think about concepts like fine trigger control when your brain is screaming, "You're gonna die if you don't do something now!" or perhaps forcing yourself to look at your front sight while a violent attacker is somewhere in your line of sight.

In a perfect world, you'd attend a live, in-person self-defense training class a few times a year and fill in the gaps with weekly practice. In the real world, you have things like family and jobs to worry about instead.

There are some things you can do to keep your basic gun handling skills sharp that require less time.

Dry Fire

Keeping to pure shooting skill, there is one thing you can do right at home, in minutes per day, that will improve your shooting skills more than any other activity. In fact, you can consider this a money-back guarantee. What is it?

Dry firing.

Dry firing is operating your handgun without the use of live cartridges. It involves practicing your stance, grip, and aim, pressing the trigger and following through to track where your "virtual" shot landed. It's that simple. The extra benefit is you can practice dry firing right at home, provided you relentlessly follow basic safety procedures.

Remember earlier when we discussed the number one challenge of accurate handgun shooting? The force required to operate a handgun trigger is almost always more than the gun's weight, so according to the laws of physics, it tends to want to move as you press the trigger. Your job, and a learned and practiced skill, is to keep the handgun perfectly stationary before, during and after the trigger press.

Dry fire practice (repeatedly pressing the trigger while holding your handgun on target) gives you essential practice in mastering this difficult skill. Better yet, you can practice without all the associated distractions in a live shooting scenario: noise, recoil, other shooters and worrying about where your shots land on the target. In effect, you can isolate the singular skill of a perfect trigger press. So it's focused practice—and free. Minutes per day will develop your trigger press—and accuracy—from novice to expert in no time.

Why isn't everyone an expert shooter since this is so easy and beneficial? Virtually no one does it regularly, and if you do, you'll stand out from the crowd.

There is a big self-defense benefit to dry fire practice, too. By practicing the most elementary of shooting skills until it's subconsciously perfect, you've removed the requirement of conscious brain activity when you pick up a gun to shoot. Muscle memory kicks in, and your body knows how to get accurate shots on target.

Dry Fire Practice Steps

Safety is the most important element of dry fire. Dry fire practice offers no excuse for violating the four gun safety rules. Even though we're going to go to great lengths to verify the gun is unloaded, we're still going to treat it as if it is loaded. And we'll exercise strict trigger finger discipline and muzzle control while making sure we're pointing at a safe target and backstop. By following the rules, we can ensure that if a stray round of live ammo ends up in your practice area, the only damage will be to your pride and perhaps a piece of furniture.

Step 1: Remove all live ammo

Remove all ammunition from your gun. Remove it all from your revolver's cylinder or the magazine in your semi-automatic. If you have a semi-automatic pistol, clear the round from the chamber. Inspect your gun—twice or more— then insert a finger to ensure chambers and magazines are clear.

I like to remove the cartridges from the magazine and place them next to my dry fire target. The one by itself is the cartridge from the chamber. It's a visual cue the gun is really empty.

I like to set the removed ammo near my dry-fire target and backstop, so I can clearly see it. This serves as an additional cue that the ammo is not in the gun. If I remove a magazine, I'll set the loaded magazine in view and stand the extra round from the chamber next to it, again, to visually verify that both the magazine and chamber are clear.

While this may sound excessive, just do it. Too many distractions in our daily lives may create a "pause and resume" scenario during a practice session. If you stop, reload your gun without thinking, then get distracted and restart your dry fire session, tragedy happens. There are too many true stories of this precise scenario.

Step 2: Target

Select your target. Ensure your target is backed by a safe backstop capable of stopping a bullet. Even though you're following safety procedures, it's essential to build in levels of extra insurance. Consider a bookshelf, solid wall, or similar.

Step 3: Position

Get a comfortable stance and find your natural point of aim. This is a great time to also practice front-sight focus.

Step 4: Trigger press

Now, slowly press the trigger as slowly and smoothly as possible. The goal is to complete the full trigger press until the gun's action releases—without moving the sights off target. When I say slowly, get a timer or buddy and literally drag that fraction of an inch trigger movement out over two full seconds. Part of what we're trying to do is exercise the "timing the shot" demon from your bank of bad habits. Focus on "slow" during practice—as your skills improve, you'll be able to press the trigger as fast as needed without moving the gun off target.

Step 5: Follow through

As the hammer or striker releases, watch your sights on target while continuing to keep the sights stable and on target. After the "click" sound is long gone, see if the sights are still on target. If so, that's where a real shot would have landed. Because there's no recoil, dry fire sessions are an excellent opportunity to train your eyes to see the sight picture after the gun "fires." Eventually, you'll know where your shot hit without looking at the target. You'll be "calling your shot."

Step 6: Reset your handgun action for the next shot

After your first shot, the process to reset or cock the handgun will vary depending on the type of your gun.

Revolver (Double Action)

Double-action revolvers are the easiest type of handgun to fry fire. After you complete the first dry fire "shot," you don't have to do anything to prepare the gun for the next shot. Get your body, grip and sight alignment back in place, aim at your target, and press the trigger again.

Whether or not your revolver has a hammer, always practice it in double-action mode. That is, press the trigger without first cocking the hammer. That's how you should use the revolver in a defensive application anyway, so you might as well get used to it in practice.

Semi-Automatic Pistols (Double / Single-Action)

With a double-action pistol, you can configure your dry fire practice depending on what you want to accomplish. You can always press the trigger to simulate a full, double-action firing sequence like a double-action revolver. However, in real life, after that first double-action trigger pull, your handgun will cock itself, so the second shot only requires a light, single-action trigger press. Since you're dry firing and there is no automatic cycling of the action, you'll have to pull back the hammer manually to prepare the gun for a single-action shot. So it's up to you to simulate a first double-action shot, followed by a series of single-action shots or some other scenario. Practice double-action shots immediately followed by single-action shots. The transition from heavier to lighter trigger takes some getting used to.

Single-Action Pistols and Revolvers

If you shoot a 1911-style handgun or a single-action revolver, dry fire practice is pretty straightforward. You must cock the hammer after each shot. With a single-action revolver, you want to make the hammer cock part of your dry fire sequence, as you'll have to do that in real life. With a single-action semi-automatic pistol, you don't want to build a habit of cocking the hammer each time you pull the trigger. Remember, when you shoot live ammunition, the gun will cock itself after each shot, so you don't have to. To help overcome building "bad muscle memory" when dry firing a single-action pistol, I like to fire the first shot, aim at a different target and simulate more trigger presses against an inactive trigger. After a few of those "shots," I bring the gun back from the firing position, cock the hammer and repeat the exercise.

Striker-Fired Pistols

If you shoot a pistol that's striker-fired, like a Glock or similar model, you have to cock the gun after each shot. To do this with most striker-fired pistols, you must rack the slide, at least partially, as there is no hammer. Pull the slide back ¼" or so, and the striker mechanism will reset. Experiment with your gun to see how little of a partial slide rack you can get away with. Like the single-action pistol scenario mentioned above, you don't want to build a habit of racking the slide after every shot, so vary your firing sequence accordingly. Some specialty magazines will configure your pistol to simulate repeated trigger presses.

With striker-fired pistols like these, you'll need to rack the slide, at least partially, to reset the trigger between dry-fire shots.

.22 Handguns

If you shoot a .22 pistol, you're probably better off not dry-firing. Most rimfires do not react well to dry firing due to how the firing pin is placed—repeated dry firing will cause damage to the firing mechanism. Most centerfire handguns are perfectly safe to dry fire. Always check your owner's manual to see what the manufacturer recommends.

Add some complexity!

Once you've mastered basic dry fire practice, you can add variety to get more training value per practice session.

1. Draw from your holster! You've got an unloaded gun in safe conditions. What better time to practice your holster draw? Mix in more complex sequences where you draw your gun and dry fire one or more times. Be creative!
2. Practice magazine changes. Dry-fire your gun and pretend that was the last shot in your magazine. Then, practice dropping that magazine, pulling a new one and reloading your gun. **Be extra careful that all magazines you use are empty!**
3. Practice malfunction drills. When you dry fire, pretend your gun didn't go bang. What do you do? Practice the malfunction drills appropriate for your type of handgun.

Don't rush your dry firing. That's bad form and will help you develop rotten habits. Your brain is a fantastic thing that will build muscle memory of your actions regardless of the speed at which you complete them. Focus on completing your dry fire sequence slowly and perfectly every time. If you do that, speed will take care of itself. Remember Karate Kid... wax on... wax off...

If you want to get serious about practice at home, you might consider investing in a practice pistol. Companies like Next Level

Training and LaserLyte make dedicated, non-function practice pistols. These cannot fire any live ammunition, so they're safe to use at home. They are also equipped with lasers that indicate where your shot "hit" so you can get immediate feedback on your technique and progress. LaserLyte makes targets that react to the laser "strike," so your practice sessions can be fun.

Make the Most of Range Time

While there's nothing wrong with making a range trip all about mindless fun, know it won't do much to make you a better shooter. As a structured skill, practice aimed (see what I did there?) at making you better must be structured and goal-oriented. Don't panic; there are plenty of ways to mix actual practice with a bit of fun.

Measuring your progress doesn't have to be complex. You can do that simply by using a standard round target with scoring rings. Pick a reasonable distance, like five to seven yards, for starters. Fire ten shots at the target. Add up your scores and write them down with the date. Next time you shoot, do the same thing. Pretty soon, you'll have a progression of scores from your range outings to track your progress.

Let's discuss a couple of structured routines that will help develop your skills.

Raise and Shoot

Here's the most effortless skill-building routine you can do, and it works on any range. It's also perfect for dry-fire practice at home.

From a low ready position (gun pointed diagonally at the ground or bottom of the backstop), methodically raise your gun to target, acquire the sight picture you want, and fire a single shot, focusing on a perfect sight picture and trigger press. Be sure to follow through, trying to keep the sights on target through recoil. Do this slowly and deliberately, focusing on the details. Repeat. A lot. And do this every time you go to the range. Use a draw from concealment instead of starting with a low-ready position if your range allows or when dry-firing at home.

This simple motion builds practice reps of bringing your gun onto the target, finding the sights, aligning them with the target, and then breaking a perfect shot, complete with follow-through. Here's the neat part: After you do this enough times, you'll be astounded at how you can complete the same routine at much greater speed and without concentration while knocking the center out of your target.

The 45 Drill

Here's one that's simple and fun! It'll also help improve your practical shooting skill—getting shots on target accurately and quickly.

It's called the 45 drill because all you have to remember are four "5"s.

1. Five-inch target. We'll cheat and say paper plates of roughly similar size. Odds are you already have some, they're cheap, and they're small enough for basic shooting practice.
2. Five yards. Position the targets five yards downrange.
3. Five shots.
4. Five seconds.

The goal is to get all five shots to hit your five-inch paper plate target in five seconds or less from a distance of five yards.

Pretty simple, right? Ideally, you'll do this drill by drawing from a holster, so the five-second time limit includes your draw. Many ranges don't allow you to draw from a holster, so you can adapt by starting from a low-ready position. Just hold the handgun in front of you at about a 45-degree angle aimed toward the ground. At the start of your five seconds, raise the gun, get on target and commence firing.

To simplify the time tracking, you can have a friend do it using "Start" and "Stop" commands. If you want to get fancy and have a smart-phone, free shot timer apps are available. These have features that sound a starting beep and then listen for shots. The shot timer will show the number of seconds elapsed between the buzzer and the last shot it heard. You can also set a "par time," which means you designate an interval, like five seconds, and the timer sounds a starting and ending beep.

The Dot Torture Drill

If I had to pick just one practice routine, it would probably be the Dot Torture exercise. The Dot Torture drill makes productive and structured use of a 50-round box of ammo and exercises various shooting skills.

As far as I can tell, this drill was designed by David Blinder at personaldefensetraining.com and modified by Todd Louis Green at www.pistol-training.com. Credit where credit is due!

It might be this one if I had to pick just one practice drill. It exercises all of the basic shooting skills with one 50-round box of ammo.

The drill has you do slow and accurate fire, rapid single shots from a draw, multiple shots from a draw, single-hand shots with each hand and even reloads. And the whole 50-round string of fire is scored so you can track your progress over time. Visit www.pistol-training.com to print the targets on standard notebook-size paper. Detailed instructions are on the target itself.

Get a Shot Timer

Smartphone timers are OK for casual use, but a dedicated shot timer is worth the investment. With microphone sensitivity calibrated for the loud noise of nearby gunfire and logic to help filter more distant shots from other parts of the range, a proper shot timer can provide valuable quantitative feedback on your shooting performance.

In a basic scenario, a timer can help you develop your speed, such as drawing from a holster and getting a shot on target, split times between shots on target, transitioning to other targets, etc.

A shot timer like this Competitive Edge Dynamics 7000 is a great training tool.

To me, the biggest value of a shot timer is the pressure it creates during your practice session. You'll be amazed at how much stress that starting "beep" combined with a running clock adds to your practice routines. Early on, you'll fumble, rush, and make mistakes—all things beneficial to do on the practice range.

It's great to have in your shooting bag and a valuable tool for dry fire practice, too.

Competition

Competition, not even IDPA (International Defensive Pistol Association), doesn't help you develop fighting skills or tactics. In fact, many competition moves might be outright dangerous in a self-defense encounter.

However, competition can help you become really, really good at handling your gun, drawing from a holster under stress, shooting and moving, getting sights on target, and shooting accurately at speed. It's also a great way to practice handling reloads and malfunctions. The clock is always running, and while that and an audience don't create nearly the same stress level as a fight, it's still valuable conditioning.

Human nature and our desire to outshine our buddies and strangers means that any gun competition will soon become a gaming-the-system arms race where competitors will latch onto any equipment advantage to shave fractions of a second off their times. Even in IDPA events, where the whole idea is to compete with realistic carry gear and clothing, you'll see plenty of folks trying to bend the intent for a slight advantage.

If you're more serious about becoming better at personal defense than moving up the results rankings one or two places, consider competing with your carry gear, dressing and preparing precisely as you would when headed out for the day. The gamer might beat you by a few tenths, but you'll gain valuable skills while having fun in a friendly match.

11

DEFENSIVE MINDSET

L et's establish expectations right off the bat. Reading this, or any other book, won't prepare you to defend yourself and others in the real world.

That may sound strange coming from the author, but I think we'll quickly find common ground. Moving from zero to proficient in any skill, especially a life-altering one, is a process. Learning and the ability to act proficiently and consistently require time: various learning inputs, demonstration, practice, critique and more practice are just some elements of a successful learning program.

A book like this one will undoubtedly help you get started, but live training events are essential to reach the finish line. Until you put theory into motion and learn from inevitable mistakes, no amount of book knowledge will adequately prepare you for a real-life defensive encounter.

As part of my profession, I've been fortunate to have the opportunity to train with excellent instructors across the country. I've made countless mistakes (and continue to do so) on the range and under the eyes of qualified instructors that would likely have gotten me hurt or killed in the "real world." I've been even more fortunate to have been shot (with simunitions and airsoft guns) lots of times in training scenarios and exercises. Had you asked me before these training runs if I would prevail or get perforated, I'd have told you odds were approaching 100% I'd ace the exercise. Humility resulting from failure is an excellent learning aid.

Scenario training with qualified instructors in invaluable.

I relate these points to illustrate that brain knowledge is one thing, but you will not have markedly improved your skills until you put it into action, make mistakes, experience successes, and learn from both.

As you study defensive skills in this book, remember that it is imperative to reinforce what you learn with live training and practice in a defensive training environment.

Finding A Reputable Defensive Training Program

Finding a reputable defensive shooting instructor or school begins with recommendations from reputable people.

With the explosive growth in gun ownership and concealed carry, schools and itinerant instructors continue to pop out of the woodwork. Some are great, many are OK, and others are to be avoided. As a prospective student early in the concealed carry learning journey, it's difficult to sort wheat from chaff. Enter referrals from past students.

If you don't know people who have engaged in defensive training (not "shooting" training, but holistic personal defense), a great place to start is with local law enforcement. If you know any officers in your area, start with them. If you don't, ask your friends if they do. When you find a law enforcement contact, ask them who does safe, responsible, credible, and practical training in your area. Ask them where they refer friends and family for training. After all, it benefits them for concealed carriers in their jurisdiction to be well-trained.

If you have friends who have taken training classes, that's another source of recommendations—with a caveat. If they're high on one program or instructor, be sure to ask them how many other classes they've taken at other places and what was different to make the recommended one special. If one starts from a position of little knowledge and learns from a facility or instructor with something more than zero knowledge, it's not that hard to impress.

As you search your network for recommendations, be sure to ask many questions. Why was it good? What could have been better? What do others have to say about them?

Gun stores can be a source of training or referrals, but do your vetting. I've taken classes from large, dominant-in-the-local-market stores that were absolute garbage and others that were outstanding.

Training classes are not cheap, but the cost of lousy training, should you ever have to rely on it, can be life-shattering.

Mission: Escape

Your job is to protect your family. Yes, that certainly encompasses the idea of preventing physical harm or death. But protecting your family also means continuing to be there for them. No matter what your role is in the family "business," you are not "succeeding" in protecting your loved ones if you go and get yourself killed in the process.

It's called self-defense (and not the ninja games) for a reason. Your job is to defend yourself and those you care about, not to be society's police force. Accordingly, your self-defense strategic and tactical plan should be developed around one core objective.

Survive a violent encounter.

The word "survive" is carefully chosen. Is "winning" a defensive encounter any less successful if the outcome is escape rather than killing or wounding your attacker? Before you toss that statement in the proverbial trash as "weak" or perhaps "defeatist" in nature, let's discuss the concept in more detail.

First, consider the ultimate violent encounter scenario: you and your family can altogether avoid it. Perhaps you see or sense risk and change your plans accordingly. Maybe you don't walk down a street that's a bit shorter to your destination but feels fishy. Maybe that guy in the convenience store gives off bad vibes, so you turn around and get back in the car. Sure, since you've alerted on something, your odds of prevailing in a conflict might be pretty good. But stop and think: do you really want a conflict at all? I'll help. No. You. Don't.

Know that any armed conflict can be a lose-lose situation. Even if you "win" by surviving, you may lose. It may cost you your life savings and then some to "prove" you're the good guy. And that's before your opponent's family files their lawsuit. You may spend days, months or years in jail. There's a great chance you'll lose your job. People will look at you differently, possibly for the rest of your life. And, last and certainly not least, you might have to live with the fact that you took a life.

It's not hard to find hundreds of stories about armed citizens who did the right thing and suffered beyond comprehension for years after a violent encounter. Read some of those case studies. You really, really don't want to have to use your concealed carry gun—ever.

Even if you're able to survive a defensive encounter by drawing but not firing your gun, you still might face a slew of troubles. Brandishing a firearm is often taken seriously in our legal system. If your "bad guy" develops a credible story about how you threatened him for no apparent reason, you might find yourself playing defense in the legal system. Don't get me wrong. If you have no other option but to draw your gun, do what you must. Just do everything in your power to avoid that course of action if you can.

By no means does the " survival " goal mean you won't ever fight. Sometimes, that's the only way to survive a defensive encounter. You fight to survive if you have no other option.

Case Study: You Were Right! You Lost Everything...

On October 29, 2011, Jay Lewis was driving home from his job at an IRS call center in Des Moines, Iowa. He encountered a Ford Taurus driven by James Ludwick, driving four other people home from a Halloween party. Ludwick engaged in that road rage game of passing Lewis and slowing down. Unknown to Lewis, Ludwick was a convicted felon and was drunk at the time, with over 2.5 times the legal limit in his system.

Not surprisingly, an accident occurred, and Ludwick and another passenger began beating on the windows of Lewis' car. Lewis pulled out his .380 ACP pistol and screamed for the attackers to stop and get away from the vehicle. The two men backed up, and Lewis exited his car to inspect the damage. When Ludwick and another continued approaching, Lewis called 911, so the remainder of the encounter was caught on tape. Lewis repeatedly told the two men to "get back" and "stay where you are." He was recorded saying those commands 11 times.

The next sound on the 911 tape was that of a single gunshot. Lewis fired and struck Ludwick once in the chest. Police arrived and arrested and charged Lewis— not Ludwick.

Lewis could not make the $225,000 bond and had to rely on the Public Defender. As a result, he remained in jail until his trial. During his four months incarcerated, Lewis lost his job, was evicted from his apartment, and all of his possessions were thrown in the street.

The prosecutor ultimately ended up dropping most of the charges except for a reckless use of a firearm complaint. Once the case got to a jury, Lewis was quickly acquitted of all charges because they felt he acted in apparent self-defense.

The legal system eventually declared Lewis innocent, but by then, he had lost literally everything.

Lessons

The lesson is simple. You can win in court, but getting there can cost your savings, assets, and career. Also, don't count on the system to look out for you. In this case, the police gave no credence to Lewis' actions, and neither did the District Attorney. It wasn't until a jury got involved that Lewis was cleared of wrongdoing, but by then, it was too late.

Mental Defense

Earlier in the book, we discussed the importance of being aware of your environment. The best way to prevail in a personal defense encounter is to avoid it entirely. While high levels of awareness can't guarantee you'll never encounter trouble, it certainly does sway the odds in your favor.

Now, it's time to consider strategies and tactics for those times when awareness and avoidance have not been enough.

The most important tool in a self-defense encounter isn't your gun. It's your brain. And the effectiveness of your brain in a fight for your life depends solely on how you've prepared and trained it.

When someone throws something in the direction of your face, you instinctively move your head or perhaps whip your arm up to catch or deflect the object. What you don't do is stop and think, "Hmmm. There's an object headed my way, and if I do nothing, it's gonna hit me in the face. I should evaluate what my options are, then decide on and implement the best course of action."

Instead, you act instinctively and without conscious thought because from early childhood, stuff like that has happened in one form or another a million times before, and your brain has learned an avoidance or deflection behavior. It just acts and directs your muscles to do pre-programmed things because it's pre-wired to do so.

If you can do hands-on defensive training, by all means, do so. There's no better way to teach your brain how to respond to a violent scenario than actually doing it. Before live training, you can begin engaging your brain with intentional planning, evaluating "what if" scenarios and visualization.

Planning

The purpose of advance planning is to free your brain from evaluating decisions that could have been made earlier. When planning a trip, I always start a simple list on my computer of everything I need to bring a couple of weeks in advance. Actually, I cheat by resurrecting and editing the list I made for a previous trip, but it's still *planning*. Doing this removes all stress and pondering from the actual packing process. Over some number of days, I add items to my list as I think of them. By the time I'm ready to break out the suitcase, there's no more wondering what I might need to pack. It saves a lot of time as I eliminate all the wondering and decision-making when I'm about to head out.

The same concepts can be applied to your self-defense lifestyle, too. The more decisions you make about your concealed carry strategies in advance, the better. Again, you're freeing your brain at the time of action from making so many fundamental decisions.

For example, you can make advance decisions about when you will always carry and when you will not carry. You could "plan" a policy of carrying every time you head out to visit a store or restaurant. You could plan a policy of never carrying when visiting the kids' school. Removing a new decision process when you're headed out the door will only improve your overall effectiveness by ditching deci-sion-making in the moment. You'll avoid that temptation to leave the gun at home because you'll "only be at the store for a few minutes." You'll be less likely to forget and bring your weapon into a school (assuming it's prohibited in your state) because you've made it a mental rule during advance planning.

You can, in advance, plan your carry methods for different situa-tions. With the luxury of time, you can carefully evaluate the pros and cons of different carry rigs and guns for running, winter weather, dress clothes, etc.

You can plan foundational strategies without getting into detailed scenarios (we'll cover that next). You might plan priorities with your significant other. "Our priority will always be to get away. Since I'm carrying, assume you will go first, and I'll cover you as you escape." Or maybe you'll create an emergency code word to let your family members know something bad is happening, and they need to focus and pay attention to you. You might plan to start identifying emer-gency exits as soon as you enter a store or restaurant. You get the idea.

What-Ifs

You can start a lifelong game of "what if" strategizing without being paranoid. It's perfectly normal behavior in many aspects of life. Sports is a great example. If you ever played softball or baseball, you likely did all sorts of what-if planning. "OK, there are two outs and a runner on first, so if the ball comes to me, hitting the ground first, I'm going to throw to second base."

"What if" planning for defensive scenarios won't give you all the magic answers because every situation is different, with ever-changing variables. It will save precious bandwidth for the computer between your ears in times of stress and paralyzing input. If you've already thought through a what-if scenario, you can likely save your brain a couple of steps and start your on-the-fly decision loop ahead of where you would have been with no what-if planning. Let's consider an example.

What if you opened the door at your local stop-and-rob because you wanted a Coke? You see a guy holding a gun at the counter, shouting at the cashier to hand over the money. You might ponder this in advance and figure out your best option, if possible, is to back right out post haste, get to a safe place, and call 911. By making a tentative plan for a scenario like this, you've allowed your gray matter process to skip the whole, "Gee, this place is getting robbed. I wonder if I should intervene, hit the floor, hide, or try to escape?" Instead since you've already determined a tentative plan of getting out of Dodge, your brain can jump straight to step two: action. Can I make it back out the door without being seen or being shot? You've saved a lot of wondering and processing when fractions of a second matter.

When you have the luxury of time to consider and maybe even "walk through" a situation, you can ponder and strategize a near-infinite number of what-ifs to determine the best response.

What if the guy behind me in line pulls a gun and tells everyone to get on the floor?
What if I'm in my car at a red light, and someone taps on the window with a pistol?
What if someone gets too close to my personal space on the street and asks for time, money, or a light?
What if I'm in the mall and hear gunshots?
What if, when driving, I encounter a bunch of police shooting it out with a suspect?
What if I'm at dinner with my spouse, and an angry man comes in yelling for the manager?
What if my back door shatters in the middle of the night? What do I do about the kids?
What if I'm the first person on the scene of a car accident, and one of the passengers is bleeding profusely from his leg?

We could go on all day. This short list represents real, not hypothetical, events people like you and I have had to process in the heat of the moment. Why not create a list as you go about your daily life and consider what-ifs you might encounter? If you never experience them, great! If you do, you might save a life by considering some of your options in advance.

Playing simple what-if scenarios not only helps you in the event of encountering the actual event in the future, but it also keeps your brain engaged in a proactive, defensive mindset. You'll find yourself more alert and tuned in to possible risk areas in your daily travels.

Visualization

Mental exercises can never fully replace the value of live, hands-on training followed by practice and repetition. Still, they can assist the process of instilling habitual responses in your brain.

Some of the all-time best running backs in the NFL have used intentional visualization techniques to improve their performance on the field. When riding in a car, taking a walk, or chilling on the front porch, they'll bring up mental pictures of past plays, recalling images of the offensive and defensive player positions and movements. By "watching" these memories repeatedly, they're exercising the brain to evaluate past runs and consider alternate ways to execute the same play better. When asked how he consistently foresees where defenders will go, one player responded, "I've seen these plays and my anticipatory moves in my head a thousand times. I just do what my brain tells me."

In the competitive shooting world, you'll see this all the time. Competitors will mentally walk through stages of fire with their empty hands in a shooting position, cataloging the movements they want to make, where they'll change magazines and reload and in what order they'll engage targets. They're telling their body precisely what to do by visualizing shooting the stage in advance. When the buzzer goes off, there's less thinking and planning and more "doing."

With a bit of imagination, and without even using a gun, you can help condition your brain to perform specific defensive textbook skills. For example, beginning to move when you draw your gun is almost always beneficial. Why not visualize and practice it in advance to break the bad habit of standing there like a target in advance?

Action vs. Reaction

Let's talk about tailgating. Yes, it's incredibly annoying when you're the one being tailgated, but I promise, this isn't an opportunity to rant. We're going to make an important point about action and reaction.

Suppose you're following the car in front of you too closely. You don't care the guy in front of you is ticked because you have genuinely epic driving reflexes; you're Jeff Gordon hyped up on Mountain Dew. You're on the highway going 70 miles per hour and following your victim a car length or two behind.

For whatever reason, the guy in front of you slams on his brakes. All you see are rapidly approaching bright red lights. You are now in reaction mode to a visual stimulus—the lights going on and the other car rapidly slowing.

Here's what you need to know about human reaction to a visual stimulus. It takes a human brain about one-quarter of a second to see and process that signal—for the rods and cones in your eyeballs to detect the visual change of brake lights and transmit information through the optic nerve and to your brain. Then, your brain sends a telegram to your foot to stomp on the brakes.

Since your reflexes are fantastic, guess what? You might shave a few hundredths of a second from the average person's biological performance. What you are not doing, even with your awesome reflexes, is defying biology and physics and reducing that quarter of a second to near zero.

If you were cruising along at 70 miles per hour, your car traveled just under 50 feet before your foot even touched the brake pedal. No matter how good your driving skills are, there's no getting around that. Of course, the guy in front doesn't stop instantly; he's decelerating, and so are you. But the fact remains, you didn't even start slowing down until you'd traveled 50 feet. The moral of the story is that reaction time matters, physics enforces immutable laws of the universe and motion within, and you will hit him. Physics always wins. Just ask any of those people you see by the side of the road getting a ticket for rear-ending the car in front of them. Can you tell I have serious issues with tailgaters?

Using Reaction Time to Your Advantage

In one of the more enlightening and thought-provoking exercises I've done in a training session, we experimented with the concept of action versus reaction in a dramatic manner.

Envision an attacker and a victim. The attacker is armed and holding a gun on the victim. The victim is unarmed and, in normal circumstances, is at the mercy of the attacker. To illustrate just how decisive aggressive action can be, the instructor set up the following scenario. You believe the person holding the gun on you is about to kill you—no ifs, ands or buts. Giving up your wallet or car keys won't help you with this exercise. After some instruction in a last-ditch, low-probability-of-success evasion (really distraction) technique, we took turns trying an aggressive drop and lunge move, ducking under the aimed handgun and side-swiping the shooter, ideally starting the long-shot process of drawing and using our own gun. The "attacker's" job was to shoot you when he saw your movement. For this illustrative exercise, we used inert training pistols in a "no firearms" environment.

Let's make a hard stop here to avoid any possible confusion.

This is not a tactics recommendation, nor was the exercise "practice" for a defensive tactic.

This does not imply that you can do some Ninja move to escape a gun-at-your-head situation. Some people can with reasonable odds of success, but that particular skill is not something you will learn by reading a book. This technique would not have great odds of success in the real world, so don't think you can do this and become some evening news hero.

This admittedly unrealistic drill's only purpose was to test and demonstrate the concepts of human action and reaction.

So, how did things work out? The more athletic in the group averaged about a 50 percent success rate, meaning they didn't get shot during the initial duck and lunge move. All the attacker had to do was press the trigger. The defender had to dive for the floor while lunging forward towards the shooter or to the side while drawing their own gun. That's a lot of body movement. Yet, about half the time, the defender "won" in the initial move contest by dodging the shot and starting to "shoot" back.

The "victim" (left) initiated an aggressive move in a last-ditch attempt to turn the tables on this bad situation. It was an enlightening way to demonstrate the advantage of action over reaction. Photo: H&K Firearms and WOFT Training.

Why? The attacker had to see the movement, process what was happening, and then send a brain signal back the other way to the shooting hand to adjust aim and fire. For most people, that round-trip process takes about a quarter of a second. During that fraction of a second, the defender was able to (for a moment, at least) get out of the line of fire and change the status quo.

Again, this is not a recommendation or training technique. It's just an example of how aggressive and proactive actions can be used tactically. Given the choice between being the one initiating action and responding to action, you're always better off acting and forcing your opponent to react.

Stepping back into the real world of tactics, this is precisely why movement is such a vital part of one's self-defense repertoire. By definition, defense always involves reacting to someone else's action. Like the attacker in the above exercise, the real-world aggressor knows what they're going to do and executes their action. You're forced into the disadvantageous position of reacting to whatever they do. Now consider in an armed robbery, assault or whatever, the attacker has planned their moves and objectives well in advance, and when the time comes, they are simply implementing a chain of actions. You must respond to each one, always being at a disadvantage.

But what if you could take action and disrupt their plan? This leads us to the famous OODA Loop concept.

The OODA Loop in Practical Terms

As you might have guessed, OODA isn't a kind of cheese or a new yogurt. It's an acronym for Observe, Orient, Decide and Act. Put into tangible words by Air Force Colonel John Boyd, it describes the decision processes. Somewhat the renegade, Colonel Boyd was a national asset for many reasons outside of his codifying the OODA Loop concept. He pioneered the energy-maneuverability theory of fighter aircraft tactics and was quite the successful fighter pilot due to his understanding of fight dynamics. In fact, one of his nicknames was "Forty Second Boyd." From a position of disadvantage in an aerial dogfight, he claimed he could "kill" his opponent within 40 seconds. Judging by his first-in-class finish at Fighter Weapons School and subsequent invitation to become an instructor there, there must have been some truth to the boast.

Anyway, part of Boyd's theoretical work was documenting the OODA concept. Like many theories, this one looks like solid common sense when dissected. OODA postulates four stages of action based on new information. In the experiment we discussed in the previous section, let's define the OODA process from the attacker's perspective.

Observe

What is happening? The attacker sees the victim moving downward aggressively and without warning.

Orient

During this stage, we try to make sense of the observation based on various factors and life experiences. In this example, possible explanations for the sudden observed movement might range from the victim having a heart attack to a physical defensive maneuver. Based on the attacker's life experience, he'll likely reach the "this guy is trying not to get shot and might even be trying to attack me" conclusion during the orientation stage.

Decide

Since this defensive move by the potential victim was unexpected, the attacker now has to decide what to do about it. He observed it and then evaluated the move in the orient stage. Now, he must decide how to respond. Should he try to re-aim and shoot? Should he step back? Should he leave and run away? Should he try to grapple with the victim with his non-gun hand until he can attempt to shoot again? Or something else altogether?

Act

Only after all this has happened can the attacker act and implement his chosen response, whatever that is.

Of course, all of this happens in a fraction of a second.

Lots of self-defense-minded people get all wrapped up in Boyd's OODA loop, memorizing the stages and drilling into each step. At the risk of committing concealed carry strategy heresy, I say hogwash. Don't worry about OODA loops and what each stage means. I'll bet a year's supply of Reese's Peanut Butter Cups, none of us are going to think about OODA loops in the middle of a mugging or active shooting situation.

Instead, let's boil it down action and reaction. If you act, the other guy has to do all that OODA reacting. As we discussed in the previous section, that benefits you or at least places you in a position of less disadvantage.

It's funny how the concept covers so much common sense ground. Even in a scenario as complex as an active shooting, the response strategy of somehow disrupting the attacker's plan is a step in the right direction.

As a real-world example, consider the nightmare of an active shooting. During the Virginia Tech incident in 2007, five different classrooms were attacked by a psychopath intent on murdering innocent people. Students and professors in two of the classrooms took proactive action by barricading the classroom doors when they heard gunshots nearby. In those two rooms, one professor and one student were killed. In the other three rooms, a total of 27 professors and students were killed. Why the difference? The people in those two classrooms acted, thereby forcing the shooter to react. By disrupting the attacker's pre-existing plan, many lives were saved. Sometimes, delay is all that's needed for an effective defensive strategy. In almost any imaginable situation, we're always better off finding a way to prevent an aggressor from carrying out their plan unimpeded.

As you proceed through this section, you'll read about the importance of learning to move and shoot. Why? Moving represents action, and any action that disrupts the plans of your attacker might make the difference between a successful defense and failure.

Action vs. Reaction In a Shooting Exercise

In a self-defense encounter, you start well behind the power curve. In other words, you begin the confrontation at a distinct disadvantage by having to react instead of act.

Here's an illustration of how the initial actor usually wins the race. In 2011, Dr. J. Pete Blair, a Criminal Justice professor at Texas

State University, set up an interesting experiment. To quantify the risk to police officers from armed suspects, he had officers enter rooms with a training (non-lethal) pistol in the ready position. At various points, he stationed other officers acting as criminals who had their training guns either pointed at the floor or their own heads, as in a suicide scenario. The "criminals" were instructed to aim their guns and shoot at the responding officers at a random time of their choosing. It is important to note the responding officers, once they saw the "suspects," pointed their guns directly at them and were ready to fire. Blair recorded the times of these simulated gunfight interactions.

Here's the surprise. The "bad guys" took an average of .39 seconds to raise their gun, aim it at the responding officers, and fire. The responding officers, who already had their guns pointed at the bad guys with fingers on the trigger and ready to fire, took .38 seconds to process what was happening and press the trigger. Even though the "bad guys" were at a significant disadvantage, having to raise the gun and aim first, they took the same time to get the shot off.

The results? The two sets of volunteers ended up shooting each other. Not one responding officer in this experiment was able to shoot the bad guy first. The learning from an exercise like this reinforces the "action beats reaction" concept. The time the responding officers' brains took to see and process what was happening was nearly equal to the time required for the bad guys to raise their guns, aim and shoot.

For you and me, the lesson is simple. If we start off "even" with the bad guy, we lose because we'll always be reacting to whatever they have decided to do. That's why we spent so much time talking about strategies to see trouble coming and avoid it at the beginning of this book.

There's another way to look at the cost of having to react. If you can shoot at an outdoor range, try this experiment. While facing a target with a holstered gun, have a friend stand beside you, **facing away from the target**. Instruct them to start running away from you and the target in the opposite (safe) direction whenever they feel inspired.

A quick reiteration here for safety. At no time is your friend in front of you and your gun—they are to run AWAY from your target in the opposite direction.

When you see them start to run, draw your gun and fire at the target. When your buddy hears the shot, they have to stop running. After you shoot, safe and holster your gun and only then turn around to see how much ground your friend covered before you were able to draw your handgun and fire at the target. Most people will find that the runner covered 20 or 30 feet—usually more.

So this is an interesting exercise, but what does it mean? Let's review. You were standing there ready to go, and even still, someone initiating action could cover 20 or 30 feet in the time it took you to respond. Imagine if that person was running towards you rather than away. In that case, a person that was 20 or more feet away could reach you and do something bad before you could do anything about it, and that doesn't count the decision loop in your brain evaluating whether it's a real threat that justifies drawing and shooting.

When you start to think about how someone acting (not reacting) can reach you that quickly, it changes your perspective on the importance of maintaining awareness so you don't get caught in that situation.

Does that mean that you should start drawing your gun on anyone who approaches within 20 feet? Not at all. It reinforces the importance of learning to draw your weapon quickly and efficiently. It also reinforces the importance of immediately moving when you detect danger headed your way. Even if you start backing up at a slower rate than an attacker is running towards you, you're still adding distance and time until you meet.

12

BASIC DEFENSIVE SKILLS

Here's something we can all learn from, and I'm not picking on anyone here; I'm simply observing more of that sometimes dangerous human nature. Often, while at the range, I'll see a couple of buddies shooting at targets, perhaps testing a new gun. While evaluating a perforated target, one will comment to the other along the lines of, "Well, that'll do just fine if anyone ever breaks into my house." The defensive scenario varies, but the importance of the underlying false assumption remains the same. Being eternal optimists and having a natural belief we'll always rise to any occasion, we associate a half-respectable range target with our ability to prevail in a potentially lethal encounter. Would we expect to be prepared to race the Monaco Grand Prix after "training" by regular drives back and forth to the store?

While range practice presents an (unrealistic) picture of you standing there and methodically picking off potential attackers, a real encounter is a bit different. Some factors that make defensive shooting more unpredictable than plinking away at paper targets include but are not limited to:

- The element of surprise. You will not be expecting to be attacked. You will not be, at that moment, prepared to be attacked. If you were, you wouldn't be at that place at that time.
- You'll be reacting, not acting. As the aggressor and perpetrator, your assailant is, by definition, ahead of you on the power curve. He or she has already planned a course of action. He or she already knows their next steps. You don't. From the get-go, you're in a position of having to react to actions you don't yet know are headed your way.
- Your attacker will likely be moving while trying to rob, harm, or kill you. Unlike the paper target at your range, your real-life target will try hard (like you) not to get shot.
- If you're doing your job, you'll also be moving at full speed, trying to escape and not get shot.
- You may not know if you've hit your attacker until if and when they decide to stop doing whatever they were doing. Unlike paper targets, you may not see hits or holes, at least not right away. Unlike at the range, you'll have to trust your training and skills to know you're getting hits on target.
- Your assailant may not even react to being shot, again, at least not right away. Real crime encounters are chock full of stories about aggressors continuing to fight after being shot multiple times.
- You may find yourself physically fighting your attacker with one hand while trying to retrieve your defensive firearm with the other. If you're fortunate, you may have time to draw your gun. Or you may not.

Sound like chaos? That's precisely the point. It's so easy to develop a completely unrealistic mental picture of how you'll be able to defend yourself should you ever find yourself in a self-defense encounter. Time and time again, survivors say that they "never saw it coming." Most encounters are up close and personal, not methodical dueling contests where the contestants are 10 or 20 yards from each other.

It's essential to recognize that there are shooting skills and fighting skills. They overlap at some points, but learning to hit bullseyes on targets isn't enough to improve your odds of prevailing in a dynamic and chaotic defensive encounter.

Speaking of fighting, how's your physical conditioning? Are you in shape enough to physically fight someone for 10, 20 or 30 seconds? How about a minute or two? Can you run, full out, for 100 yards wearing your everyday clothes and shoes, perhaps carrying a child?

Case Study: A "Non-Range" Situation

> At about 3 am (nothing good ever happens after midnight, right?), a Chicago man was driving in his BMW on the south side Loop when another man in a Volkswagen rear-ended him. The driver exited his car to inspect the damage and turned to retrieve his phone from the BMW. At that point, the VW driver drew a gun and pushed the man back into his BMW. As it turns out, the victim was a concealed carrier. At some point in the process of being forced at gunpoint back into his car, he drew his handgun and fired one shot at the carjacker, killing him in the process.

Lessons

A defensive shooting situation rarely, if ever, resembles anything that happens on the range. In this case, the victim was attacked in the middle of the night. Details are unclear, but when he had to defend himself, he was either in the process of getting into his car or already seated there. That's probably not a situation one would generally practice at the range.

There's another lesson to be learned from this story. Carjackers have used the "bump" and assault tactics for years to trap victims in a location of their choosing. Whether the motive is robbery, rape, or murder, it's proven to be an effective way to choose a victim and perpetrate the crime on their terms. After a fender bender, the last thing on the victim's mind is that the "accident" was staged. In this case, it seems the victim turned his back on the carjacker when retrieving his phone. That provided the window of opportunity for the criminal to draw his gun and get down to the business of carjacking.

Myths or Strategies?

More than anything else, I sincerely hope this book imparts the seriousness of deciding to carry a firearm for self-defense. It's no game. It's a lifelong commitment. It requires you to make changes to your daily routine. It requires ongoing learning, practice, and repetition of core and advanced skills. It also requires rigorous study and analysis without reliance on hearsay wisdom freely available online.

With that said, let's consider some of the more common topics and beliefs. Do they reflect wisdom or sound strategy? We'll present them here. You can make your own decision as you consider the angles.

Warning Shots

There's an exception to every rule. However, in the case of examining whether warning shots represent sound strategy, there are very, very few examples where warning shots turned out to be a good idea.

The goal sounds great, at least in theory. If things turn ugly, and you're legitimately in fear of death or serious bodily harm, you draw your gun and fire in a harmless direction. In the perfect outcome, whatever threat is on your horizon figures out you're serious about defending yourself and decides to go forth and find an easier target. Can it work? Maybe. And there have been times when it has. And there are other times where it made a bad situation worse. No police department I'm aware of even allows warning shots, much less encourages them.

The reasoning is simple. You draw a gun at one time and one time only—when not doing so will result in immediate death or serious bodily harm. That's it. Put more simply, in a perfect world, you should keep your gun safely holstered until you need and intend to use it.

There are many ways a warning shot strategy can go wrong.

Once you draw, everyone present knows you are armed. If the threat you're focused on has a buddy, you just became a target for someone you may not have known about.

You're responsible for the destination of the bullet you just fired. It's not hard to find cases of shots fired into the air striking others when they come down. The landing rate for shots fired upward is 100 percent. Every year, people are killed in the "one-in-a-million" scenario of a bullet returning to earth.

If the threat in question is also armed, they may not be impressed by the fact you just made a loud noise with your gun. Perhaps they're amped up on drugs or adrenaline. Or maybe they're an experienced criminal, and this isn't their first rodeo involving gunplay. You just continued the lethal force back-and-forth routine while doing nothing to prevent a response by your attacker.

In many states, brandishing a firearm is against the law in itself. If you draw and fire a warning shot, you're not directly defending yourself from imminent death or harm (because you had the opportunity to do nothing but threaten and make noise). An aggressive prosecutor may decide to make a great example of a vigilante citizen.

The list goes on, but you get the idea. A firearm isn't a whistle, air horn, pepper spray or Taser. It has potentially lethal consequences, and its use is for potentially deadly situations.

Racking the Side as a Deterrent

The "strategy" of racking a slide, thereby making a scary noise that is sure to frighten off an attacker or intruder, has many of the same downsides as a warning shot. Yes, you are preparing your gun for use, but if you intend to send a message, you might be asking for trouble.

One thing consistent with after-action debriefs and interviews is that during adrenaline-fueled incidents, participants often don't hear everything happening. Many people involved in gunfights report not even hearing the shots they fire. When fighting for survival, the brain does a marvelous and sometimes annoying job of filtering out extraneous information. So, right off the bat, a wound-up attacker might not even hear your best Hollywood "I'm coming after you..." sound effects.

Depending on the situation (perhaps the proverbial noise in the middle of the night), you might just be alerting someone else to your presence and location.

By definition, since you're racking the slide, your gun isn't really ready to use. This leads us to the next myth...

Carrying with an Empty Chamber is Safer

The strategy of carrying a handgun with an empty chamber isn't the least bit new or uncommon. Entire militaries have adopted it as standard practice at various points past and present. In the United States, 1911-style pistols were often carried this way. The practice was, and may still be, a common doctrine in Israel. In that case, the reason was more likely the smorgasbord of small arms types that comprised the country's beginning weapons stockpile. All those different action types required some sort of procedural standardization, even if suboptimal.

I don't favor the practice for defensive purposes. Why? Because your gun isn't fully ready for use in a dire and time-critical situation.

Remember, by definition, we're talking about semi-automatic pistols here. If the chamber is empty, all cartridges are in the magazine. To make the gun ready to fire, one has to vigorously rack the slide back and allow it to strip a round from the magazine, force it into the chamber and cock or partially cock the hammer or striker.

You'll need both hands unless you resort to a one-handed method, like racking the slide on a belt or nearby object.

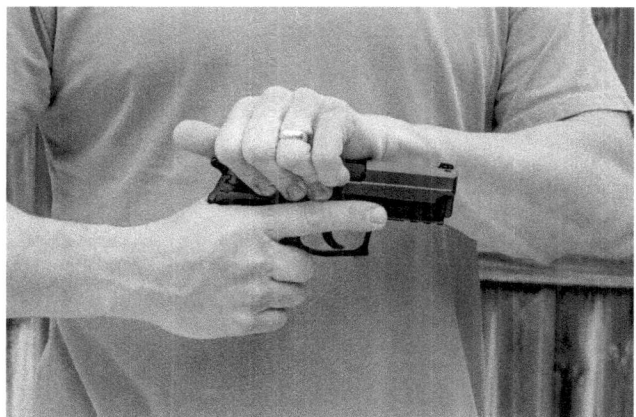

There are some techniques where you can rack a slide with one hand, but they can be finicky. Generally, two hands is the reliable way to go.

Many empty-chamber carriers brag about how quickly they can draw and rack the slide, but they miss one critical point.

You don't get to decide if you have both hands available during a defensive encounter. That decision belongs to your attacker and the circumstances of your encounter.

Most defensive encounters are up close and personal. Hands-on physical altercations are common in many armed scenarios. You may be fighting off an aggressor with your support hand while frantically trying to access your gun. If it requires a slide rack, good luck! Or perhaps you're carrying a child or shoving a loved one out of the line of fire. The point is there are a million reasons why you can't assume you'll have two hands available to perform administrative functions on your handgun.

As for concerns about safety and inadvertent discharges, most modern firearms are designed NOT to fire without deliberate movement of the trigger. Different models use active and passive safety systems, including trigger leaves, manual safeties, double/single action and grip safeties. Do your homework and try a few models at your local gun range to see what you're comfortable with. You'll also find that the more experience you develop with handguns, the more you learn to trust the inherent safety designs and the more you'll trust the ultimate safety—your brain. Remember, without operator action, no gun "goes off" on its own. Strict adherence to the safety rules at all times is the real safety.

Caliber Choice

Gun enthusiasts will argue for one caliber over another to the death despite whatever statistical evidence exists. Somehow, human nature always results in one or a couple of anecdotal analogies to determine the "real truth." And arguably, part of the "which caliber is best" argument results from there being some truth to the smaller vs. larger caliber debate.

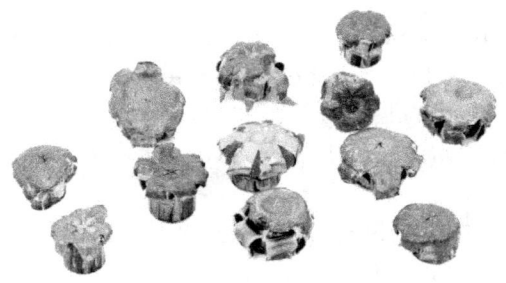

Modern defensive bullets are designed to behave like this when hitting organic targets. These improved hollow points result in a lesser performance difference between handgun calibers.

Statistically, over time and compiled from thousands of actual shootings, there is very little difference in measurable results. Metrics like the following work out about the same for standard defensive calibers: .380 ACP, 9mm, .38 Special, .357 Magnum, .40 S&W and .45 ACP.

- One shot stops

- Number of shots to stop the aggressor
- Percentage of shootings that did not result in incapacitation

Over the long haul, there is relatively little material difference between the major calibers. Yes, I know, that's heresy.

Modern defensive ammunition, not the full metal jacket round-nose stuff used for practice, has leveled the playing field immensely. That's one of the reasons so many law enforcement agencies have moved from larger calibers back to 9mm. If you can expect similar results from an easier-to-control platform with more capacity, what's not to appreciate?

Although it will take some range time and maybe a few gun rentals or borrowing from friends, deciding which caliber to use should be easy. Find the gun you like and can shoot well. Choose the largest caliber you can adequately control. For many people, especially those newer to shooting, that'll be something in the .380 ACP, 9mm or .38 Special ballpark.

Open vs. Concealed Carry

I hope you're a Second Amendment advocate if you're reading this book, regardless of your other political views. Without it, we wouldn't be having this conversation at all, and carrying a gun to defend yourself and your family wouldn't be an option.

I mention gun rights here for one reason. The defense of gun rights should not be confused with a sound defensive strategy.

Many people choose to open carry in states where it's not prohibited by law. We're not here to argue the constitutionality or lack thereof of said laws. If someone wants to open carry to make a statement or help normalize ownership and carry of firearms, that's their business. It makes no difference one way or the other to me.

However, if your primary objective is protection rather than political activism, then perhaps consider the pros and cons of open versus concealed carry.

If you carry openly, you may be presenting a deterrent factor. Some potential aggressors may choose to find an easier target or less dangerous environment. Or, they may view the carrier as target number one. Perhaps they see an opportunity to grab a brand-new gun. To my knowledge, statistics on this aren't available, so I can only tell you my opinion. I do see too many folks wearing a gun, in full view, using a holster with no retention capability. Any person behind them in the fast food line could grab it in a split second.

I always choose to carry concealed under the simple reasoning I don't want anyone to know I have a gun until if and when I need to use it. I choose to retain exclusive control over the decision of if and when my firearm becomes a factor in a defensive situation. Call it whatever you want: the element of surprise or the possibility of throwing an unseen wrench into an aggressor's plans. If my gun is clearly visible, I am part of an event whether I like it or not.

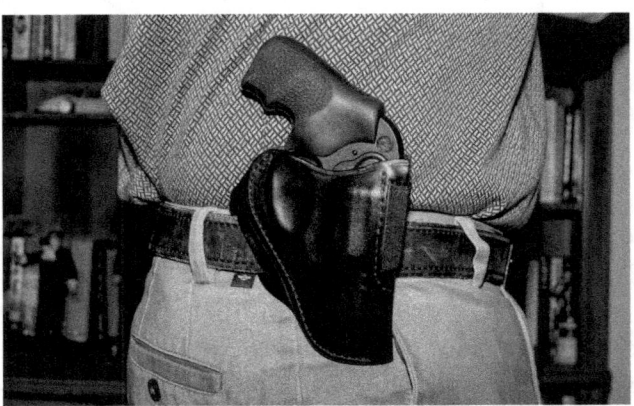

This is a great holster when used with a covering garment for concealment, but I would never use it for open carry as your gun can be easily snatched from behind.

If you have strong feelings about evangelizing for the Second Amendment, great! Consider taking people to the range. I have yet to bring an anti- or gun-neutral acquaintance who failed to have a positive experience. Without exception, they always want to come back.

Gun Control and Operations

At a local shooting competition some years ago, I witnessed "burned-in" gun awareness and control habits in action. An action-pistol competitor was dashing across the shooting bay, moving to the next designated set of targets.

Halfway to his destination, he caught a toe on something and tumbled head over heels, eventually half-rolling, half falling back into a standing position. During the unplanned gymnastics floor exercise, we all noticed his gun remained pointed down range and his finger off the trigger throughout his acrobatic routine.

I can guarantee you that as he started his headlong flight, he wasn't thinking about his gun, its muzzle orientation or his trigger finger. Instead, he'd spent so many hours and repetitions worrying about such things as muzzle and trigger discipline that his reptile brain took over and delivered those actions. It was no different than stomping the brake pedal when a child runs in front of your car—it all happened without conscious thought.

Here's the thing. Achieving this level of autonomous habit with basic gun operation and control skills is not hard to do. All it takes is the repetition of the proper habits. You won't create the necessary muscle memory by reading about it or watching it on YouTube. Thinking about it will help some—remember the power of visualization. Literally going through the motions is what it takes.

Think about these types of operations and your current level of automatic proficiency with each...

Have you ever fumbled with the safety (if applicable), wondering if it's on or off? Have you ever had to look at it to see what the visual indicator says?

When your gun goes click instead of bang, what do you do in the following fraction of a second? Are you thinking about why? Wondering where you got the ammo? Looking for someone else to figure out what went wrong?

If you have to make your gun "safe," do you have to stop and think about the steps?

Do you instinctively know if your gun is ready to fire (or not) at any given moment?

Have you ever noticed your finger is still on the trigger when you're not firing?

If someone calls for your attention while at the range, do you maintain muzzle discipline without thinking while you turn around to see what they want?

You get the idea.

There are lots of .22LR conversion kits that will quickly convert many standard pistols to rimfire. It's a great way to practice for a lot less money.

The good news is that all these actions and habits can be cemented in your brain and muscles by having fun and going to the range! If you're worried about the cost, splurge on a .22 handgun that operates exactly like your defensive gun and use that. Not only are .22s great fun to shoot, but the ammo is much less expensive.

Shots on Target

Once you're comfortable with the basic operations of your firearm, you'll want to move on to mastering shooting performance. The goal is simple: put shots on target with "good enough" accuracy without mentally processing all the steps like sight alignment, grip, stance, trigger control and follow through. You won't be skipping those steps; they'll be automatic, like applying the brakes in your car: see the child in the road, process the correct response, figure out where your foot is, move it to the brake pedal and apply pressure.

While the ability to hit a quarter at 25 paces is desirable, putting shots quickly in a designated "target area" is more important for defensive shooting.

Guess what achieves this goal? More shooting! Also, believe it or not, *not shooting* is an even better way to refine those skills, and you can do that right at home. Refer back to the section on dry fire practice for more details.

Earlier in the book, we discussed the components of firing a good shot in detail. Now, it's time to begin making those steps a natural and instinctive action. Rather than trying to focus on all four major components at the same time, you might consider a building block approach.

Start with the proper stance as outlined previously. While the odds are you won't be shooting from a conventional "range" shooting position in a defensive encounter, you need to feel this foundation and, more importantly, the benefit it provides of controlling your gun instead of letting the gun and its recoil control you. During your next few trips to the range, focus on checking your stance before every shot. Is your weight distribution proper? Are you using your bone structure and big muscles to align with the target and create a solid shooting platform?

Once you get that burned into a natural habit, shift focus to your grip. Before each shot, ensure your hands are in the correct position on the gun. Double-check to ensure the grip pressure balance is right between your firing and support hands. How about those thumbs? Are they in the correct position? Check the pinkie pressure. Remember that's a great way to make leverage work for you to control muzzle flip. Before long, you won't have to think about all the elements of your grip constantly—it'll just happen naturally.

Sight pictures sound easy, but even they require some habit-building. I like to repeat the process of having my eyes pick up the front sight first, then allowing the rear sight to settle into the correct position.

Finally, when all else feels automatic every time you shoot, focus on your trigger press. We won't repeat it all here (refer to the Basic Shooting Skills section), but focus, focus, focus on a smooth trigger press, disregarding the slight movement while you're doing so. Your goal is to train your finger to make a consistent press every single time. Break that habit of trying to time the shot and focus on the motion perfectly. Arguably, freeing your brain from managing the details of every trigger press is the most important habit you can "burn into" your brain and muscle memory.

Once you've made habits of the components of making good shots on target, remember to perform reminder checks on every range visit. Ensure you continue executing the four primary components faithfully and without sloppiness. Over time, you'll be amazed at how quickly, smoothly and effortlessly you can raise your gun to target and score an accurate hit.

One-Handed Shooting

It's human nature to practice what we're already good at. If we're honest with ourselves, it's no fun to go to the range and practice things like shooting with your support hand. You miss a lot; it doesn't feel right, and the target looks more like Swiss cheese than a sheet with one ragged hole in the middle. The visible results are unimpressive. Instead, most of us head off to the range and leisurely perforate targets using a solid two-handed grip, yielding the most satisfying outcome.

There's one potential gotcha to learning how to shoot proficiently with a two-handed grip. You don't necessarily get to decide if you'll have two hands available for shooting during a self-defense encounter.

If you're serious about self-defense, you need to convert at least some of that range time to structured practice on relevant skills—especially the ones where your performance is weak. That means one-handed shooting, using both the dominant and non-dominant hands.

Note how my support hand is pulled in close to my body, keeping it well out of the line of fire.

Most people will "lose" a degree of accuracy when shooting one-handed thanks to reduced stability and the related increase in the difficulty of keeping sights precisely on target. Then, there is the trigger press. You still have to move the trigger through several pounds of motion without moving the gun, but you now only have a single hand to keep the gun stable.

The bottom line is obvious. Rounding out your defensive shooting skills will require becoming proficient and comfortable with one-handed shooting and gun manipulation. Here are some tips to help you become better. Before you practice, establish a consistent routine for your support hand position. You won't have options in a fight, but for practice, you want to ensure your support hand is well out of the way.

Footwork

When shooting two-handed, your feet will likely be in a "fighting stance," with the support side foot slightly forward. You might find more overall stability when shooting one-handed with the opposite positioning. Move your firing hand-side foot forward to see if it gives you better stability. Again, practice and repetition will eventually translate to automatic response in a stressful encounter.

Geometry

If you're having trouble keeping your handgun reasonably stable on target, try rotating the gun 10, 20, 30 or even 45 degrees toward the center of your body. Instead of being aligned perpendicular to the ground, the base of the grip will be skewed to the outside of your body while the sights are angled slightly toward your center. This small muscle and bone geometry change helps many with one-handed grip stability. Just don't rotate too far—that horizontal gangster grip you see on TV does not lead to improved shooting!

Grip Pressure

When shooting with two hands, it can help to use less grip pressure with the firing hand and more with the support hand, thereby freeing up firing hand flexibility for more trigger finder control. When shooting one-handed, you may need to increase grip pressure with your firing hand and accept the tradeoff of improved overall stability at the expense of trigger finger control.

You can also keep one of those grip-strengthening tools, or even a tennis ball, handy to build your grip strength in both hands.

I get more stability shooting one-handed if I rotate the gun about 30 degrees. Your mileage may vary, so experiment!

Distance

When live-fire practicing one-handed shooting, start close to your target. Three to five yards is ideal. Statistically, you're more likely to need that one-handed skill at closer ranges. Also, the closer range gives you some positive reinforcement on which you can build. Take the small "accuracy successes" at three yards while you improve your skill. You can gradually move your target farther away as you get more consistent with hits at close range.

Use Your Available Time

When shooting one-handed, your gun is going to move more under recoil. You'll see more muzzle flip and need to apply more correction to get your sights back on target. That's just physics, as two hands provide more recoil control than one. When practicing at the range, take your time and don't shoot again until your gun is stabilized and back on target. In a self-defense encounter, you don't have the luxury of time, but on the other hand, *you can't miss fast enough to improve your outcome.* You'll naturally increase your speed as you practice perfectly, taking the time you need to get shots on target.

All Thumbs

Your thumb position may also vary with a one-handed grip. When shooting two-handed, your thumbs may be horizontal to the ground or, with some techniques, pointed upward. Shooting one-handed with your firing hand thumb curled downward may improve grip pressure.

When at the range, experiment with different techniques to find what works for you, and most importantly, force yourself to allocate a percentage of your ammo budget to one-handed practice—from both hands. Practice one-handed dry firing at home. This, more than anything else, will build proficiency. You'll develop muscle control and strength without the distraction of recoil and muzzle flip. Getting used to manipulating the trigger while keeping your sights on target before, during and after the trigger press will translate to less flinching and more accuracy when firing live ammunition later.

Drawing Your Gun From Concealment

Earlier in the book, we reviewed the proper steps for drawing a handgun from a holster. To quickly review, in an ideal practice or range environment, the five primary steps are:

1. Clear your support hand; Establish a firing grip.
2. Raise your gun from the holster.
3. Rotate your firing arm.
4. Join firing and support hands.
5. Extend to the target.

In a self-defense situation, you may not have the luxury of completing all five steps as you would on the range, so it's important to focus on the absolute necessities.

For example, let's consider the very first step: clear your support hand. Prevailing over an aggressor certainly won't be any easier if you manage to shoot your non-firing hand, so no matter what, you have to make sure it's out of the way of the muzzle. There's only one way to build a "thoughtless" habit to clear your support hand: repetition. Don't think about tens or hundreds of practice draws over time; think in thousands. Before long, you won't think about clearing your support hand—it'll just happen. Besides, in a stress-fueled fight for your life, you won't have time or inclination to repeat the steps to a safe draw in your head.

Another difference is that you'll almost certainly be drawing from concealment for self-defense. Unless you open carry, some type of clothing will be in between your firing hand and your handgun. You've got to get that out of the way long enough to remove your gun without a time-robbing snag or other draw hangup.

Let's assume you've adopted the most common "type" of concealed carry and are using a holster somewhere in the hip or appendix position area. Using an inside-the-waistband holster, all you need to hide the exposed grip of your revolver or pistol is a shirt or similar top garment. With this general carry placement, you can design your "Step 1" for range practice using a similar motion required to access a covered handgun on your belt line. Instead of moving your support hand straight to your sternum, bring it to somewhere near your beltline, grab a handful of shirt, then raise to your lower chest area.

The fabric grab's location will depend on where you place your gun on the beltline. If you carry behind the hip bone, you'll need to grab your shirt somewhere in the 2 o'clock vicinity (for right-handers) to obtain enough clearance. If you carry more in an appendix location, the grab will be closer to your centerline. Experiment with slow practice draws using a verified unloaded gun until you find the right location and motion that avoids the gun getting caught up in clothing. Be sure to experiment with different types of shirts, sweatshirts, etc. Various types and weights of fabric behave uniquely. You'll also need to practice moving your covering clothing well over the height of your holstered gun to provide enough clearance and avoid tangles during the draw.

Instead of going to the sternum, the support hand goes to the beltline to grab a handful of shirt and pull it out of the way.

Your procedure will vary if you carry under a jacket or other open-front clothing. Since the objective is to move the gun side of your coat back behind the holster and out of the way, you'll likely end up with a one-handed clearing motion—it would be difficult to reach all the way across your body with your support hand to move an open jacket out of the way!

Try extending your firing hand thumb straight out, hooking the jacket front as you vigorously move your hand backward to access your handgun. Especially if your jacket has a bit of weight, you can fling it back long enough to remove your gun unobstructed. With this type of draw, your "range" draw motion of moving your support hand to your chest still works just fine. You might also try keeping something with a bit of weight in the jacket's gun-side pocket. This will help your jacket to swing and stay out of the way long enough to retrieve your gun.

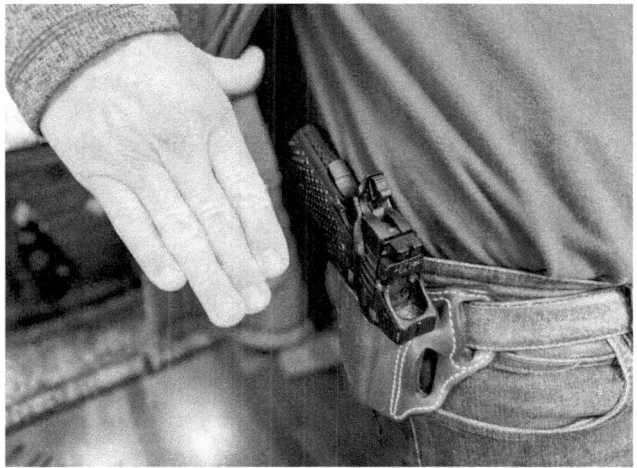

When using open-front clothing like a jacket or blazer as a cover garment, try using your thumb on the firing hand to clear as you reach for your gun.

You'll also want to learn to draw one-handed from shirt or pullover concealment. Remember, you don't get to decide whether your support hand will be available during an encounter. Circumstances and your attacker make that decision. Be sure to practice one-handed draws from concealment, too. A similar technique for clearing an open jacket can be used to raise a shirt using that extended thumb.

The most important thing to remember is the importance of practicing draws from concealment. In the midst of conflict, you can never count on rising to the occasion based on what you've read—physical repetition to build muscle habits and smoothness is a must. I always do this with an inert or unloaded gun to allow for experimentation and fine-tuning of your motions.

Moving

One of the mantras of defensive encounter strategy is... Move! So, why is that? There are several reasons why movement will at least improve your odds of a successful outcome.

Action Instead of Reaction

By definition, if you are the potential target of an attack, your attacker has all the advantages. They have a plan. They have calculated in their mind how events will go down. They have the advantage of initiating physical motion first. The bottom line? You're starting the encounter from a significantly disadvantaged (losing) position.

By beginning to move, you're interrupting the attacker's planned sequence of events and forcing them to enter their own OODA loop cycle. They need to detect your motion, try to figure out what your objective is, and what they're going to do about it. In effect, while you're still under a planned attack and still disadvantaged, you're turning the tables in a slightly more favorable direction. Your ability to interrupt "the plan" may buy you time or a more favorable position from which to respond.

You Become a More Difficult Target

Shooting, hitting, or stabbing a stationary target is not all that difficult. Hitting or otherwise damaging a moving target is orders of magnitude more complex. If a defensive encounter has already gone to guns, your movement offers no guarantee you won't still be shot, but it does shift the odds in the right direction, especially if you've practiced shooting back while you're moving.

Like every other skill we've discussed in this book, this one requires lots of practice. Ideally, you'll add instinctive movement to your draw routine practice. When practicing your draws from concealment, consider taking a step sideways while you're doing it to get your body used to initiating movement as soon as you begin responding to a threat.

The next skill to add to the movement category is shooting while moving. There are lots of techniques being taught that encourage unnatural movement, like sliding the lead foot forward, backward or sideways, then dragging the following foot to follow. The theory is to avoid tripping over your own feet. I can't speak for you, but I find this method extremely awkward, and even with lots and lots of practice, not something my brain would revert to in a moment of high stress. Millennia of human fight or flight response would have your brain screaming, "What's this shuffling? Run!" I prefer something without so much inertia to normal and natural movement. Try moving in the desired direction smoothly, almost like a fast walk. You can develop rapid movement with lots of stability by treating your body like a tank and turret, with your lower body twisting in the movement of travel so you don't get tangled up in your own feet while rotating your upper body to engage the target.

If you have access to a range that allows, practicing shooting while moving in a controlled manner is invaluable.

You Buy Time

Earlier, we discussed the concepts documented by Tueller of how an attacker can cover a surprising distance, perhaps 21 feet or more, in the time it takes for a skilled shooter to draw a firearm. However, consider the benefits of your own movement. If you begin moving backward or sideways when you detect the incoming attack, even if your rate of travel is slower than that of your attacker, you are adding time to the "intercept." They're still getting closer to you but at a decreasing rate. Those extra seconds or fractions may make all the difference in implementing your own response.

Finding Cover

By definition, nothing is shielding you from an imminent threat if you've gone into defensive mode. Immediate movement might be a valuable tool to start the process of getting something, anything, in between you and the danger.

Getting Assistance

Your defensive encounter might benefit from safety in numbers, depending on the situation. A perpetrator of a more personal crime might decide that the risks outweigh the benefits if you can steer the location toward possible assistance from others.

Forget About Your Gun?

Sometimes, the right thing to do is to move right at the threat. Rather than get locked in on a response of accessing your gun at all costs as a first tactic, your best option, if things are already up close and personal, may be to engage the threat physically first.

The shooting in West Freeway Church of Christ in Texas provides a case study. Hindsight is brutally unfair, but in this case, church security volunteer Richard White may have been able to survive his encounter with a shotgun-wielding attacker had he forgotten about trying to draw his gun and instead went straight to hands. Separated by a couple of feet, the murderer turned his shotgun towards White, who was frantically trying to retrieve his pistol from a belt holster under his jacket. No doubt about it; the situation was lousy and perhaps unwinnable for White. Perhaps had he lunged to control the shotgun barrel aggressively instead of trying to outdraw and shoot the attacker just in front of him, the situation might have ended differently.

Communication

The only way to develop a 100 percent winning record for defensive encounters is to avoid them in the first place. Clearly, there are many encounters you can't simply avoid. Think of an active shooter scenario or a targeted attack where someone intends to rob, rape or murder you.

Sadly, there are too many avoidable "escalations" where a calm head and verbal de-escalation skills could have prevented violence. How many road rage or street fight stories have you heard where a gun comes into play? As discussed earlier in the book, part of the carry lifestyle is becoming (if you're not already) the most polite and relaxed person you can be. The reason you want to work so hard at avoiding trouble is precisely because you choose to carry a firearm as a last resort defensive measure.

Unfortunately, you cannot control some situations, and your verbal tactics toolkit requires a more offensive component. Societal norms and our natural desire not to be "weird" are powerful things. Think about how strange it would be to publicly yell at someone at the top of your lungs when you desperately want them to do something. Similarly, when preoccupied and in survival mode during a defensive encounter, will you think about communicating clear and concise instructions about what you want or need to happen?

If you can demonstrate a sufficient defensive response, combined with an instruction like "Stop!" "Get back now!" or "Drop the gun!" who knows? Perhaps you'll deter the encounter. At the very least, you've made public that you're the intended victim, not the aggressor. Witnesses or bystanders in hearing range will get at least a partial picture of the events and your role.

The late Tiger McKee of the acclaimed Shootrite Academy was famous for his insistence that students on the range shout out commands while practicing draw-and-shoot exercises. Why? You guessed it. We won't do this arguably unnatural thing without physical practice and repetition. You know what to do.

Changing Magazines

In a perfect world where you had nothing else to do but train for self-defense, you'd practice all sorts of things, regardless of the probability of needing that skill. In the real world, we've all got plenty of other things to worry about, so we must prioritize which skills we're willing to invest limited training and practice time in.

Changing magazines is one of those skills that warrants learning and practice. That's because you might need to change a magazine during a self-defense encounter for two different and unrelated reasons.

First, you'll need a fresh magazine if you run out of ammo. Sure, statistics show that reloading for this reason is rare. On the other hand, if your particular encounter involves more than one assailant or is some active shooter scenario, you might be surprised at how quickly you can empty your handgun.

The second and far more likely scenario is rectifying a malfunction. In a semi-automatic pistol, the magazine is the weakest link in the chain and the most common cause of pistol malfunctions. Whether from use or hitting the ground, those relatively thin stamped metal feed lips on magazines can become bent, and it doesn't take much for that to lead to a feeding jam.

I practice magazine changes regularly, and I recommend you do the same. They are awkward, and to do them smoothly and reliably requires repetition.

Magazine Change Basics

The first step to smoothly changing magazines in a semi-automatic pistol is consistent storage of the spare magazine(s). Carrying a spare mag in a pocket is less than ideal for emergencies. You never know the orientation of the magazine flopping around in your pocket. It will pick up pocket lint, potentially causing a malfunction. It might get jammed up with other items in your pocket. All the moving around might result in one or more rounds working their way out entirely or partially. Using a proper magazine carrier is worth the trouble so you know exactly where the magazine is, how it's oriented, and that it is protected and ready for use.

A belt carrier, either inside or outside the waistband, placed in a location easily accessible by your support hand, is ideal. Make sure to orient the magazine so the cartridges inside are facing forward.

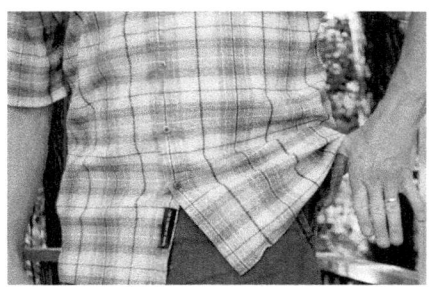

Like drawing while moving a cover garment with the same hand, the "thumb" technique can be used to access a spare magazine since your gun hand will be busy.

Now that you're equipped, you can consider two scenarios for magazine changes. The "speed reload" is primarily used to replace ammo in your handgun when you run empty. The "tactical reload" is intended to replace a partially-used magazine with a new full one.

Speed Reload

When your handgun runs dry, the priority is to reload it. In this situation, the magazine in the handgun is empty, so it's of no further use to you in a defensive encounter—it's time to replace it with a fresh, fully loaded magazine. Here are the steps.

1. Drop the Empty Magazine

Before doing anything, get your finger off the trigger and rest it along the slide well outside the trigger guard. With the handgun barrel parallel to the ground (normal shooting position), depress the magazine release button and let the magazine fall freely. If it doesn't fall of its own accord, use your support hand to rip it out and then drop it on the ground. Since we do things under stress the way we've always practiced them, I also do this on the practice range. Yes, your magazines may get dirty or scratched. Also, yes, you can clean them. They are tools, not museum pieces.

You don't want to find yourself in a gunfight gently removing an empty magazine and setting it on a nearby table or taking time to put it in your pocket. Dump it. Don't laugh at this scenario! There are lots of stories where police officers have found their pockets full of spent cartridge cases from revolvers after a street shooting incident. Why? That's what they did on the practice range. When the revolver ran dry, they would retrieve the empties from the cylinder and pocket them so they wouldn't have to pick them up from the ground later. Practice like you want to perform in real life.

2. Retrieve a Fresh Magazine

The next step should be done in a speed reload situation parallel to the first step—dropping the empty magazine. In most cases and with modern guns, you can operate the magazine release control with your firing hand thumb. Since your support hand is not presently occupied, why not start the process of retrieving a fresh magazine from the opposite side?

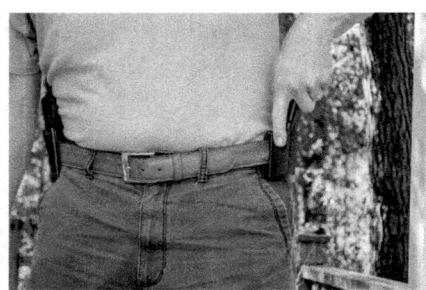

Align your index finger with the front of the magazine to help guide it into place. Your brain is very good at "driving" the index finger without looking!

There's a reason for making sure the cartridges face forward in your magazine pouch. With your support hand, reach for the new magazine by using your index finger to find the leading edge of the new magazine. Allow your index finger to slide down the front of the magazine, grip the body with the rest of your fingers, and withdraw it, bringing it up toward eye level.

3. Use Your Visible Workspace

After the empty magazine falls free, start bringing your gun up in front of your face while slightly angling the magazine well toward your support-hand side. End up with your handgun pointing forward and up, with the grip rotated toward the magazine you're bringing up to meet.

With practice, you can "find" the gun's magazine well without looking. That's part of the reason for aligning your index finger with the front of the new magazine—your brain does an excellent job of positioning your fingertip without looking. You want to get this operation right with no fumbles, hence the benefit of doing all this in your visible workspace. By bringing the gun up to eye level, you can see the magazine and guide it into place while keeping visual awareness of whatever may still be happening in front of you.

4. Aim Your Index Finger

Let your index fingertip ride up the front of the magazine well while you insert the magazine. Your thumb will ride along the side of the magazine, and the magazine's base will be planted in your palm.

Perform the magazine change in your "work area" so you can see it easily. Better to get it right the first time by looking. Note the index finger guiding it into place.

5. Seat the New Magazine

When the new magazine is fully inserted, smack the base of the magazine sharply into the handgun to ensure it's fully seated and locked in place. One of the most common causes of malfunction is improper or incomplete magazine seating.

As the magazine is placed, let your palm smack it into place, ensuring it's properly locked in. Note that the trigger finger is still in a safe position.

6. Chamber a Round

By definition, using the speed reload scenario means there is no round in the chamber, and in most cases, your handgun's slide will be locked open. You're not ready to fire again until you chamber a round. The easy way to do this is to operate the slide lock lever with your firing hand, thereby releasing the open slide, chambering a round and putting the gun in ready condition. You can also perform a slide-rack maneuver to accomplish the same thing. In a minute, we'll discuss the pros and cons of using the slide lock as compared to racking the slide.

Tactical Reload

Sometimes, reloading before the magazine in your gun is empty may be beneficial. Perhaps there's a lull in the encounter. Maybe the encounter appears over, and you want to top it off as a precaution. Assuming the magazine in place is still functional, there's no reason not to save any remaining ammunition in case you need it later.

There's not much of a decision process behind whether or not to attempt a tactical reload. If you have cover and a safe opportunity, you might consider freshening up your ammo supply. If you're not able to at the moment, you'll know!

There are two primary ways to reload a fresh magazine while retaining the existing one.

The Serial Method

Since there are two distinct actions here, unloading and retaining the existing magazine and retrieving and loading the fresh one, the fail-safe method is to perform these things one after the other.

Just as with a normal speed reload, get your finger out of the trigger guard, then hit the magazine release button with the gun oriented so gravity is in your favor, but place your support hand under the grip so you can trap the falling magazine. Instead of trying to put this partially empty magazine back in your magazine carrier, stow it in a pocket. That's a cue that it's not a full (fresh) magazine.

With your support hand now free, you can resume the same process as a speed reload. Retrieve a fresh magazine from your carrier, insert it and smack it into place to ensure it is secure and properly seated.

Here's the important part! Remember, by definition, your gun is already prepped to fire. There's a round in the chamber, and it is cocked and ready to shoot—there is no need to rack the slide. If you do, you'll simply waste valuable time while ejecting a perfectly good round of ammo. Also, being loaded and ready, keeping your finger off the trigger and your muzzle pointed in a safe direction throughout the entire magazine change process is critical.

The Parallel Method

As the name implies, this method calls for removing and securing the partially spent magazine and inserting the new one simultaneously. It's arguably faster and more efficient but at the expense of reliability. As you'll see, it takes much more coordination (and practice) to do it without error.

You know the drill: finger out of the trigger guard first. Then, step one is to retrieve a fresh magazine from your carrier or pocket, depending on where you store the extra. Grasp it as usual, ideally with the support hand index finger aligned along the front of the magazine body.

Before ejecting the existing magazine, retrieve a fresh one as normal.
Note the index finger placement.

Now, the difference...let the index finger slide to the thumb side of the magazine body. This will effectively place the fresh magazine between your index and middle fingers, with its base still resting in your palm close to the base of your fingers. You'll notice your thumb is free. Hold that thought...

By dropping your index finger along the side of the magazine, you can now support it between your index and middle fingers.

Bring the fresh magazine up to your pistol, both in your line of vision and the muzzle pointed safely downrange. This is not the time to inadvertently shoot yourself or a companion when you're fumbling with a loaded gun and two magazines.

Eject the magazine into the same hand holding the fresh magazine so that your thumb and the thumb-side of your index finger catch it. The thumb gives us the unique ability to grip, so use it to get a firm hold of the exiting magazine.

Now, you can drop the "old" magazine into your palm between the thumb and index finger.

Now, you can guide the fresh magazine between your index and middle fingers into the gun, allowing those two fingers to ride outside the gun's grip and use your palm to smack the new magazine into place.

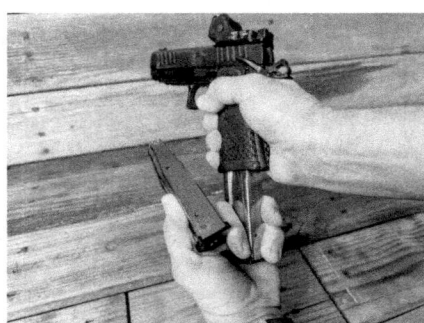

Now, you can shift your hand and insert the fresh magazine between your index and middle fingers while retaining control of the used one between your thumb and index finger. Smack it into position with the middle of your palm.

Again, just like the serial method described earlier, your gun, by definition, is ready to fire, so no racking or slide release is required. Stow the partially used magazine in a pocket and get back to the situation at hand.

As you can imagine, this is complex stuff. You'll fumble plenty when trying these techniques for the first time. And to be fair, the odds of you having to perform this in a self-defense encounter are low. But odds are not certain for a reason, so I prefer the "be prepared through practice" mentality.

The good news is you can practice these motions anytime using an empty pistol and empty magazines.

Slide Lock Lever or Rack the Slide?

So, to lever or not to lever?

When reloading a semi-auto handgun, assuming you shot to empty, ejected the spent magazine, and loaded a new one, you'll need to do one of two things: release the slide lock lever or retract and release the slide. Which operation should you practice? As always, there are pros and cons. We'll review them here so you can make an informed decision as to which method suits you best.

Slide Lock Release

Without a doubt, the slide lock release is the fastest and most efficient if your hand size and gun design allow you to do it without modifying your grip. Ideally, you can use your firing hand thumb to reach the lever and apply enough force to disengage the slide, allowing it to slam forward, load the chamber, and make the gun ready to fire. If you have the reach and thumb strength to do this without moving your hand from a firing grip, great!

Of course, you can also use your support hand to operate the lever. Since you just used that hand to reload a magazine anyway, it's available to flip that lever while returning to the proper two-handed grip position. This can be useful for guns with a tight lever, as you can adjust your hand to create more leverage.

This Beretta pistol has an elongated slide lock lever with a generous activation pad, so it's easy to reach and operate with the firing hand thumb, assuming right-handed operation. Other pistols may have more difficult lever placement, so the racking method may be preferable.

Some criticize the slide lock method for creating unnecessary wear and tear on the parts. However, given that we're talking about self-defense applications here, that is among the least of my worries.

Slide Rack Method

Rather than operating the slide lock lever, you can pull back the slide a fraction of an inch from its locked open position and let it slam home. The result is the same—you load a new round in the chamber and prepare the gun to fire. The nitpicky among us point out that this method fully uses the recoil spring power as the slide is fully retracted that extra fraction of an inch before beginning its forward travel. Whatever. I've been unable to measure a reliability difference between the slide lock and slide rack methods.

There are some obvious disadvantages of the slide rack method. First, it requires two hands, and as we've pointed out, you may not have two hands available in a defensive encounter. Second, it's slower than using the slide lock. More motion equates to more time. Although you can become very fast with practice, racking the slide will always take longer than using the lever.

On the benefits side, the slide rack method works on any semi-automatic pistol. If you have multiple guns in your household, you don't have to worry about the different positions of slide lock levers on different guns. If your pistol is one of those with a "Hulk strength required" slide lock, the racking method may be your best bet. Last, there are times when the slide does not remain in the locked open position. Perhaps one of your thumbs pressed against the lock lever when firing the last shot in the previous magazine. When you insert a fresh magazine and the slide is closed, the lever release won't help you—you'll need to rack the slide.

If you choose the slide rack method, you can always use the lever if your support hand isn't available. Over the years, I've gravitated toward this method, but only because my job requires me to use different guns, and it always works.

Reloading a Revolver

Let's establish a couple of assumptions here. We will discuss revolver reloading in the context of double-action revolvers like the classic "snubbies" or larger models from companies like Smith & Wesson, Ruger, and Colt. While one can use a single-action (think cowboy sixgun) revolver for concealed carry, it's not the most practical option.

Once you open the cylinder, you can hold the revolver using your left hand. Note the left-hand fingers through the frame holding the cylinder fully open. Now, the right hand will be free to unload and reload.

As revolvers almost always have the cylinder release on the left-hand side of the frame, we're going to describe the process using "right" and "left" hand terminology rather than "support" and "firing" hand. If you're a left-handed shooter, you'll most likely find yourself shifting the revolver to your right hand and then beginning the process described here.

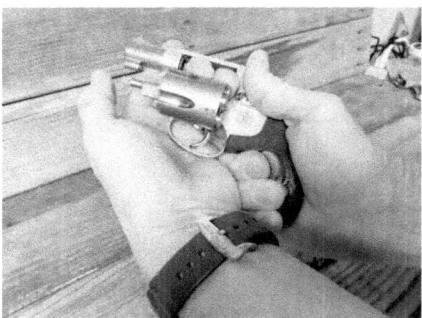

You can use your left thumb to drive the empties out with the ejector rod or use your right hand to smack it if more force is needed. I don't really need my right hand to support the revolver in this picture, but since this one ejects easily, I chose to leave it in a firing grip with my finger out of the trigger guard.

Using your right hand, activate the cylinder release latch or button (depending on your brand of revolver) using your right-hand thumb. At the same time, press the cylinder out of the frame to the left using your trigger finger. This gets your trigger finger out of the trigger guard and creates space in the frame for your left hand middle and ring fingers to reach through and hold the cylinder fully open. Keeping the gun near eye level as you would reloading a semi-automatic, tilt the muzzle upward to get a gravity assist. At this stage, you can hold the revolver, with the cylinder open, entirely with your left hand, freeing the right for unloading and reloading.

Using your left thumb, vigorously press the ejector rod to drive the empties out. Ideally, the upward muzzle angle will help cartridge cases to fall free. Depending on your revolver's grip style, there may not be a lot of room for all cases to fall clear, so practice making sure the cylinder is fully open and your ejection motion is smooth.

Once the cylinder is clear, use your right hand to retrieve new cartridges. At this point, it helps to tilt the muzzle towards the ground to get a gravity assist for dropping new cartridges into the cylinders. Using your right hand, load the fresh cartridges into the chambers. When finished, snap the cylinder shut and resume your firing grip.

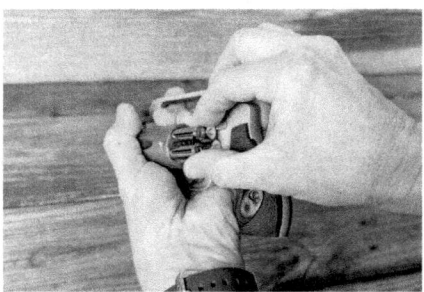

Being careful to hold the cylinder wide open with my left hand, I can load fresh cartridges. This model uses a moon clip system, so all five can be loaded at once.

Speedloaders, Speed Strips and Moon Clip Revolvers

For faster reloading, rather than one cartridge at a time, you can use a speedloader or even a speed strip. A speedloader is a cartridge holder made to fit the diameter and cartridge count of the cylinder of your specific handgun model. These devices "hold" all cartridges at once, allowing you to insert them into the cylinder in one motion. Once inserted into the chambers, a twist or mechanical release feature "let's go" of the cartridges.

Speed strips store spare revolver rounds in a row to fit easier in a pocket. With practice, loading two rounds at a time into the cylinder is easy.

Speedloaders are a great way to carry spare ammo, and you can only perform one loading motion rather than a half dozen, give or take.

Speed strips are rubber or silicone strips that hold cartridges through tension in a row. They allow you to load one or two at a time by inserting and twisting the strip off the cartridge base. So, you can perform three 2-cartridge loads rather than six individual loads to achieve the same result. The speed strips are also easier to carry as they are flat rather than cylindrical.

Some revolvers have their cylinders cut to accept moon clips. These springy, flat metal discs hold all the cartridges (tightly). You load the whole assembly into the revolver, leaving the moon clip in place. When all cartridges are fired, you simultaneously eject the whole mess (clip and cartridge cases). It's the fastest way to reload a revolver. The only catch is your revolver has to be modified for this type of operation. Many newer models come that way right out of the box.

This Smith & Wesson snubbie revolver has a cylinder cut for use with full moon clips.

As always, practice and repetition are the only things that will build proficiency in reloading a revolver under stress. Add adrenaline, panic, and big muscle focus by the brain, and this simple action can become a real challenge. The more you can practice, ideally using inert snap caps, the better.

Go Fast, But Don't Miss

One defensive shooting instructor offered a piece of sage advice about speed. It went something like this.

 Do the non-critical things as fast as possible, but slow down for the essentials.

Let's break that down for clarity. Moving your cover garment and getting your firing hand on your gun without error is important, but it doesn't directly resolve your problem. While raising the gun to a reasonable firing position is important, this motion won't fix your problem on its own. Getting a good sight picture before you fire is essential. You can't miss fast enough to help yourself. Pressing the trigger without moving the gun off target is also essential. Moving the gun off-target is surprisingly easy with a rushed and sloppy trigger press.

The bottom line? Hurry up getting your gun out and in a position to act. Slow down to aim and fire.

Case Study: Unarmed Fighting Skills

 A Vicksburg, Virginia, man returning from work at 8 am to the apartment he shared with his mother and sister found the back door ajar. Upon investigating, Malcolm Robertson, armed with a handgun, came out of a bedroom and confronted the resident. Robertson had previously dated the resident's sister but had a restraining order.

A fight ensued, and at some point, the resident gained control of the firearm and shot Robertson, who later died from his injuries.

Lessons

A firearm won't always be available should you run into trouble. This Virginia man certainly wasn't expecting to find an armed intruder in his residence at eight in the morning, but he did and had to make do with what he had—his hands.

13

ADVANCED DEFENSIVE SKILLS

As the saying goes, your primary defensive "weapon" is your brain. While physical skills, training, and repetitive practice are all critical components, your thinking and planning are the most likely to save your life. Let's discuss some advanced defensive concepts and skills.

Cover and Concealment

The first step to prevailing in a self-defense encounter is to minimize the degree to which you get hurt. In other words, job one is not to get shot. That's where concealment and cover come into play.

While often used interchangeably, concealment and cover are very different concepts. Let's explore each in more detail and how to use them effectively.

Concealment

Concealment is precisely what it says and no more substantive—literally. Concealment is something that hides or obscures you or your position from the person causing you grief. It has nothing to do with barriers or protection against bullets, edged weapons or flying debris. Technically speaking, a bedsheet hanging from the ceiling can offer concealment.

I once saw a video of a gunfight in a convenience store. The two participants chased each other through the store, each vying for a position to shoot the other. Running through aisles of beef jerky, chips and various other snacks, each would pop up above the top of the display racks looking for the other. When they were below the "snacks aisle" line of sight, there was no shooting going on, even though they knew their opponent was just feet away on the other side of the snack cakes.

Stop and think about this for a second. Two people with guns, trying to kill each other, were foiled by a foot or two or plastic bags filled mostly with air. Any shot would have gone right through to the other guy without obstruction. Why didn't one or both fire a shot or two right through the displays? Given the short range, they would have almost certainly scored hits.

In fairness, I can understand this. In the heat of the moment, our brains are processing something like, "If I can't see him, I can't aim at him. So don't shoot yet." When they weren't popping up for a look like Whack-A-Moles, these guys subconsciously took advantage of concealment. Nothing in the store would have stopped a bullet, but the "concealment" offered at least temporary protection.

Don't get me wrong. I'm not in any way, shape or form saying you'll be safe hiding behind something that a bullet can easily perforate. All I'm saying is that if there are no other options, concealment can aid in your defense. Perhaps it will, if nothing else, buy you a bit of time because it's harder for someone to attack what they can't see. You might say concealment is one part of the run, hide, fight methodology.

There are plenty of examples of concealment in our daily environments. As we've just seen, stores are full of concealment options. The walls in your home arguably offer concealment more than cover because while they can hide your position, a bullet can pass through most interior walls fairly easily. Plants, bushes, tinted windows, soft furniture and myriad other things offer potential concealment in part or in full.

This "coffee shop" set up for training with Simunitions shows a few concealment options but not much real cover. Photo: H&K Firearms, WOFT Training.

Remember, concealment is a "better than nothing" option. If an aggressor is not aware of your presence at all, concealment might be sufficient. If your presence is known, concealment may offer you a brief opportunity to throw a bit of confusion and reaction requirement back toward your attacker while you work on improving your situation.

One of the primary reasons for developing movement as an automatic skill is to seek concealment, or better yet, cover...

Cover

Cover refers to something that will stop a bullet from getting to you. Typically, cover also offers concealment, but not always. Have you ever visited a convenience store or bank in a higher-crime area? Those bullet-resistant windows offer cover but not concealment.

Examples of cover in everyday life include buildings, trees, vehicles (at least the part behind sturdy stuff like engines), bookcases, machinery, and many other heavy, dense objects. For this discussion, we'll avoid going down the rabbit hole of which types of cover stop projectiles from which kinds of guns and ammo. For now, remember that (generally speaking with infinite caveats) rifles are more powerful than handguns, so "heavier" cover objects will be required.

While every defensive situation presents its challenges and ideal responses, a primary objective is almost always to get to a position of cover. Remember, we're talking about the defense of self and family here, so if you can get to a place that provides cover, you're already on the way to winning.

Consider some tips for using cover to your advantage.

Think Three-dimensionally

All sorts of unusual things in the world around you can be used as cover. Our logical brains tend to think vertically, probably because we stand upright on two feet. There are plenty of horizontal options out there, too. In a jam, flopping down on your face behind a curb might be a better option than standing around. An anecdote from the story *Blackhawk Down* illustrates this point perfectly. During the fight, at least one experienced special forces operator took advantage of cover in the middle of an empty street. Considering his position and that of the enemy, the slope and curve of the slight hill in the road made him untouchable with traditional line-of-sight weapons like rifles and machine guns. He would pop up to fire, then lay back down to take advantage of cover. No walls or barricades required.

Our everyday world is filled with objects and structures that can provide a little help. The next time you're walking around in public, note how many walls, ledges, staircases, benches and other objects are available to use in a pinch.

Some Cover Is Better Than No Cover

There's a great scene in one of my favorite all-time moves. In *True Lies*, Agent "Gib" Gibson (Tom Arnold) is chasing terrorists down a Washington, D.C. Sidewalk. The bad guy turns and fires at him.

Arnold quickly hides behind a lamp post, which doesn't exactly hide his husky frame. Being a Hollywood movie, Arnold isn't hit, and the post stops rifle bullets. Unrealistic? Of course. But that doesn't mean that partial cover is useless. Presenting less of a target is always an improvement.

Sure, my cover preference will always be the inside of an Abrams tank and, if that's not handy, a bank vault. However, I'll take what I can get. Even partial cover can save your life by shielding vital organs. If caught between standing in the open or behind some partial cover, take what you can get!

Unless you're also using substantial furniture, most home and apartment interior walls are really "concealment," as bullets will pass through them easily.

Don't Crowd Your Cover

If cover is a barrier between you and a gunshot, you do not need to be up close and personal with your cover. Bullets travel in straight lines except in bad spy movies, so you can't be hit if something solid is between you and your attacker—it doesn't matter whether or not you're right up close to it.

There are potential disadvantages to getting too close to your chosen cover. First, you may need some elbow room to shoot back. If you're up close to a wall or corner, you may not have the space fire from a half-decent position. The closer you are, the more you'll have to worry about fragments from incoming fire hitting you. If someone else is shooting at your cover, you may be subject to injury or death from the bullets or other fragments.

Note how this shooter isn't crowding right up against the available cover/concealment. By standing farther back, you can better control what you see and how much of yourself you expose.

The other benefit of allowing space between you and your cover is improved visibility. You can see more precisely what's on the other side if you back off and allow some space. You'll also find that you can expose less of yourself as you look or shoot from behind cover if you take a position a little farther away. Allowing some space creates more sensitivity in your ability to position yourself.

This is one of those concepts where some trial and experimentation can be enlightening, and you don't even need to use a gun. Using doorways or objects around your house, experiment with distance, checking your visibility and what you look like from the opposite direction.

Cover as a Brace

There are few absolutes in defensive shooting. The right strategy almost always depends on the circumstances, and "it depends" answers abound. The conventional school of thought regarding the use of cover is to stand well behind it to avoid ricochets and reduce exposure. On the other hand, there are situations where charging right up to a protective barrier may be the correct response.

Consider whether creating a stable or braced shooting position is worth the tradeoff of being too close to your cover. If you're shooting at a distance, using the cover object to stabilize your gun may offer a favorable risk/reward. Or perhaps there are multiple threats in different positions in front of you. "Crowding" your cover may be the only option you have to protect against multiple angles. This is yet another reason to ponder scenarios when out and about in your daily routine.

Sometimes, using cover as a brace may be advantageous, so the "don't crowd your cover rule" may not apply.

Using Lights

Weapon lights are great inventions—provided they're used correctly. In the concealed carry market, they're more commonly used on home defense handguns as they're a little more challenging to carry concealed. Still, we're seeing more "carry-friendly" options with small but powerful and reliable lights and compatible holsters.

The purpose of a gun-mounted light is to clearly show you what you are actively shooting at or what you are willing to shoot at. They are not for searching or looking around for the source of the proverbial "bump in the night" or anything else. Remember, a gun is, by definition, pointed at everything your weapon-mounted light is directed towards. You don't want to be lighting up things you aren't willing to shoot using a weapon-mounted light.

A hand-held light is the proper tool for seeing, looking and searching. Period.

Until you've decided to shoot, a light separated from your gun is the safest way to avoid negligently shooting something or someone you didn't intend to hit. Over the years, people have developed multiple ways to use a hand-held light and handgun together. Let's explore the three most common methods.

These Streamlight models are high-quality weapon lights. Mounted to the front rail on a pistol, they illuminate what you intend to shoot.

FBI Technique

The FBI technique is perhaps the most flexible way to simultaneously carry and operate a hand-held light and handgun. Ideal for flashlights equipped with a tailcap switch, this method allows complete independence between your flashlight and firearm hands.

The FBI method provides more independence between your light and shooting hands.

Use an icepick grip with your support-hand thumb on the flashlight tail cap and the lens extending past the pinky finger. With this orientation, the light is near your shoulder, and you can move it closer or farther from the body as desired. Your handgun can be holstered or in a low-ready position. If you need to shoot, the idea is to go completely one-handed with no assist from the support hand holding the flashlight.

Besides creating independence between looking and shooting, the theory is you can hold the light farther from your body, ideally drawing attention (and an aiming point for the bad guy) away from your body. I'd say there is some validity to this theory based on the number of times I've perforated bad guy targets right in their gun hand in shoot house exercises. There is a very real subconscious tendency to aim and shoot directly at the visible threat, which in this case would be a light beam. On the negative side, you'll rely solely on your one-handed shooting skill.

A variant of this technique involves holding the light similarly but anchoring it on the collarbone or against the neck. Your upper body becomes "tank-like," moving and rotating the light and your corresponding shooting position as the light moves in different directions. Of course, you lose the benefit of moving the light source away from your vital areas.

Harries Technique

The Harries technique is frequently seen on television, presumably because the actors can make it look cool and dramatic. The method is geared more toward actual shooting than searching, as the gun and flashlight hands are anchored together. It's difficult to avoid pointing your muzzle at whatever you're illuminating without temporarily breaking the position.

The Harries technique is more natural, and while it doesn't help control your gun during recoil, it can add some stability.

Like the FBI method, you hold the flashlight in a reverse icepick grip, using your thumb to operate a tail-cap switch. However, instead of positioning the light on the support side of your body, you lower the light hand to a near-horizontal position across the front of your body. The gun hand's wrist rests on top of the flashlight hand's wrist. The idea is to move your hands together, keeping them anchored to each other at the wrists.

While this technique provides some stability to your shooting hand, like the cup-and-saucer grip technique, it does nothing to control your handgun's recoil. That's the price of using a gun and a hand-held flashlight simultaneously.

Surefire Technique

Some tactical hand-held lights are designed with "grip assistance rings" along the flashlight body. One reason for this design is to use the Surefire (and other similar) light techniques. Also intended for shooting rather than looking, the idea is you hold the flashlight between two fingers of your support hand, then wrap your support hand around the handgun grip. It's awkward and requires plenty of practice, but the method does provide a much better shooting platform. I'd describe it as somewhere between shooting solely one-handed and a conventional two-handed grip.

The Surefire technique definitely requires practice, and a purpose-built light also helps lock it between your fingers.

Gotchas and Weapon-Mounted Light Considerations

Separating "searching" and "shooting" is far preferable from a safety perspective. How many stories have you seen of a homeowner accidentally (negligently) shooting a family member, friend, or neighbor while investigating that "bump in the night" scenario? As the various techniques illustrate, there are ways to use a hand-held light and handgun independently, thereby avoiding aligning your muzzle with your light.

With that said, with proper thinking, planning and practice, a weapon-mounted light can be a valuable addition to your defensive handgun configuration. But remember, *a weapon-mounted light is not a substitute for a hand-held light.* Instead, think of it as an additional tool. You should still always use a hand-held light for looking and evaluating. If you need to shoot, you can activate a weapon light if the situation allows and either drop the hand-held light or shift to one of the techniques we discussed. Dropping a valuable tool in a moment of stress is unnatural, so ponder that strategy on your own to decide whether it makes sense for you.

You also might want to consider (and try, using an unloaded gun) some potential "gotcha" scenarios. The first time I had to change magazines due to a malfunction during a dark conditions exercise, I found out just how hard it is to do while holding a flashlight. It's not impossible, but it's not something you want to learn for the first time during a self-defense encounter. Is this a high-probability scenario? No. Is it something you should train for? Probably not. But it does bring up a valuable point. Consider things you might need to do while operating a gun and light: open or close doors, hold or direct a child or family member, carry and operate a cell phone to call for help, and so on. It pays to think about such things in advance.

Case Study: Two Is Better Than One

A husband and wife duo ambushed and killed two Las Vegas police officers in a CiCis Pizza restaurant. After stripping the dead officers of guns and ammunition, the pair went into a nearby Walmart store, firing a shot and yelling about a forthcoming revolution.

An armed citizen, Joseph Wilcox, was in the store with a friend returning a product and decided to take action. Approaching the husband, Wilcox confronted him, apparently not knowing about the killer's wife, who was trailing behind. At that moment, the wife shot Wilcox once in the chest, killing him. During a shootout with more arriving officers, the wife shot her husband and then turned the gun on herself, ending the incident with Wilcox and both murderers dead.

Lessons

Our brains have eons of survival programming that tells our senses to focus on the threat. We tend to develop tunnel vision and auditory exclusion during a fight-or-flight response. The problem is that we may not recognize immediate threats outside of that narrow view. In this case, Joseph Wilcox didn't see or recognize the danger presented by the second killer, and it cost him his life.

This brings up another topic to discuss with your significant other: monitoring for other potential threats.

Team Defense

Most of this book so far has been about developing your individual skills, tactics and strategies for becoming self-defense aware and proficient. That's great! But much of that value goes out the window when you introduce companions into a self-defense situation. Consider this analogy. An aspiring football player grows up tossing a football through a tire in their backyard. They become a freak of nature, able to do this on demand from any distance, even while running full tilt. They've got impressive individual skills. Send them onto the field with ten other players, never having run a single play together, much less practiced as a team. How's it going to go? That group won't be winning many games.

Team defense in this context refers to nothing more than being on the same page regarding defensive strategies with your significant other and family. It's about communication and planning. Do other members of your circle know what you'll do in a self-defense situation? Do you know what they will do?

With so many people recording on their cell phones, it's easy to see examples of team defense strategies' successes and failures. We can learn from this.

Consider one recent example: the assassination attempt on President Donald Trump at the Butler, PA political rally. There's plenty of freely available footage of the event, and given the layout of the audience behind the podium, we can see how dozens of individuals and families reacted. Some sat and watched the entire event unfold, even as incoming gunfire was headed their way—as if the event was something being watched from safely behind a TV screen. Some, surprisingly few, dove for the floor. Some assumed protective positions around their significant others.

I think the most significant lesson from these video clips is that most people have tremendous inertia when taking any immediate action in response to an unfolding event far outside their life experience. You can almost see their brains trying to process something that "just can't be happening." What is that noise? It can't be gunfire—that just doesn't happen in my daily life. Did that person near me just get shot? What is going on? You get the idea. Most of our brains aren't programmed to immediately digest and accept a situation like that, and precious time is wasted trying to reconcile with the unfolding reality. That lag can mean the difference between life and death.

Again, considering this one representative example of a violent event, wouldn't you rather be one of those people who immediately dove for the floor or took other appropriate action at the first hint of danger? Like most other topics discussed in this book, improving your odds relies on planning and preparation.

Pre-Planning

Earlier, we discussed the importance of pondering possible scenarios as you go about your daily life. The more you consider and plan for "what ifs," the better you can respond when a "what if" becomes a "what is."

The first step in team defense is expanding those "what if" conversations to your significant other. Discuss possible roles in an emergency. We can't provide recommended answers to every scenario, so consider general approaches and discuss them with your companion.

What is your general strategy if you end up in a robbery situation? Who talks? Do you immediately comply or try to delay? Is one person primarily responsible for trying to remember descriptive information about the attacker?

Who is responsible for calling for help when possible? Does that person understand the basics of how to talk with a dispatcher? Will they remember to describe their partner as "the good guy" and mention whether or not they are armed? Wouldn't it be nice for responding authorities to know something like, "One of the victims is a man in a blue jacket. He's armed and has a concealed carry permit?"

Does one of you try to escape the situation while the other defends?

What's your objective if some violent encounter breaks out that doesn't involve you directly? Wouldn't it be nice to know in advance if your goal was to get the heck out of dodge? If something bad starts in a restaurant, wouldn't it be nice for everyone to know the objective, if possible, is to escape through an alternate exit?

You get the idea. Advance planning is invaluable. The more you can minimize decision-making in the moment, the better.

Trust

Parents have long used "safe" words with their children. If some adult uses the "safe" word, the child knows to trust them and do what they say. The classic example is a school pickup by someone the child may not recognize.

This trust concept applies to adults, too. If you and your significant other have discussed defensive response strategies, you'll both know there might be a time when you need just to obey your partner —right then, no questions asked. For example, my wife and I both know that if the other says something like, "We need to leave right now," that means no discussion and no looking around to figure out what's happening. Just. Do. It. Now. So be it if that means dashing through a crowded restaurant and into the kitchen.

When two or more are involved, coordination and communication are essential. Working with someone else under stressful and evolving conditions is a learned skill requiring much practice. Photo: Gunsite Academy.

Our tendency to follow rules and norms and not be publicly weird is a strong force, but it can be overcome with advance consideration. Suppose your partner issues a command like this. In that case, you know not to worry about getting in trouble, upsetting the manager or worrying about other patrons watching you because it is a life-and-death situation.

Communication

Except for toddlers, we're not accustomed to narrating our own planned actions to the rest of the world. However, nothing is more important in a dangerous situation than mutual understanding of what each party is doing or plans to do. Clearly, this falls under the "if the situation allows" category, as you can't be strategizing with each other in the middle of a mugging. But you certainly can in many different scenarios, like during the chaos of the Butler, PA, event described above.

Communication during chaos is unnatural, so you need to not only think about it ahead of time but do it. Live training is a great way to learn this skill with your partner. Consider the low-hanging fruit like this:

I'm going to (fill in the blank); you call for help!

I need to reload!

Move the kids over there; I'll (fill in the blank)!

I'm going to help this person; you (fill in the blank).

And so on...

Communication also applies to bystanders who aren't with you. If you're ahead of the response curve and already in the take-action phase, there's no reason you can't issue instructions to bystanders who are still in denial about what's happening. "You! Call 911 now and tell them (fill in the blank)!"

Who's the Boss?

On a related topic, you'll be amazed at how hard it is for two people to coordinate during a dynamic situation unless they've practiced together. We all see things through a different lens and develop our own picture of appropriate actions to take in response. Add stress, and those challenges get worse.

Sometimes, your partner may not see what you see, and there's no time for discussion. This might be the time for forceful "encouragement" to ensure that they know what needs to be done. In this case, the right answer was to leave as the other two individuals were about to exchange gunfire.

In past team tactics training events, one thing was consistent in after-action discussions looking at what went right and wrong: we really had no idea what the partner was thinking, at least in the beginning stages of working together. One person might have gone right at the threat because of a perfectly valid reason in their mind, while the other focused on escape for an equally valid reason. One might have seen possible second or third threats. You get the idea. Teamwork doesn't come naturally. That's why team sports coaches focus on repetition of the fundamentals over and over.

While training and practicing together is the ideal long-term solution, establishing a clear "leader" can help reduce confusion.

In the Home

Team tactics in the home are much easier to pre-plan as there are a limited number of potential scenarios, at least compared to what you may encounter in public.

Think about basic things you might want to do in a home emergency.

What are the possible entry points into your home?

Where is your bedroom in relation to those?

What is your plan for any children in the house? Is one of you responsible for getting to them? Do they know what to do in various situations? Where are the kids' rooms relative to your bedroom and possible entry points to the home? For example, if your front or back door is between your room and your kids, how will you handle that if there's an intruder?

What objects throughout your home provide concealment? How about cover?

Who is primarily responsible for calling 911? Do they know what to say, such as describing all the home occupants and locations? Do you keep charged cell phones at your bedside? I keep mine on a charger on my nightstand, along with a flashlight.

Are there exits from your home that could be used in certain situations?

What is your rallying point in the event people get separated during a home emergency? Perhaps a neighbor's home or other land-mark nearby?

Active Shooter Situations

There's a fundamental theme throughout this book. Planning and preparation can save your life. Becoming a tactical ninja certainly won't hurt your odds of being low on the potential victim list, but most of us aren't going to get to Delta SEAL school anytime soon. On the positive side, much of personal self-defense involves avoidance and making sure you're not the easiest target.

Let's consider some statistics to set the stage for ways you might survive an active shooter event. The numbers might vary from study to study, but the approximations are similar.

- About 75% of active shooting situations end in five minutes or less.
- About two-thirds of active shooter events end before police arrive.
- Only about 15% end without the use of force.

- About half of active shooters killed themselves during the event, many when first confronted by an armed citizen or law enforcement.
- In incidents where an armed citizen was present, they were successful in stopping the mass shooting about 75% of the time.
- Most active shooter incidents take place in gun-free zones, so armed citizens generally are not present.

Looking at past incidents, we can see some learnings we can apply.

Harder Targets

In numerous events, potential victims who somehow made themselves a more complex or time-consuming target to reach survived the encounter. For example, in the Virginia Tech mass shooting, an attacker targeted five classrooms during an 11-minute event. In two classrooms, professors and students barricaded doors and created entry barriers. In these two rooms, two people were killed. In the other three rooms, a total of 27 were murdered—immediate resistance action matters.

Time Matters

Mass killers seem to understand time matters and that they have a limited time in which to inflict maximum damage. In case after case, we see examples of murderers bypassing locations and groups of people who have created some form of "time obstacle" for the killer to overcome. Like prudent planning to make your home or self a less appealing target that requires more time and energy to burglarize, erecting difficulty barriers can be an effective strategy during a mass shooting event.

Think Disruption: You Don't Have to "Win"

Mass killers know the clock is ticking, and police will arrive in an average of four to nine minutes. This time pressure can work in favor of potential victims as a "winning" strategy doesn't have to include defeating the attacker in an outright gunfight. If you consider survival as winning, delaying or otherwise thwarting the attacker's plan can lead to a more positive outcome. Think back to the discussion on the importance of interrupting an attacker's plan as a way to regain some advantage in the conflict.

Take, for example, the 2012 mass shooting in Clackamas Town Center Mall near Portland, Oregon. A 22-year-old shooter (we won't use any of their names here) entered the mall armed with a semi-automatic rifle and numerous full magazines and started shooting. After killing two people and seriously wounding a third, an armed citizen, Nick Meli, drew his Glock 22 and aimed at the shooter. He did not fire, as there were innocent bystanders behind the shooter. At this point, the killer ran to a stairwell, where he killed himself. It is believed that Meli's efforts disrupted the plan enough to end the rampage. While Meli, armed with a pistol, was seemingly prepared to take on a shooter armed with a rifle, it appears disruption was enough—he didn't have to prevail directly in that very mismatched gunfight.

One can never rely on a scenario ending like this one, and that's not the point here. The fact is this: time is life. When people are dying every few seconds, introducing delays and disruptions into the mix can make a big difference in the outcome.

14

AFTERMATH

If you ever have the misfortune to be involved in a self-defense incident, know that the process is just beginning when the smoke clears. The good news is you survived the encounter. The bad news is there may be a new battle in the works, and you're once again the primary target.

Fortunately, there are things you can do to prepare for the inevitable aftermath. Knowledge is power, so we'll spend a few minutes talking about things you might expect to encounter. Then, we'll talk about actions you can take to make your life easier during the post-event process.

Case Study: Getting Shot By the Police

 A gunman walked into an Amarillo, Texas, church service. A group of attendees disarmed the gunman while fellow congregant Tony Garces managed to take the invader's gun. The good samaritan then proceeded to hold the perpetrator at gunpoint until police arrived.

When responding officers arrived, they ordered Garces to drop the gun. Fearing the loaded gun would go off, Garces proceeded to lower the gun toward the floor, at which point an officer shot him in the chest. Fortunately, Garces survived.

Lessons

Responding officers don't yet have full knowledge of what events have just transpired or are still in progress. Nor do they yet know who the good guys are and who are not. As they're presumably amped up by responding to a potential mass shooting event in progress, it's a situation ripe for disaster.

In an ideal situation, the armed citizen would do well to make sure the firearm is safely out of hand as police enter the scene. If it can't be holstered, one can always place it on the floor and step on it to keep it secure.

It's a difficult situation with inherent risk. Other cases have ended with similar tragedies when different officers gave conflicting commands to the armed citizen, again ending with the citizen being shot during the resulting confusion.

On the Scene

One thing that will make the process go a bit smoother is understanding the responding officers' situation. Remember, they are showing up to a chaotic scene involving gunfire and possibly injuries or death. They'll be amped up like you. They arrive on the scene and see people with guns, blood on the floor and who knows what else. If you're not careful, they might see an "unknown person" (you!) standing there with a gun. Do you see a dangerous moment in the works here?

Remember, they don't have the benefit of having been present when things transpired, as you were, so they won't have much of an idea of what happened until they methodically rebuild the sequence of events through evidence and witness interviews. You know you're innocent, but they don't, at least not yet. And remember, these people hear "I'm innocent!" a hundred times a day from virtually everyone they encounter, including some of the worst society has to offer, so forgive them if they don't immediately take your word at face value. There will be plenty of time for the truth to become clear.

First, be sure you are safe. If not, get to a safe place to begin the reporting process. Then, think in terms of what respondents will see and act accordingly.

Report First!

Given the confusion over who did what that's just now beginning, it pays to be the first to call for help from the authorities. Think about it. If the other guy (the aggressor or someone sympathetic to them) calls first, they get to structure the starting narrative. "That crazy guy over there went nuts and started shooting! I was minding my own business!" It's not as far-fetched as it sounds. I'm sure most of us have faced similar stories from the guilty party for lesser incidents. I once had a guy who rear-ended me at a red light, telling officers I backed into him. That was fun to sort out.

Right, wrong, or indifferent, people tend to lean toward the first story presented as being closer to the truth. It also begins to paint a picture of who is innocent and who is guilty. An innocent person would report a self-defense event. A guilty one isn't going to be motivated to call the police for much of anything. It's far preferable to be the one initiating the call for help or reporting an incident that is already over. You want to establish the truth as succinctly and factually as possible as the starting point in reconstructing events.

You may not always have the luxury of being the person who dials 911. You may be injured, occupied restraining an attacker or any number of things. Depending on who is present, you can always verbally instruct someone there to make the call on your behalf to start the process.

Whether you make the call or instruct someone else to, consider describing yourself so responding officers start to develop a picture of who is who. Keep it short and straightforward, and do not try to relay the entire narrative of what just happened. Think in simple terms. "I was attacked. The scene is safe now. I'm six feet tall and wearing jeans and a plaid shirt. I'm armed, and my gun is holstered." You get the idea. Officers with guns will be storming the scene in minutes. If it helps to let them know who you are, consider doing so.

You also may still be in danger and unable to summon help. If you can get away and call for help from a safer location, do so. Think of the classic road rage disagreement. Priority one is to get away. Priority two is to call and report the incident.

Bottom line? You are the good guy or gal. Act like it.

Plan for First Responder Arrival

You just survived a fight for your life. You may have just shot or even killed someone. You are probably shaking like a leaf and wondering what the heck just happened. Regardless, it's up to you, and you only, to get your act together to prevent further tragedy. When you are safe and the threat is no longer imminent, it's up to you to shift mental gears and start thinking about what will happen next.

Police will show up. They will have guns drawn. They will have little, if any, information about what's going on. They may have no clue who is a good guy and who is a bad guy. They will have an immediate priority in securing the scene. That means that everyone holding a gun will be considered a threat until they can sort out the details of what happened. They will, by necessity, view you as a potential threat until proven otherwise. You telling them that you're the good guy will mean absolutely nothing in the heat of the moment. You know what happened, but they don't.

So, it's up to you to start securing yourself as soon as possible. Part of that process is taking all necessary actions to make yourself as visibly non-threatening as you can.

Secure Your Gun

Step one is to secure your gun as soon as you are safely able. If you're using a proper holster, you should be able to do this with one hand. If you can't, or you're using a holster that requires multiple steps to reholster safety, you can always set your gun on the ground and stand on it. Whatever you do, take all possible measures to make sure there is not a gun in your hand when police come through the door. To be clear, this isn't to be sneaky; it is to do everything in your power not to look like an obvious threat.

If you can't reholster your gun, safe and and place it on the ground like this. It's still secure but not an obvious threat to first responders. Be sure to tell them what you're doing and why.

Here's another reason why building good gun handling habits at the range is so important. When things go bad in a self-defense shooting, the last things you'll be thinking about are details like re-engaging a safety lever or de-cocking a double-action pistol before placing it back in your holster. Trainers harp on building muscle memory for actions like keeping your finger off the trigger, reholstering safety, and de-cocking (or applying the safety) immediately after firing. In addition to basic safety, this is another excellent reason. In the heat of a lethal force encounter, these "habits" might save your life.

Hands Up and Cooperation

Once your gun is secured, you should do everything possible to appear compliant and non-threatening. That means clearly showing your hands. If you are able and the situation is secure enough, keep your hands raised, visible, and in the air.

Now is the time to cooperate, not argue your point of view. Follow instructions and make life easy for all involved. There's a great chance some or all of the following might happen.

You may be handcuffed. This is routine. The police must secure the scene, including participants, to ensure safety.

You might be placed in a patrol car. Again, routine. Go with it. You'll have time later to help sort things out.

Officers will take possession of your firearm for obvious reasons —disarming people at the scene, and it may be future evidence. Don't plan on getting it back anytime soon.

You might be taken to the police station. Again, this is not the time to argue or resist, even if you feel like you're being treated unfairly.

These actions may seem aggressive and unfair since you're not the bad guy here. But stop and think. How often does resisting and throwing a fit at the scene resolve anything? Have you ever seen a police officer stop an arrest in progress and say, "Oh, sorry, I didn't realize you were going to argue and get really mad about this? Never mind, you can go now." Again, you'll have time later when everyone has calmed down to share the truth.

To Talk or Not To Talk?

And here we are at the question that has caused more arguments than the debate over whether .45 is better than 9mm. Should you or should you not talk in detail to responding officers about what happened?

First, I am not a lawyer qualified to dispense legal advice. Even if I were, statutes and procedures are different in every state, so there's no one-rule-applies advice to be had. Second, every situation is different, so it will boil down to a judgment call on your part. You are the responsible party and will have to live with the consequences.

I will, however, share some personal thoughts, opinions and observations to help you start down the path of answering this question for yourself.

We all tend to be unnecessarily binary. With this debate, you'll hear something like this one one extreme. "All you should say is, 'I was in fear for my life; I won't speak to you until my lawyer arrives.'" Conversely, you might hear advice to share all possible details since you're the innocent party. Innocent people have nothing to hide, right?

Like most things in life, the best answer likely lies somewhere in the middle ground. Making it clear you were the victim is usually a good thing. Making it clear you were facing death or severe harm is usually a good thing. Clarifying that "the guy over there" attacked you is a basic fact you might want to share.

On the other hand, trying to recount lots of details at that moment has landed an awful lot of innocent people in trouble. As just one example, during the chaos of a self-defense fight, you likely will have no idea of how many shots you fired. The majority of people get it wrong after the fact. Even witnesses can't reliably account for such details and they weren't the ones fighting for their lives. Recognize that you were under the influence of a major adrenaline dump and that your brain was occupied with things other than tracking details. Details you share in the heat of the moment might come back to haunt you later if you get it wrong.

There may also be a happy medium between cooperation and allowing time to settle down and get help before sharing your whole story. You may consider telling responding officers that you want and intend to cooperate fully, but you're just emerging from a stressful incident and need time to settle down. You may consider telling them some basic facts and then requesting to get into more detail when your lawyer arrives.

Speaking of lawyers, now is the time to find one and make an arrangement. You'll need to know that number, and the person answering will need to know who you are when you make that call from the police station. How many cases have we seen where people who did the right thing are dragged through the legal process, demonized and sometimes imprisoned for political reasons? It happens—a lot. Part of protecting yourself and your family is making sure you have good legal representation on standby. You can interview lawyers with self-defense experience on your own or explore options from the growing network of defensive liability plans.

Case Study: Subway Good Samaritan or Villain?

A 26-year-old Marine veteran intervened on a New York City subway car when a 30-year-old homeless man began acting erratically and threatening other passengers. Daniel Penny restrained the man in a chokehold. Later, Jordan Neely became unresponsive and died.

Testimony was varied. Many on the train hailed Penny as a hero for protecting them from Neely. At least one wondered why Penny restrained Neely for so long. Some testified that Neely was alive and breathing after being let out of the restraint hold. Others indicate responding officers didn't take proper action to help revive Neely.

Penny was later charged with second-degree manslaughter and criminally negligent homicide, finally being acquitted in December 2024.

Lessons

It's doubtful Daniel Penry began his day hoping to murder a stranger. In fact, much testimony and public opinion hailed him as a hero for intervening in a threatening situation. Yet Penny endured arrest, murder charges and a year-and-a-half legal battle to avoid prison. His acquittal was met with mixed reactions—some saw justice finally done, while others considered him a racist killer.

The lesson is this. The Monday morning quarterbacks in the media, legal system, and public will question your actions ruthlessly using the benefit of hindsight. And most of the criticism will come from those with the least practical knowledge of self-defense. It is not likely to be a fair process. This is one reason why so many self-defense experts preach avoidance and escape. As an armed citizen, you are not the police or society's designated protector. Your primary mission is to protect yourself and your family. Even your actions within that limited scope might land you in ruinous legal trouble.

What Happens Next

In a perfect world, when the dust settles, police and the District Attorney's office will determine your actions were consistent with justifiable homicide (or lesser) and send you on your way. One would think this would be the norm in an actual self-defense case. And it does happen. Sometimes, Police Chiefs or Sheriffs stand at the podium, talking about how a brave and selfless citizen stopped a violent crime in progress. But don't count on this outcome.

Sadly, politics, power and ambition add other factors to the justice equation. How many cases have we seen on the news in which an ambitious District Attorney is preparing for the next election or higher office and wants to make an example of someone caught in a bad situation?

You can do all the right things and still lose, and many armed citizens have.

Arrest and Incarceration

After a violent encounter, there is a good chance you might be arrested and charged with a crime. In that eventuality, you will spend at least some time in jail. Even if you are granted bail and are able to meet the terms, it will take some time to navigate the process.

This is why it's important to think about the worst "what if" scenario before you need it. No one plans on being caught up in a violent self-defense encounter, but if you have that misfortune, it'll help you immensely if you know what to expect and who to call to aid your cause.

Bail

If you have to make bail, you have two choices. You can pay the full amount in cash. If you can afford that, you'll get it back, assuming you don't flee and show up for future court proceedings.

The other option is to use a bail bond company. Suppose your bail is set at $500,000, and you don't have quite that much money stashed away under the sofa cushions. You can go to a bail bondsman and pay 10 percent of that amount, $50,000, and that company will guarantee to the court that you'll show up. If you don't show up for your trial, the bail bonds company is on the hook to the court for the $500,000. That company will also send distinctly unfriendly people to chase you down so they don't have to write that half-million-dollar check. If you do follow through and attend your trial, you don't get any of your $50,000 bail bond fee back. That 10 percent is the bail company's compensation for taking the risk and guaranteeing your adherence to the rules.

When you use the services of a bail bond company, they will want all sorts of collateral to protect their investment. Be prepared to supply access to any assets you have.

Criminal Charges and Civil Lawsuits

As discussed in the Daniel Penny case study, the first big hurdle in a self-defense case gone bad is fighting criminal charges. After you make bail, the actual process starts. If you don't make bail, plan on losing your job, followed by your home if you're the primary bread-winner in the household. Even if you do manage bail, you still might lose these things as you'll be branded a "killer."

If you're charged with some form of murder or manslaughter, you'll need a defense team. Not a lawyer, but a team. We're talking lawyers, paralegals, investigators, expert witnesses and more. That all costs a fortune. Costs of mounting a legal defense quickly move into six-figure territory, win or lose.

Even if you manage to win a criminal case, after living with that incredible stress for years, you then may face civil proceedings. The family of your attacker has something to say in the process, too. You'll see a public sympathy PR campaign complete with elementary and high school pictures of the person you hurt or killed. You'll likely get sued for incredible amounts of money. The worst part is that civil liability cases have lower burdens of proof than criminal cases, so you can win in criminal court but lose the civil case. Just remember the OJ Simpson trials. He won the criminal case but lost the civil case. Oh, and don't forget to add another six figures to the running legal tab.

Remember, all of these things may happen even if you did nothing wrong. Our legal system is far from perfect, and it's often not about real justice but about playing the game. Are you starting to see the picture of why you really, really, really don't want to draw a gun in self-defense unless you have absolutely no other alternative? The next time you hear an internet commando talk about how they would have intervened in some situation, think about the aftermath. Remember, you're not protecting your family if you're in prison because you prematurely chose to get involved in someone else's conflict.

You might hear ad nauseum the gun counter apothegm, "I'd rather be judged by 12 than carried by six." That's not wise; it's foolish and shortsighted. You really don't want to be judged by 12, either. Let's focus on doing everything in our power to avoid both of those scenarios.

Self-Defense Liability Protection

Love it or hate it, health insurance is (in theory at least) a way to plan for managing the risk of significant expenses. Paying a certain monthly fee, you (again, in theory) are "covered" if something terrible happens and you face massive health care bills.

While not technically insurance, there are similar solutions for self-defense liability protection. We won't get caught up in the insurance or not insurance terminology here, but we will note that it looks similar from a high level. For a monthly fee, you "pre-pay" for assistance in the event you need legal and other assistance after a self-defense event. Most (probably all) of these plans do require your case to be clear self-defense. If you pick a fight and are considered the aggressor or violate any laws, you won't get the coverage benefit. Otherwise, the plan helps you with a broad array of services and benefits, including things like:

- Lawyers are on call for immediate consultation after an event.
- Bail assistance and payment.
- Trial lawyer representation costs for criminal and civil cases.
- Expert witness assistance and compensation.
- Loss of wages.
- Liability judgment coverage.

Benefits, terms and conditions vary with plans, so do your

research to see what works best for you. Here are some established options for consideration.

———

Armed Citizens Legal Defense Network: armedcitizensnetwork.org
    US Concealed Carry Association: usconcealedcarry.com
    US Law Shield: uslawshield.com

15

PARTING SHOTS

If nothing else, I hope this book has shown you that carrying a concealed firearm is a decision that affects your entire lifestyle. Carrying a gun is the easy part, but the significant changes required are in how you approach your daily life.

While everything covered in this book is important, I'd like to leave you with a short list of closing thoughts...

Carrying a gun isn't a change that allows you to move about life with less trepidation or concern about potential trouble. In fact, the opposite is true. The fact that you carry a firearm provides every reason to avoid trouble and be the person who walks away from confrontation. Your new goal is to become the most publicly polite person you know.

Think and plan realistically. Many people who buy a gun for protection give a cursory thought to being able to handle a defensive scenario the same way as a paper target on the range. Study cases, read, watch videos, and most importantly...

If you choose to carry a gun for protection, get training. It's not cheap, and it'll cost you time out of your busy schedule, but there is nothing more important than live training upon which you can build a long-term practice routine.

You guessed it. Keep your skills sharp. Whether awareness in your daily life, non-lethal techniques or tools, or gunfighting skills, practice and repetition are the only things that will help you perform adequately in a life-or-death situation.

Involve your family or significant other in your decision. They need to understand the defensive lifestyle, too and, at minimum, know what to do in the event of a self-defense situation.

Find a lawyer, or better yet, engage with a legal self-defense network. You can do this for the price of a couple of gourmet coffees per month.

Now, make your decision. Just because you read this book doesn't mean you should buy a gun and start the process. Carrying a concealed weapon isn't for everyone. If you find yourself questioning your commitment to the lifestyle, don't do it. If you're ready, get to it.

You now know what to do!

ABOUT THE AUTHOR

Tom McHale is an author and Editor of American Handgunner magazine. He's published eight books to date. During the past 15 years, Tom has published nearly 2,000 articles across a variety of publications.

Tom McHale also serves as Director of Public Policy and Digital Media for the American Constitutional Rights Union and ACRU Action Fund.

Prior to his writing career, Tom spent 25 years working in the technology industry as a marketing executive. Tom is a graduate of Emory University with a major in Economics and a minor in Computer Science. He completed his Master's Degree in Business Administration at the University of North Florida with a concentration in Finance and Marketing.

tom-mchale.com

ALSO BY TOM MCHALE

The Practical Guide to Guns and Shooting, Handgun Edition

The Practical Guide to Reloading Ammunition

The Practical Guide to the United States Constitution

The Practical Guide to Gun Holsters for Concealed Carry